Endgame
WINNING CLOSING ARGUMENTS FROM GREAT GEORGIA CASES

Endgame
WINNING CLOSING ARGUMENTS FROM GREAT GEORGIA CASES

Pearl S. Schaikewitz
Editor

PUBLISHED BY THE
DAILY REPORT
AMERICAN LAWYER MEDIA, L.P.

Fulton County Daily Report, 190 Pryor St., SW, Atlanta GA 30303
American Lawyer Media, L.P., New York

©1994 by American Lawyer Media, L.P.
All Rights Reserved
No part of this work may be reproduced or copied in any form or by any means without prior written permission of the publisher.

Printed in the United States of America

ISBN-1-879590-65-4

Cover Design by J. Allan Stagg
Cover Photography by Susan McCarter

Contents

Foreword i

Introduction iv

Negligence, Wrongful Death
Chapter I: Just a Good Woman 2
By Roy E. Barnes

Chapter II: Death of a Football Coach 14
By Lowell S. Fine

Chapter III: Mother and Daughter 38
By W. Carl Reynolds

Negligence
Chapter IV: A Tree Falls in the Forest 66
By W. Wray Eckl

Chapter V: Touching a Power Line, Striking a Chord 90
By Philip C. Smith

Chapter VI: Soft Tissue, Solid Recovery 120
By Charles W. Stephens

Medical Malpractice
Chapter VII: Tragedy at Birth 140
By Don C. Keenan

Chapter VIII: A Paralyzing Case of Pneumonia 172
By Thomas W. Malone

Product Liability
Chapter IX: Trading Lives for Profits: The Mustang II Case 216

Chapter X: Sounding Forth the Trumpets: *Moseley* Reprise 240

FELA
Chapter XI: Derailing a FELA Case 258
By Edgar A. Neely Jr.

Acknowledgments 285

Foreword

Great trial lawyers will tell you final argument is the most important phase of the case. Closing argument is the last opportunity of the advocate—the trial lawyer—to put forth the best of his or her ability and experience as a true professional. Simply put, it is the ultimate opportunity to win your case.

Closing argument is the time to use the advocate's skill as a teacher, salesperson, and speaker. It is the phase of the case when the artistry of the lawyer's accumulated education, experience, intelligence, and ability can and should exhort the strength of the case or the validity of the defense.

After the evidence is closed, the jury enters the jury box with a sense of anticipation. It can be felt in the atmosphere. You can see it in the jurors' faces. They are ready for the lawyers to help them decide the case. Now is the time for the human voice to paint in the minds of the jurors the drama of the incident, to bring back the witnesses and the evidence to form a picture of the case.

The facts can be made vital, emotional, sympathetic, or compelling. Your tools may be wit, sarcasm, logic, or ridicule. Claims can be shown to be exaggerated, meritless, or absurd. Now is the period to bring the common sense of the jury into play to support your position or to chill your opponent's claim.

Now is the time to cement the identification of the fact finder with the client and obtain the justice sought.

All your efforts in closing argument are for naught if you do not respect the fact finder. If you fail in this attitude toward the jury or the judge hearing the case, it will come through, it will be felt, and your efforts will fall on deaf ears. Sincerity is the cord that will hold your case together.

Your case should have had a theme, and you should have emphasized strong points of your theme throughout the trial. Now is the time to capitalize on the strength of your theme and the weakness of your opponent's position. You should do it with sincerity and candor. Never appear slick and opportunistic. Do not appear verbose, arrogant, stuffy, selfish, or condescending.

You, the lawyer, are also on trial. The fact finder sees the client through you. Do not be a pompous bore. Do not drone on and on. Say what you have to say and then stop. You will gain favor with the jury and the judge.

Never, never fawn over the jury. The jurors took an oath to do right and they mean to so do. Slobbering obeisance toward the fact finder will only get you resentment or contempt. It will not get you a verdict or favorable finding.

When you filed your case or your responses, you should have then begun to think about and prepare your final argument. When the moment comes you will have little time for reflection on what you have to say. When the evidence is closed you must resist the natural feeling that, "I have put up my case. The evidence is all in. Shortly the court will give the charge, and we will await the jury deliberations." The case is not over for the trial lawyer. Do not relax; this is your golden opportunity.

Your closing argument should be sincere, clear, vigorous, and logical, and should appeal to the common sense and fairness of the jury. It should personalize the witnesses and the parties. It should make your position appear correct and fair. It ought to convince that you ask for the right thing. It must ring with conviction.

Many trials will have an event, a witness who says something—frequently unexpected—some incident that will give the trial a spark. Use it and let it fuel your final argument whenever you can. It is likely the most memorable point in the trial. Grasp its strength for your position.

It is important that you be yourself when you plead your cause. Don't attempt to adopt the style of some famous lawyer. It will appear artificial and will not serve you well. Develop your own method of presentation. Your own personality and style will enhance your sincerity and conviction for your cause.

Whatever your technique may be, remember to whom it is addressed. The style of your argument and its content should never fail to reflect whether it is addressed to the court or to the jury.

Tell the fact finder what you want, why it is right, and sit down.

The Honorable Harold L. Murphy

Judge, U.S. District Court
Northern District of Georgia

Introduction

In the great chess match that is civil litigation, victory is determined after the last witness leaves the stand, when the only remaining pieces on the game board are plaintiff's lawyer and defense lawyer. In chess, this final test of wills is called the endgame. At trial, it is called closing argument. It is, as Judge Murphy in his foreword says, "the ultimate opportunity to win your case."

In assembling a sampling of great closing arguments, we looked to some of Georgia's biggest verdicts, some of the state's more renowned defense victories, and ultimately to some of its most experienced trial lawyers. This anthology is neither exhaustive nor definitive, but we hope it is instructive. In that respect, *Endgame* also serves as starting point. Building upon the collective experiences and wisdom contained in the chapters that follow, the reader, we hope, will be able to improve his or her own advocacy skills and in the process advance the craft of courtroom oratory.

Endgame begins with Marietta lawyer Roy E. Barnes's study in brevity. With the defense admitting liability on the eve of trial, the entire case came down to a few hours' presentation of evidence and then closing argument. For what amounted to a half-day of court time (including the jury's deliberations), Barnes and his clients walked away with a $1.6 million verdict for the death of a mother of four who never worked outside the home.

"If you award anything less than $2 million, you will have besmirched the memory of [the decedent]," he tells the jury. "You will have sent out a word throughout the nation, throughout the highways and byways, that a good woman is not worth much, so be careless if you drive a tractor-trailer truck. . . . I think that you will award a fair and adequate amount. . ., because a good woman is worth more than gold. She is worth more than silver. She is worth all of the love in the world."

In Chapter II, Lowell S. Fine demonstrates the finesse required in defending an insurance company. His is the first of three defense verdicts represented in the book. Here, he had to defend an insurance company against a suit brought by the widow of Jim Luck, a beloved Georgia Tech coach killed when a tractor-trailer truck jackknifed and collided with a campus police car carrying the coach. Making Fine's victory that much more remarkable, his insured's truck driver had already pleaded guilty to vehicular homicide.

In Chapter III, W. Carl Reynolds shows how he successfully persuaded a jury in federal court to award $10 million for the wrongful death of a working mother and $13.2 million—including $5 million in punitive damages—for the catastrophic injuries sustained by her young daughter. The mother encountered a tractor-trailer stuck across the road as she was taking her children to day care; the top of her car was sheared off as it passed under the truck.

Reynolds makes much of the truck driver's ignoring a bystander's suggestion that he put out emergency reflectors to warn oncoming traffic. Reynolds argues, "Maybe he felt it was more important to do whatever he needed to do . . . to get his load delivered than to protect the motoring public who might be maimed and injured and killed. . . ."

In Chapter IV, W. Wray Eckl tells how he successfully defended a wood-chopper sued after a fallen tree limb cracked the skull of a little boy. Mindful that he was in a small town, the Atlanta lawyer uses a folksy manner, and a soft touch, to argue the case: "Homer has been doing this for sixty-five years. Do you think he would have been where he was if [he] perceived any danger to anybody?" Deflating the plaintiffs' most compelling argument, Eckl devotes some of his own summation to reviewing the seriousness of the boy's injuries. It was the worst day of his client's life, he confides in the jury, but adds: "This was an accident. It was not anybody's fault. It was tragic that it occurred, but the law says there can be no recovery for an accident because nobody is really at fault."

Chapter V presents Philip C. Smith's $28.9 million victory against Georgia Power Co. for a man who was nearly electrocuted when he touched an uninsulated guy wire. Although the plaintiff endured tremendous pain and suffering, his medical expenses were only about $10,000, he lost no wages, and he made a complete recovery. Smith repeatedly makes the point that the jury must assess huge punitive damages to force the defendant to make an economic decision in favor of safety and prevention: "What would it take to get Georgia Power to pay attention? . . . Twenty-five million dollars? . . . [B]y sending such a verdict you'll do something constructive. You will get their attention and send a message they cannot ignore." Note the "send a message" theme; it appears in other chapters as well.

In Chapter VI, Charles W. Stephens explains how he won $720,000 in a Toccoa, Georgia, case involving only soft-tissue injuries, a loss-of-consortium claim, and $150,000 in medical specials. Stephens's case, he says, hinges on winning the credibility battle—making the jury believe that his client, Danny Yearwood, suffered a discernible injury that necessitated repeated doses of painkillers. The defense argued that Yearwood exaggerated his complaints in order to get more medication, playing up the unseemliness of the plaintiff's drug dependency. Stephens turns the issue to his own advantage, using it to make his client seem more sympathetic: "For almost three years now, Danny Yearwood has been in a deep, dark hole, and his family has been desperately trying to . . . pull him out. At times, they have almost been sucked into that hole themselves, and it has truly been a window into hell."

In Chapter VII, Don C. Keenan describes the tragedy of a baby born with severe brain damage because of the doctors' failure to perform a cesarean section. Medical malpractice trials tend to evolve into battles of the experts. In showing the jury how the medical testimony stacked up, Keenan keeps it simple: "I submit to you, they couldn't find anybody they didn't have a string on to get on that witness stand and contradict the two Emory doctors and the three nationally acclaimed experts we had. They had to resort to friends. They had to resort to people that they had a hook in. . . ."

From a tragic birth, we go to the case of an elderly patient who entered a Savannah hospital with a case of pneumonia and ended up paralyzed. To win the $1.95 million recovery, Thomas W. Malone had to overcome testimony from his client's treating physician, who insisted that the 71-year-old woman would live no more than seven years after the trial.

Chapter IX sets out Foy R. Devine's argument in his $9.3 million verdict against Ford Motor Co. for the design of the Mustang II. His clients were the parents of a teenage girl, a rear-seat passenger who burned to death when a rear-end collision exploded the 1975 Mustang II's gas tank. Devine uses internal memoranda to make Ford look like a company willing to trade lives for profits, punctuating his point with the transcript of a conversation in which a well-known Ford official asks then-President Richard M. Nixon to lean on regulators to "cool it" on safety requirements.

Chapter X, reprinted from the 1993 Daily Report book *Side Impact*, presents the argument responsible for the $101 million punitive damages portion of the record-breaking verdict in *Moseley v. General Motors*. Like the Mustang II case, *Moseley* involved a teenager incinerated in a postcollision gas-tank explosion. Here, the fuel tank was located on the side of the vehicle, outside the vehicle support rails. GM, like Ford, claimed the accident resulted not from any defect in design, but from the high speed of the other vehicle.

Plaintiffs lawyer James E. Butler Jr. waged his case like a holy war. He tells the jury he woke up at three o'clock in the morning "with a tune in my head, and it was about trumpets." Then, quoting from the "Battle Hymn of the Republic," he asks the jurors in effect, to "[sound] forth the trumpets that shall never call retreat."

In Chapter XI defense lawyer Edgar A. Neely Jr. displays the timeless art of Old South oratory. In dissuading a jury from finding against his railroad client, he mixes in homespun expressions, describing the neurological evidence in the case, for example, with the phrase, "everything is chicken down in Dixie."

Except in the few cases where we indicate otherwise, the speakers wrote their own introductions and annotations to the closing arguments that follow. Their versions of the facts were shown to opposing counsel for corroboration. The chapters have been edited for style and continuity.

Pearl S. Schaikewitz

Editor

Pittman v. Sims
No. 1-87-CV-2155RCF (N.D.Ga.)

Result: $1.6 million verdict
Plaintiff's Counsel: Roy E. Barnes of Barnes, Browning, Tanksley & Casurella (Marietta)
Defense Counsel: Kent T. Stair of Webb, Carlock, Copeland, Semler & Stair (Atlanta)
Judge: Richard C. Freeman
Trial Date: November 16, 1988

Chapter I

Just a Good Woman

Introduction
By Roy E. Barnes*

Two of the most difficult cases for a trial lawyer are the wrongful death of a minor child and the wrongful death of a housewife and mother. Logically, mothers and children should have great value to a jury. However, practice has taught that unless a jury has an economic basis upon which to compute damages, most wrongful death cases of children and homemakers yield small verdicts.

This case arose out of a horrendous collision. On August 13, 1987, Johnnie Pittman was killed instantly in a crash with a tractor-trailer on Georgia Highway 92 at its intersection with Cannon Drive in Douglas County. Johnnie, who was forty-five years old, had been married for twenty-six years to Jimmy Pittman. The couple had four children, two daughters who were married and two younger boys who were almost grown. At the time of her death, Johnnie was on the way to visit and care for her sick mother.

Jimmy Pittman filed suit on September 30, 1987, against the driver of the truck, Richard Sims, and the rig's owner, Tennessee Commercial Warehouse, Inc. In their answer, the defendants denied liability. However, when the case came on for trial, the defendants admitted liability, thus preventing Mr. Pittman from introducing into evidence the gory details of Johnnie Pittman's death.

To make matters even more difficult for the plaintiff, the defendants used their peremptory strikes against women, ensuring that an all-male jury was chosen. Such was permissible in those days before discrimination in jury selection was prohibited in civil cases (see *Strozier v. Clark*, 206 Ga. App. 85 (424 SE2d 368) (1992)).

Since Mrs. Pittman's husband, four children, and pastor were the only witnesses who testified about the value of her life, the trial was extremely short. In fact, the presentation of evidence lasted only a little over two hours. Defense counsel did not put up any evidence or cross-examine the plaintiff's witnesses.

In his closing argument, defense counsel suggested $250,000 as an adequate amount of damages for the wrongful death of Johnnie Pittman. In fact, the highest pretrial offer to settle the case was $750,000, not an unreasonable amount considering that the deceased was a homemaker.

However, there are some cases in which the family of the deceased makes the case. This is something that only experience teaches. Which plaintiffs the jury will like and which plaintiffs they will dislike is a mystery trial lawyers confront every day. Jimmy Pittman was a good, hardworking man. Neither he nor his deceased wife was formally educated to any great extent, but they never complained about the hand that life had dealt them. The Pittmans also had four good, well-mannered children. When you talked with them, you could tell that they had been taught all the principles of life at their mother's knee.

Trial lawyers take gambles every day, and a good trial lawyer knows when to gamble and when to settle. It is a trait that I am still seeking to learn. In any event, I felt that the jury would like Jimmy Pittman. I knew they would like the children and

I thought they would be warmed by the story of Johnnie Pittman. Nothing extraordinary, nothing great, nothing historical, just good, hardworking people. Just a good woman.

And so, I constructed an argument on what the value of a good woman was to society, and I sought not to overstate the case. Rather, I presented the case concisely and succinctly, and relied primarily upon the closing argument to make the point of the value of a good woman. Evidently, the jury agreed. The jury was only out forty minutes before returning a verdict of $1.6 million. Later, two jurors apologized to me for not being able to return the full $2 million I had asked for in closing argument.

Closing Argument
Johnnie Pittman Has Only Me Here Today

MR. BARNES: May it please the court and gentlemen of the jury:

For the last two days you have heard and seen a brief glimpse into the life of Johnnie Pittman. I always feel inadequate and incompetent to try to explain in a brief period of time what a life means— what the life of Johnnie Pittman means.

I wish I were a member of a large firm like that of my opponent and had the resources to better present this case to you. I wish I were as talented as my opponent and the literally hundreds that are in the defendants' law firm to better be able to assist and present Johnnie Pittman's case. Johnnie Pittman has only me here today to try to explain her side of the story because her voice has been silenced forever. No longer will she see the husband who loves her or the four children who count on her counsel and guidance and love. Her life was taken prematurely, and she has only me to stand up for her—and I feel incompetent compared to this well-experienced and large law firm that represents the trucking company. I hope and pray that you will not penalize Johnnie for my inadequacy. I must depend on you to make up for my failings.[1]

At the beginning of this case, the defendants stood up and

even though for over a year that this case has been filed and pending in this court, for the first time, the defendants admitted in open court that they were liable for the homicide and death of Johnnie Pittman. We were here with witnesses ready, willing, and able to present evidence as to how the defendant drove a tractor-trailer truck carelessly, recklessly, negligently into the automobile of Johnnie Pittman and pushed her vehicle across the road and killed her instantly. Yet, with these witnesses standing in the wings, the defendants, after a whole year of denying any fault or liability, finally said, "We agree that the defendants negligently caused the death of Johnnie Pittman."

Why did they do this? Why is it that lawyers with the expertise, training, and experience of [Webb, Carlock, Copeland, Semler & Stair] wait until the day of trial before they finally decided that the defendants had killed Johnnie Pittman? Why were Jimmy Pittman, Johnnie's husband, and her four children put to the worry and expense and concern of having to prove what they knew in their hearts was true—that the defendants killed their wife and mother.

I will tell you why. I will tell you why the defendants knew that they must admit liability, that they must admit fault, that they could not deny negligence, and that is because they knew that not one juror drawn from the entire Northern District of Georgia, which stretches over all of north Georgia, could be selected to believe a ridiculous story that the defendants did not cause the death of Johnnie Pittman. They had the right to admit liability and they utilized it. But at the same time, the callousness that they have [shown in deciding] whether to admit liability and fault in the death of Johnnie Pittman also goes to temper what they will tell you about the worth of Johnnie Pittman's life.

Rolling Death

In fact, the defendant Richard Sims did not even have the decency to show up in court and face the husband whose wife he had taken and to look at the four children of Johnnie Pittman and tell them why he drove a tractor-trailer truck into the side of their mother's car. A tractor-trailer truck—we all see them. We all know them. Not one of us driving down the road has not been affected by a tractor-trailer truck that passes us and, with the speed that only a freight train can accomplish, almost blows us off the road. We have all held onto the steering wheels of our automobiles feeling the rush of the wind of a tractor-trailer truck being driven by a driver who cares not for those who are on the highways and byways with him, but worries only if he will deliver his goods at the appointed time.

I believe that there ought to be a law that requires to be painted on the front of every tractor-trailer truck the words "Rolling Death" because rolling death they are and rolling death they become. An automobile has no chance against a loaded tractor-trailer truck, speeding down the road in disregard of every traffic law and ordinance. Rolling death—that's what they are. Rolling death they are, and as you are going home tonight from this courtroom after you deliberate and reach a fair and impartial verdict, if you look in the rearview mirror of your automobile and see a tractor-trailer truck on your bumper, the law should require to be blasted upon the front of that truck, "Rolling Death," because if you come in contact with that tractor-trailer truck, surely death will result and the truck will roll on, roll on, roll on.

Only you can stop "Rolling Death." Only you can set the conscience of those who drive these tractor-trailer trucks on the roads and byways. Only you have the right to say, "Enough is enough. We demand all of the Richard Simses and all of the tractor-trailer trucking companies to obey the laws of the land, not to speed, not to blow us off the side of the road, to be our friend rather than our antagonist."

Liability has been admitted in this case, and so the Court has instructed me not to comment further on liability other than that which I have already stated. But I do want to comment on one other matter that is within your common understanding and knowledge. There are six men on this jury, and that is not by mistake, happenstance, or accident. Just as the defense lawyers waited until this case was called for trial before they admitted liability—admitted that the defendants killed Johnnie Pittman—so they also made sure that there was not one woman on this jury. They chose and made sure that their strikes were utilized to take every woman off of this jury.

I believe you can be fair and impartial. I believe that you, as men of human experience and understanding, realize the worth of a good woman, because Johnnie Pittman was a good woman. But it is not without happenstance, not without plan, that first the defendants wait over a year before they can decide whether they are at fault and then they make sure that when the defendants come to court only men sit in judgment of the value of Johnnie Pittman.

How Much is a Good Woman Worth?

Johnnie Pittman was a good woman. You've heard the testimony here of the witnesses. She was not an educated woman. She was not educated in the terms of formal education, but she was educated in loving and concern for her fellow human beings. She was forty-five years old. She bore four children, two daughters who were married and two sons who were almost grown. She had reached that point in life in which she could see the time that her call of raising children was to be at an end and she could enjoy the fruits of her grandchildren and the uninterrupted embraces of her husband.

You have heard her pastor testify that she was the kind of woman who could always be counted upon to help someone in need. She was the one who drove the church bus or car, to pick up children and bring them to the church. She was the one who stopped by to check on somebody who was ill or infirm. She was the one the preacher could call on to come cook and she came, without complaint and without regret. You have heard testimony that she was the kind of woman who, for over two years, cooked the breakfast of two eighty-year-old women in her neighborhood every morning without complaint, without regret, and joyfully because she wanted to help somebody else. You have heard the testimony about the fact that she was a mother hen to her children, that she and her two daughters were close and that she talked with them every day and led them through the trials and tribulations of their lives with the experience of her toils, her tears, and her strains and her trials.

You have seen each of these children. You heard testify her daughter Marjorie, her daughter Joy, her son Jimmy, and her son Chris. Four good kids, two married and with families of their own. Two working, two paying taxes. Two others, soon to be married, soon on the threshold of adulthood, all four who had never been in any trouble. How much is it worth? How much is a good woman's love worth? How much is a good woman worth? How much is it worth to raise four good children [who] have never been in trouble, [who] are taxpaying, upstanding members of society? How much is it worth for the life of a woman who never called on society to give her welfare, to give her any assistance, who took care of her own problems, and reached out to help others in need?

Then you heard the testimony of her husband. She and her husband had been married twenty-six years when she was killed. She bore him four children, really five, because an infant died in childbirth. These are good folks. They are the kind of folks that you want as your next door neighbor. They are the kind of folks who would help you in time of need, who would grieve with you when you had a loss in your family, who would bring food in to you when you were sick and would even come over and cut your grass if you were down on your luck and not feeling well. Jimmy Pittman, Johnnie's husband, works with his hands—a metal worker for all of their married life. Both Jimmy and Johnnie came from the country in the mountains of north Georgia, and they brought to Atlanta and this region a sense of pride, a sense of hard work, a sense of almost stoic bearing of their difficulties, but also a sense of neighborliness.

You heard Jimmy Pittman talk about the last day that Johnnie was in life—August 13, 1987. The day began as any other day. Jimmy got up early. He left the house at 6:15, and he went over to check on his wife who had been the flesh of his flesh for over twenty-six years. She was uncovered in her bedclothes and he covered her up and kissed her on the cheek and told her he loved her—and he never saw her alive again. You heard the testimony of her sixteen-year-old son, Chris, who testified his mother got him up to take him to Six Flags [Over Georgia] where he was working during the summer. Because he had not quite received his driver's license, she let him drive to Six Flags, and when he got out of the car, she slid across the seat and told him, "I love you." And that was the last time Chris ever saw his mother alive.

Oh, if we could call back those moments! If we knew that death was knocking at our door, wouldn't we hold the ones we love close to our breast and say, "Goodbye"? Wouldn't we apologize for all the wrongs of the years? Wouldn't we weep bitter tears on the leaving? Perhaps that's why God takes us unannounced so that the parting will be easier for us all.

Johnnie Pittman then left her husband and left her son, and where did she go? She went to Douglasville to take care of her sick mother. So much in the ken of Johnnie Pittman, that she died while she was going to care for someone else. She drove her car to Douglasville. She stopped. She put on her blinker to make a left turn, going onto Cannon Drive where her mother was living and then, as she went to make her turn, a tractor-trailer truck driven by Richard Sims, who didn't even have the guts to come here today, passed two vehicles and came speeding down the wrong side of the road and killed Johnnie Pittman. And when the smoke cleared, what were the words of Richard Sims? His words were, "Where is she? I can't even see the car." He had knocked the car so far, he did not even know where it was.

Johnnie Pittman is gone. The evidence in this case has been less than two hours—her preacher, her family, and photographs of the family have been the evidence. She did not have an income because she worked at raising good children, taxpaying children. She worked at caring for her family. Now, you will hear Mr. Stair say something to this effect, "Well, she had no income, and therefore, we can only award what Johnnie Pittman was actually earning. And if you award about $250,000 and it's invested at 10 to 12 percent, that will earn about $25,000 [annually] for the family forever." Oh, how callous! How calculated! No wonder he waited until the call of this case to admit liability, or he made sure that no women were on this jury. He is trying to pull another trick on you with such deceiving logic. How much is it worth for a good woman? Is it worth only $250,000? How much is it worth for four good children to be raised and to become productive members of this society?

A Good Woman Is Worth More Than Gold

I will guarantee you one thing: If you were to pile gold up as high as this ceiling and tell this husband and these four children, "You make the choice between the gold in this room and a living, breathing, Johnnie Pittman," there would be not one moment of hesitation in the choice because they love their wife and mother and she loved them, and no amount of money can bring her back and no amount of money can compensate for the good that she has done. But to say her life is only worth $250,000 is an insult not only to you, gentlemen of the jury, but to the memory of Johnnie Pittman. Because you see, if you award only $250,000 or $1,000,000 or $1,500,000, then you will have rewarded the defendants in this case.

The judge will charge you that the value of the life in a wrongful death case means not only the economic damages, but the joy of living—the joy of living to the deceased. And Johnnie Pittman enjoyed living, and she was in the midst of living at forty-five years of age. She was in the midst of loving. She was in the midst of caring for a husband and children.

How much is a good woman worth? I read only last week where Dominique Wilkins, who is probably one of the great basketball players of all time, had just signed a contract to play for the Atlanta Hawks; and for bouncing a basketball up and down a court for part of a year, Dominique Wilkins will earn over $3,000,000 a year. Is it not worth at least close to that for Johnnie Pittman to have raised four good kids, four taxpaying kids? Is it not worth something close to that for her to have cared for her husband? Is it not worth something close to that for her to have cared for her church and to have cooked meals every morning for those of her neighbors who were in need? I suggest to you that the value of Johnnie Pittman's life is $2,000,000—less than what Dominique Wilkins will make in just one year. $2,000,000. I don't think that is excessive. Neither do I believe that it is extreme. $2,000,000 is a good middle ground between the $250,000 that Mr. Stair suggests to you and the literally hundreds of millions that the good works of Johnnie Pittman are truly worth.

She is Worth all of the Love in the World

Now, gentlemen of the jury, I can only leave in your good conscience, I can only leave in your good stead, I can only leave in your hands what you believe is right. If you award anything less than $2,000,000, you will have besmirched the memory of Johnnie Pittman. You will have sent out a word throughout the nation, throughout the highways and byways, that a good woman is not worth much, so be careless if you drive a tractor-trailer truck. Be careless if you are a rolling death on the highways. Juries only will award a small amount, and it's just all a part of doing business, and if we do enough business, it matters not how many we kill. It matters not how many we maim, because you see, the bottom line is its still profitable. I don't believe that's right. I don't believe that you think it's right. I think that you will award a fair and adequate amount—$2,000,000— for the life of Johnnie Pittman, because a good woman is worth more than gold. She is worth more than silver. She is worth all of the love in the world.[2]

Endnotes

* Born in Atlanta in 1948, Roy E. Barnes received his A.B. (1969) and J.D. (1972, cum laude) from the University of Georgia and was admitted to the State Bar of Georgia in 1972. In 1974, after serving in the Cobb County District Attorney's office, he was elected to the first of eight terms in the State Senate. He was chairman of the Senate Judiciary Committee from 1981–82. He served as administration floor leader for Governor Joe Frank Harris from 1982–89 and ran for governor in 1990. Currently Mr. Barnes serves in the House of Representatives.

1. I am self-effacing and play up the fact that defense counsel are from a big firm because generally, jurors pull for the underdog. I always try to position myself as the underdog; that's why I say I wish my client could be represented by a member of a big firm.

2. I was inspired by Proverbs 31:10 in arguing that a good woman is worth more than gold and silver. In fact, in other versions of this argument, I have quoted Proverbs 31:10 from the Bible.

Luck v. Fogleman Truck Lines
No. 1:87-CV-1677-ODE (N.D. Ga.)

Result: Defense verdict
Plaintiff's Counsel: Williston C. White and Harvey Gray of Fortson & White (Atlanta)
Defense Counsel: Lowell S. Fine and G. Michael Banick of Alembik, Fine & Callner (Atlanta)
Judge: Orinda D. Evans
Date of Verdict: August 18, 1989

Chapter II

Death of a Football Coach

Introduction
Reprinted from the Daily Report, *August 31, 1989 (revised)*

The widow of renowned Georgia Institute of Technology coach Jim Luck lost a wrongful death suit arising from a tractor-trailer collision that killed her husband in 1986.

A six-person jury in federal court returned a defense verdict August 18, 1989, for Crowley, Louisiana–based Fogleman Truck Lines, Inc.; its insurance carrier, Liberty Mutual Insurance Co.; and Fogleman employee and truck driver Placide B. Boucher.

Shirley F. Luck sued the defendants for $6 million for the full value of her husband's life and $3,923 for his funeral expenses, according to her complaint. James Luck, sixty-three, a senior assistant athletic director, was killed in a Georgia Tech motorcade from Athens the afternoon of November 28, 1986.

A tractor-trailer driven by defendant Boucher crossed the center line of Georgia Highway 15A, colliding with a Georgia Tech police car transporting Luck and campus police Sergeant Gary Frank Beringause, according to court records. The police car was part of a Tech caravan carrying football players from a practice session at the University of Georgia in Athens on the eve of the annual football game between Georgia and Georgia Tech. The accident occurred near Nicholson, Georgia.

Boucher later pleaded guilty to two counts of involuntary manslaughter and driving on the wrong side of the road. The defense contended Boucher was driving "in a safe and lawful manner" when a car in front of him came to a sudden stop, causing him to put on his brakes, jackknife, and hit the Georgia Tech police car.

"He touched the brakes, had an unfortunate jackknife and shouldn't be held responsible for what occurred," said lead defense counsel Lowell S. Fine, who tried the case with Alembik, Fine & Callner partner G. Michael Banick.

The suit originally was filed in DeKalb Superior Court, before the defendant removed it to federal court. "We thought we would have a more conservative jury [in federal court] than in DeKalb," explained Fine. He thought more jurors in DeKalb would be Tech alumni than in the Northern District of Georgia.

Luck had been with Georgia Tech since 1955, first as an assistant football coach, then a baseball coach, and finally as an assistant athletic director. Fine added that Luck was second only to legendary Tech football coach Bobby Dodd in fame.

Commentary on the Trial Strategy
By Lowell S. Fine*

This wrongful death case presented several problems. First, I represented an insurance company, a tractor-trailer company, and its driver. Juries are notoriously biased against these types of defendants. Second, I feared inherent sympathy for the plaintiff because she was the widow of a well-known Georgia Tech coach. Third, Coach Luck was killed while riding in a Tech security car that was in its proper lane at the time of the accident. The collision occurred totally on the wrong side of the road. Finally, the driver of the tractor-trailer, Boucher, had pleaded guilty to involuntary manslaughter and driving on the wrong side of the road.

My trial strategy was to tackle these problems head-on, in both voir dire and closing argument. During voir dire I asked the jurors whether they could find in the defendants' favor even though the plaintiff was a widow and the defendants were big companies.

As for Boucher, I admitted in the opening statement that he had pleaded guilty to the charges. I contended, however, that Boucher was not negligent and that even if he were, his negligence was not the proximate cause of the accident.

The defense's theory was that Boucher was confronted with a sudden emergency that he did not create. Mr. Boucher contended that a white car had stopped suddenly in front of him. When he touched his brakes lightly, Mr. Boucher said his rig unexpectedly jackknifed and swerved across the road. Plaintiff, on the other hand, alleged that the driver of the white car had put on his blinker and pulled off the road.

Because a defense verdict seemed unlikely, I strenuously argued the liability and proximate cause issues. Also, I went into more detail than usual in trying to rebut the very high damages that the plaintiff was seeking.

Aggression Can Infuriate a Jury

The plaintiff had introduced into evidence many photographs, a blowup of the figures testified to by their economist Dr. John Brown, Mr. Luck's Purple Heart, and numerous letters and citations of awards. Also, high-level officials from Georgia Tech were brought in as "character witnesses." I thought that this was overkill and decided it called for a strong, aggressive style of defense.

This style can be effective in the right case, but I do not use it in all cases. You run the risk, with an aggressive closing argument, of aggravating a jury. I was extremely conscious of the fact that I was defending an insurance company and a tractor-trailer company against a widow. I did not want to do anything to infuriate the jury. That's why it was so important to stress to the jury that if I annoyed them in any way, they should hold it against me, and not my clients.

I had to try this case assuming that a defense verdict on liability was a remote possibility. Therefore, I vigorously attempted to hold the damages down by contrasting the plaintiff's expensive effort to obtain a high verdict with the plaintiff's failure to bring in the key witness, Ronald Holcomb, who had been driving the white car. This, too, necessitated an aggressive argument.

Still, the jury deliberated for several hours before returning a defense verdict.

Closing Argument

MR. FINE: Ladies and gentlemen, when we started this suit, I told you what an opening statement was, so I would like to tell you a little about what a closing statement is, although you have already heard about thirty minutes of one.[1]

A closing statement is only the statement of counsel regarding the evidence that's been admitted. As I told you at the beginning of the case, and I believe as her honor told you, what the lawyers tell you now or during the course of the trial is not evidence. The only evidence in this case comes from the witness stand or by way of documentary evidence that the court allows you to take into the jury room. So what I tell you now is not evidence, and what Mr. Gray tells you or Mr. White or whoever gets up next tells you, is not evidence. It's merely statements of counsel regarding that evidence.

As far as the evidence itself is concerned, you collectively have heard the evidence. The lawyers think of the next question, sometimes think of objections, so if I make a comment to you today regarding the evidence that is incorrect, let me tell you I wouldn't do it on purpose, because you would know that I was trying to fool you. Frankly, you have heard the evidence. If I make a misstatement, then I apologize, and I will try to say it the way I have heard it.²

Now, during the course of the trial, if there's anything that I have said or done or anything in the case that you feel was improper or harsh or uncalled for, hold that against me; don't hold that against my clients. I am a lawyer; I am an advocate, and I state what I believe in. So, if something goes haywire in terms of what you would expect or think to be proper, hold it against me.³

The judge's role in this case is to present the law to you, and she has the right to tell you what that law is, and she also acts as a referee in terms of the trial, as you have seen, sometimes letting certain evidence in, sometimes keeping certain evidence out, and that is her role. But when she gives you the charge of the court, you will hear no charge saying that you cannot use your common sense.

All of you have worldly experiences, you have common knowledge, you have common feelings that you rely upon in your day-to-day activities, and no charge of the court should be interpreted to mean that you cannot use your everyday good common horse sense, if you will.⁴

Let me begin with a few preliminaries and then get into the facts, if I may. The parties in the lawsuit, as her honor is going to tell you, are Mrs. Luck, who is the plaintiff in this lawsuit—she's suing my clients, Placide Boucher, Fogleman Trucking, and Liberty Mutual Insurance Company.

Liberty Mutual Insurance Company acknowledged a long time ago that it had insurance with Fogleman for this particular accident. That's not an issue. The only reason, I submit to you, that Liberty Mutual Insurance Company was added as a party to this suit was in an effort to let you know there's an insurance company involved, so that you will try to give bigger damages than would otherwise be warranted. There's no other valid purpose for that defendant being in this case. There were no witnesses subpoenaed or brought to you by counsel for the plaintiff, who are very fine attorneys, to discuss anything about the insurance coverage of the truck involved.⁵

Her honor is going to tell you that in a case like this, the burden of proof is on the plaintiff. The plaintiff has not mentioned that to you yet, but the judge will tell you that the burden of proof is on the plaintiff. And what that means is that the plaintiff has the burden of coming into court and proving [her case] to you by a preponderance of the evidence. That means—lawyers use fancy terms—but it means the superior weight of the evidence, that their position is correct, and the judge will tell you that if you find that the evidence is evenly balanced on any particular issue, then the plaintiffs have not carried their burden of proof.

A defendant in a lawsuit really doesn't have to do anything if it doesn't want to, because the burden is on the plaintiff. It takes, I don't know exactly what, but maybe $40, $50 to file a lawsuit in this court and to allege whatever one may care to allege. But you must prove [the allegations] to a jury's satisfaction by the superior weight of the evidence.

As my brother counsel mentioned a moment ago, a lawsuit is really divided into two parts, liability and damages. The judge is going to tell you that in this case, if you determine that the defendants were not liable or not the proximate cause of the death of James Luck, then you are not to consider the issue of damages. And as a lawyer who is representing defendants in this case—sometimes I represent plaintiffs—it's my job to talk to you about these two issues.[6]

So, I would like to start off discussing for a moment the accident. In the opening statement, counsel for the plaintiff made it seem just pure and simple that the driver just lost control for no reason and went across the road, fairly cut and dried. He tried to have you believe that again a few minutes ago.

The facts in this case, I believe, show exactly what I told you in my opening statement. We don't make the facts, the lawyers; the facts are the facts. And I told you in the opening that I was going to show you that the Tech caravan, if you will, was proceeding too fast; that it had its blue lights on when there was no emergency; that they were straddling a lane and preventing cars from going around them; and that they were in general creating a commotion that in part contributed to this accident. And I believe I have proven that to you, ladies and gentlemen. I believe I have proven it to you without question this morning by two witnesses, Sylvia Thomas and Connie Dalton, whom the plaintiffs chose not to call.[7]

Basically Country Folks

In considering what I have to say and the testimony of the witnesses, you may take into account, as the court will tell you, their believability, their character, and I believe that you could tell this morning as to those two witnesses probably several things. They didn't want to be here. They are basically country folks, like some of my relatives, and I believe Ms. Sylvia Thomas, whose family is made up of law enforcement officials, that it was not easy for her to have to say that basically in her opinion, the tractor-trailer was not responsible.[8]

These people told you this morning that the Tech caravan was doing what I just told you. And although there's some conflict in the testimony as to what this white car did, I submit to you that counsel for the plaintiff has failed to show you that that car was off the road as was stated in opening statement.

The truth about that car is that it came to a sudden stop, and there was only one person really on that road who had a great, close view, and that was Placide Boucher, whom I believe you have found to be a truthful and candid person. Behind him, right behind him, is Sylvia Thomas, and she says as the trailer slid around she saw a white car stopped in the road.

Now, the plaintiffs could have subpoenaed Ronald Holcomb to court, ladies and gentlemen, but they chose not to do so. I didn't need to subpoena him because the evidence was quite clear to me from the testimony that came out at trial that that man came to a fairly sudden and abrupt stop for no reason on this roadway.[9]

Sylvia Thomas told you this morning that she saw no improper driving on the part of the tractor-trailer driver. She's following that tractor-trailer for a long way. You know, I'm not naive. I know folks don't like trucking companies sometimes, and that's one reason, when you first started the case, you were asked could you be fair to all parties in the case. The judge asked you that. And I know some people don't like insurance companies, and that's why you were asked that question by the court as well, so that when you consider these facts, you can consider the parties as if they were both driving individual cars, not that one's driving a car and one's driving a tractor-trailer.[10]

But the bottom line is that the witness who saw this best saw no improper driving on the part of Placide, and she's following him all the way, said he's really going a little too slow, she wanted to get around him; she didn't see him do anything wrong; she didn't see him at fault; she didn't see him being negligent.

What happened is this: Counsel for the plaintiff has presented you with these fancy charts and they presented you with expensive aerial photographs, but I would like to show you the roadway close up the way it looked on that day.[11]

Let me show you the roadway, the way it looked. I know you haven't seen these before. This is the direction—one and two, if you will, are the direction that the Tech caravan was proceeding, and you heard about the split in the road where it becomes two lanes, and this is the first one, and then obviously you're getting a little bit closer and you see it fork off in front.

Now, more importantly—I gave you that just to give you an idea of the roadway. More importantly, this is the roadway where the tractor-trailer was coming around. You've got to remember the circumstances. There was not a heavy rain; I never told you it was.[12] It was drizzling from time to time. The main thing is the roadway was wet. And as a driver who has driven a long way—[Boucher] has driven from Louisiana to Greenville, driven for twenty years, never had a jackknife—he's coming around this curve, he sees this car come to a fairly sudden stop; he sees one tail light, not two, on the white car. And as he gets around the curve he has the incident.[13]

The point of impact, you may remember—it's hard to see what was drawn by the officer with an "X"—so, what happened was he came around and saw this car, as he got around the curve; he applied his brakes, went into an immediate jackknife, and went across the road. He was faced, in short, ladies and gentlemen, with a sudden emergency because of this caravan apparently causing the white car—[14]

With her honor's ruling, then, let me proceed. My point was that [Boucher] was confronted with a sudden emergency. There was no need for this white car to have suddenly stopped in the road.

Now, one issue that you have to decide in this case is whether the tractor-trailer was proceeding at a safe distance behind the white car. That's obviously a matter of interest to you. But there's a conflict in the testimony on that.

You have got a tractor-trailer driver [Boucher] who's driven for years and years and years, who says, I was a safe distance behind, and had I not gone into a jackknife, I would have brought my vehicle to a halt.

You have got [Sergeant Johnny Wayne] Coleman saying a certain distance—I think he said 170 [feet]; you remember better than I do; our driver saying maybe he was 70—but I think that the key point there for you to consider—Officer Coleman is a fine officer, but he told you that he's not an expert in the braking or handling or operation of a tractor-trailer; he doesn't know how many gears it has, really doesn't know how it operates, and he has never operated one.[15]

So, I suggest to you that based on the testimony of Sylvia Thomas and Connie Dalton and Placide Boucher, that he was a reasonably safe distance behind that white car.

If you believe counsel for the plaintiff that the white car was off the road, then you would have to wonder why Mr. Boucher applied his brakes. Obviously the car was not off the road. Otherwise, Placide would have just continued on down the road the way he had done for obviously hundreds of thousands of miles before. The reason he had to touch the brake was because that white car was in the center of the southbound lane blocking his way.

Clear Conscience, Guilty Plea

Now, there's been some mention of the plea of guilty, which we stipulated to—that just means we agreed to it. Basically, what that means is that [Boucher] was charged with two counts of vehicular homicide—I told you that in the opening—and being on the wrong side of the road. And the evidence by Placide, I think, was quite clear that he pled not guilty and then he did get a lawyer, and he decided to plead guilty because of the time and the money, but that he did not—he told you this—he did not ever think that he was at fault and even said when asked that he felt he had a clear conscience about it.

I think under the circumstances, considering the totality of everything and the fact that a coach was killed, that [the guilty plea] was appropriate under the circumstances and should not be considered as an admission of guilt.

As a matter of fact, the court is going to charge you that merely by pleading guilty to something—because the court understands why these things happen—that that's not conclusive evidence of negligence at all.[16]

In terms of some of the law that the judge is going to charge you, she's going to talk about negligence. Negligence is a fairly fancy word, again, but it just means failure to use that degree of care and skill which an ordinary, reasonable, and prudent person would use under like or similar circumstances. See, I made it fancy again, but I will tell you in simple terms: It means was he doing what most folks would do under the circumstances? Was he acting reasonably?

And I submit to you that based on the evidence in this case, Placide did act reasonably at the time of this incident. In considering whether someone is reasonable, you are allowed under the law to consider the circumstances. Obviously if someone has more time to think about something, then you could say maybe they should have made a different decision because they had more time to think about it. If, for example, I turned around and threw a brick over at Mike Banick and he moved to the right and the brick hit him, you could say, looking back on it, that wasn't a very reasonable thing that he did. But I think under the set of circumstances that I described, that being very quick—it requires a quick response—then I think it's fairly reasonable that he moved to the right. You could argue in retrospect he should have ducked, he should have moved to the left.

The same thing applies here, ladies and gentlemen. Placide had, coming around that curve, very little time to do anything. He did what a professional driver would do: He touched his brakes thinking that he would be able to brake to a halt.

The judge is going to tell you in this case if you find, as Sylvia Thomas said on the stand, that there was no improper driving on the part of Placide Boucher, despite the fact that there's a sad event that occurred, then you cannot return a verdict against him.

She's also going to tell you that if you consider the evidence and find that he was at fault, i.e., that he was negligent, which we vigorously deny, then you still cannot find him responsible for this accident unless you find that his conduct was the proximate cause of the death of James Luck.

I want to talk to you a minute about proximate cause because the court is going to charge you on that subject, and [Judge Evans] is going to give you a long definition which is fairly complicated, but I want to try to put it in simple terms. Proximate cause really means, what was the first event, if you will, that caused this accident? What was the precipitating event? What was it a direct result of? And I submit to you that [this accident] was a direct result of the Tech caravan, and I want you to think of it in terms of dominoes. If you stack up dominoes one by one—and you have seen this before—the first one hits the second one and just rolls on down. In this instance, the first domino was the Tech caravan, which was creating the commotion, and caused that white car, in all probability, to stop, which is the only reason the car should have stopped.

The second event was the white car stopping in the center of the southbound lane for no reason.

So, I submit to you that the proximate cause of this event was not the negligence of Placide Boucher.

And the judge is going to charge you on the law. You are to apply the facts as you see them to the law. The judge will also tell you that just because there is merely a collision on the highway does not imply fault, does not imply negligence, does not imply proximate cause; and that if an event occurs, such as a collision, which is truly an accident caused by the fault of no one, then a recovery should not be allowed in that event.

Damages: A Cecil B. DeMille Production

In terms of the damages which [plaintiff's] counsel so much wants to talk about and show you these fancy charts—I think the photo place would be very proud of this; it's almost become a Cecil B. DeMille production here—and I want to try to put it in its true common sense terms, if you will allow me to.[17]

We are dealing with the value of a life, and it's not without sympathy on the part of the defendants. It's a regrettable, sad event that occurred. I told you in the beginning that he was a good man and he was. It's a sad event that occurred.

The value of a life, though, is not the value of what others thought about James Luck or how many children he had. It was the value of life to him, as his counsel mentioned.

In terms of the damages that are to be considered in connection with the value of the life, the court is going to tell you that you are not to base your judgment—this becomes very important—on mere speculation or conjecture.

Now, counsel for the plaintiff tells you that Mr. Luck was in good health. They presented no doctor to that effect. They presented, as you may recall, only [one] witness who testified about his health—who was not a doctor—his son. And as you may remember, his son was the one who did not remember at all, until I pulled teeth to get it, that he had filed a suit against Placide [Boucher] in the Superior Court of DeKalb County.[18]

They [various Georgia Tech employees who testified about people who retire from Tech] talked to you about the age that one would [retire]. Again, I go back to common sense. Let's look at this situation. They use seventy years of age, which is pure conjecture. Only three people, maybe two, maybe four—I don't know—who ever worked at the Tech Athletic Association had ever worked past the age of sixty-five. Most people retire at the age of sixty-five.

As you may remember, the economist [Dr. John Brown] testified at a previous case for a thirty-seven-year-old man that he would work about twenty-five years until about the age of sixty-three, and that's generally the range that people work to, and people retire earlier, sixty-two, sixty-five.

The Tech plan [Mr. Luck's retirement plan], as you may remember, had or would have had, if I recall my figures—and again, I will rely on you—at the age of sixty-five, $222,000. You know that an 11 percent—I didn't calculate it—11 percent is probably something in the range of $23,000 a year that he could stop at the age of sixty-five, and his pool of money there would yield that kind of annual return to him. So, instead of making $53,000 or $56,000 or whatever, he would have that [$23,000] automatically.

Here's an area that requires your judgment as to how long this man would work, but it's understandable that he wouldn't tell people, because nobody tells their boss they want to quit until they quit. [They say] that they plan to remain forever. And the reverse is true, too, when you use your common sense. I don't say to any of the people that work in my office, "We're thinking about letting you go." We just don't do that.

I think the point that needs to be made, in short, is that there's no real evidence that he was going to work to seventy; that most people retire at sixty-five and many retire earlier.

I know and you know—because you are using your common

sense—that there are people seventy-five and older who work, but my point to you in this case is that this was a man who had no children in his home and was earning very good money, and that at the age of sixty-five, it's not unreasonable to assume that he would have decided to cash in his chips, if you will, take it easy, and have more time to do the yard work, the hunting, and the other things that he enjoyed doing.

Pit Bulldog, Hired Gun

I remember telling you at the beginning of the case about the economist, because old John Brown and I, we go back a long way. I believe John was reincarnated possibly as a pit bulldog. I'm not sure—he's chomping at the bit before I could open my mouth. He is, ladies and gentlemen, here for the purpose that I told you to begin with. Let's just call it for what it is. He's a hired gun, pure and simple; $150-an-hour hired gun who tries to come into this courtroom, use figures to put in your mind when you're capable, as counsel stated, to arrive at those figures without the aid of some gun coming into this courtroom. And you could see—I'm not going to comment much on it—you could see and you know that that man could have brought his exhibits into court.

They say that the next level below God is a U.S. District Court Judge, and I assure you that Judge Evans has access to a Xerox machine so that [Dr. Brown] could bring those in and let me look at them and let me examine him about them. And he is the type of witness—and you know it—that if I asked him, isn't it true—during a thunderstorm outside—that it's raining today, I would have trouble getting him to say yes, but he would say, "Well, it didn't rain in three prior days and it's not going to rain tomorrow." He's such a prognosticator.

I think a little bit of him like what they say about stockbrokers: If you're so smart and you know it all, then why aren't you retired?[19]

He used, ladies and gentlemen, a 1 or 2 percent discount figure [for purposes of reducing any award to its present cash value]; I think you remember my asking him that. The judge is going to tell you that the proper discount figure to be used in the State of Georgia is 7 percent, and the higher the discount figure, obviously the lower these numbers would be.

Now, in terms of what [Dr. Brown] said, I would like to comment on just a couple of things and then move on. He told you about [Mr. Luck's anticipated] social security; he told you about [Mr. Luck's anticipated] military pension. He never saw the military pension; he never saw the social security plan. He was giving you testimony on matters that had been supplied to him totally by Mr. Gray. Here's a man who has the ability to get some underlying value on when do people who are sixty-three generally retire; but he didn't bring that book [that I asked him to produce] with him. When does the military pension cut off? "Well, I don't have that information; I don't know that. Mr. Gray didn't give me that information."

I picked at him, I admit—that's why I told you earlier, if you find fault with me, hold it against me—I picked at him about household chores, I sure did, because I thought this man is just stretching these numbers to an absurdity. He's talking about $10 an hour for doing yard work, and he's talking about the loss of that. And I tell you what, I believe that you know from what you heard about James Luck that that man isn't looking for $10 an hour for the yard work he did. I don't think he was that kind of man.

When I asked him about what he relied upon for that, he said he pulled that number out of his head, and then he relied on some data from the U.S. Department of Agriculture which to this moment has not been produced. And I asked him, well, who did they interview? Did they interview 12 farmers? Did they interview 100 farmers? What does the survey consist of? That's reasonable. He doesn't know; he just knows that's a survey that he relies upon. And then when I asked him about another survey from the U.S. Department of Labor Bureau of Statistics that's put out periodically, he didn't agree with that one, but no, he's never called it to their attention.

In short, ladies and gentlemen, you got what I told you you were going to get, and unfortunately it goes on more and more, where paid professionals come over here for high hourly rates—and I hate to say it—but literally prostitute themselves.

Now, in terms of the witnesses that you heard regarding damages, I am not going to go over their testimony, but I would like to make a few comments to you, with the understanding that I'm not attacking Jim Luck—I was raised by parents who said you don't talk about a deceased, but in a court of law you have to. But I don't have anything bad to say about Mr. Luck. But I do wonder why we only heard from a few people from Georgia Tech.

You know, [plaintiff's] counsel mentioned in the beginning of the case, he mentioned something about the University of Georgia, the University of Alabama; we just didn't have anybody out of that close circle of friends of [Mr. Luck's] to come talk about him. And we didn't have anybody to come in and really say that he was a charitable man, or that he was a man who was helping the homeless, or that he was doing good public service work.

What you had in part was Mr. [Matthew] Reeves, the bus driver. You know, this was a man in the caravan. This was a man who was hired by Jim Luck, who told you that during that whole procession from Athens to the point of the accident, the cars were pulling off the road.

I don't know if this caravan was hot-dogging it or what they were doing, but they were going over the speed limit without question.

Counsel would tell you about the charges that were brought against my client, which he's already done, but what I think more importantly needs to be brought out is that [Sergeant Coleman] arrived afterwards. Yes, he interviewed all the witnesses, but he didn't charge Placide [Boucher] with following too close; he didn't charge Placide with reckless driving; he didn't charge him with going faster than is reasonable under the circumstances. These are matters for you to consider.[20]

The original lawsuit in this case, as I mentioned to you, was brought by Mrs. Luck, and in that suit the *ad damnum*—that's the amount they are asking for—was $6 million. Then we get into court and counsel [Mr. White] tells you in opening statement that now they are looking for $2.5 to $3.7 million, and I suggest to you that under the old school of plaintiff's law that you ask for about ten times more than you want.

And I want to comment a minute on the economist's figure, because I think that figure becomes fairly important. You know, I could sit here and tell you what this case is worth, but I find that a bit repulsive—that's probably too strong—I find it a bit annoying, because that's your job. My job is not to tell you what it's worth. If we were going to tell you what it's worth, we could just ask Judge Evans; we wouldn't need you folks down here. That's your job to determine liability, proximate cause, negligence, and damages, if any.[21]

The Power of Earning Interest

But I would like to comment on the economist, because it shows the power of earning interest on money. It's fairly simple—I think my kids would understand it; I don't mean to be presumptuous or arrogant when I say that—but it is the multiplication of money based on interest.

We used 10 percent, but actually Tech [the Tech pension fund], where [Mr. Luck] had such a close relationship, [offered] 10.9. If you take $300,000 and you put it in at the Tech Mass Mutual Fund at 10 percent, that fund will yield $30,000 each and every year until kingdom come. And if that's your money, when you die, that $300,000 is still there. And if you leave that money in there—I think we said 10 percent for fifteen years—I thought it was sort of interesting because [Dr. Brown] wasn't using his calculator properly—he said it was nine and a half million. I said, nine and a half million? He finally said, no, $950,000. That's what it would be: $950,000 plus $300,000 would be over a million dollars.

Let me just make two or three final points, and I'm going to sit down, because after that the ball is in your court.

The first point I would like to make is in mentioning the burden of proof, you may have wondered why counsel for plaintiff got the first strike when we struck jurors and why counsel for plaintiff gets to go up to you first at the beginning of the case and go first, and you may wonder why is it when Mr. Fine sits down that they get to go again. I mean, that's not fair in a way; I don't get to stand back up and tell you what I would like to say after Mr. White or Mr. Gray gets back up here and sort of slam-dunk me a little bit. I can't get back up and say anything. The reason is because they have the burden of proof. So, this is my last opportunity to talk to you, and I want to be sure that I do it in a proper manner for my client and with respect to the court.

I mentioned to you a minute ago about Mr. Luck and I told you, I don't believe Mr. Luck would be looking for any money for household work he did. That was something that apparently he liked to do. I don't believe that he would have really liked his Purple Heart being paraded around. Unfortunately, there are too many of those given out by our country. I don't think he would take great pride in the production of showing you those medals. Those kinds of things, as well as the charts and the blowups and the bringing in of the bulldog [Dr. Brown], were to try to get you to have sympathy for the plaintiff, try to build up some sort of bias against the defendants.

And what I ask in this case is what you told the court in the beginning: that you would be fair to both parties, that you would treat the corporate defendant, the insurance company, and Placide with the same degree of fairness that you treat Mrs. Luck, to which she's fully entitled; and I don't believe her counsel would tell you anything otherwise.

Your verdict in this case, ladies and gentlemen, must be unanimous. That is, you all must agree to it. And it can't be four and two or three and three. It can't be what's called a quotient verdict. A quotient verdict is where one juror says, for example,

I want to give $100,000, and the other five say no, I just want to give a dollar, and then you total it all together and you divide it by six. I believe you can see the inequity of that. It must be a unanimous verdict.

And the word verdict, ladies and gentlemen, really sums up to a great extent what our law is about. The word verdict means *veredicto*. It comes from Latin. It means to speak the truth. Let your verdict speak the truth; let it be a fair verdict; let it be a reasonable verdict; let it be a sensible verdict, and let it be one upon which you have used your collective common senses.

We appreciate very kindly—and I don't say this to score any points with you—your very close attention—all counsel have talked about it—during the course of this case. I know it takes you away from your family and your homes, and it's not the perfect system, but it's better than what they have in Russia and it's better than what they have in Iran, and I believe, with people like you, it's a system that will allow our country to grow and flourish.

Thank you very much.

Endnotes

*Born in Atlanta in 1944, Lowell S. Fine obtained both his A.B. and LL.B. from the University of Georgia, where he served as student bar association president and research and projects editor of the Georgia Law Review.

1. I'm referring to the plaintiff's initial closing statement, which was given by Mr. Gray. Mr. White made the plaintiff's concluding argument.

2. I made the preceding remarks because I wanted the jurors to know that I was trying to be "fair and square" with them. It had been a long trial—one week—and I wanted to tell the jury that if I made any mistakes during closing, they would not be intentional.

3. I knew that my argument was going to be aggressive, and I didn't want the jury to think that my clients had suggested that I be tough or harsh.

4. With all of the technical charges I expected the judge to give the jury, I thought the case, from the defense's perspective, essentially boiled down to common sense. For example, common sense dictated that if the white

car had not stopped suddenly in front of Boucher, he would not have had to brake at all. Moreover, if the white car had pulled off the road as plaintiff contended, Boucher would merely have continued on his way, and the collision would not have occurred. Thus, it seemed to me that using common sense, the jury could decide that the white car did something other than what plaintiff's lawyers alleged. The plaintiff's argument, of course, was that even if the white car did stop suddenly, the rig should have been following far enough behind it to stop safely.

5. I wanted the jurors to know that the plaintiff's addition of the insurer was another strategy to get them to award more damages than the case warranted. I pursued this theme throughout closing argument.

6. I said that sometimes I represent plaintiffs because opposing counsel said that defense lawyers never concede anything and throw up smoke screens. I thought it might help my case if the jury knew that I was more than just a "hired gun" for the defense.

7. Sylvia L. S. Thomas had been riding behind the Fogleman truck for about thirty minutes before the collision. She said that after the truck jackknifed, she saw the white car stopped in the lane the truck had been driving in. Ms. Thomas's father is a sheriff, her brother is a detective, and her first cousin is a police chief. She said the police cars leading the convoy were flashing their blue lights, and that she did not know whether to pull over. The next witness, Connie Dalton, lived in Carnesville, Georgia, and had never testified before. She testified that she had been following the police convoy for about twenty minutes. She said the convoy "pretty continuously" exceeded the speed limit during that time. She also said that whenever she tried to pass the convoy in a passing lane, the convoy's cars straddled the center line, and she could not get by. Ms. Dalton testified that the white car had slowed but did not stop.

8. I made the "country folks" remark to bring out that these witnesses were simply country people who had come to the big city to tell the truth. They were not enthusiastic about testifying; they simply told the jury everything they saw.

9. Ronald Holcomb was the driver of the white car. We had filed a separate suit against him, which was pending at the time of trial. If he testified, we intended to show that he was biased because of that suit.

10. Here, I reminded the jurors that in voir dire, they made a commitment not to be prejudiced against my clients. The jurors swore that they could return a verdict for the defendants if the evidence showed that the defendants did not cause the accident. I wanted to let the jury know that the judge would charge them that all parties are equal under the law.

11. Mr. Gray objected to the photographs I wanted to show the jury. The photographs were taken several days after the fatal collision. I agreed not to argue that the skid marks shown in the pictures were there the day

of the accident. Rather, I wanted to show the jury the curve in the road. On that basis, Judge Evans overruled the objection.

12. Plaintiff's counsel said that I said it had been raining heavily when the accident happened. I don't recall making that comment. The fact was it had been drizzling.

13. The photographs showed that Boucher had to round a slight curve in the road before he could see the white car stopped. Only one tail light on the white car was working; obviously, if both tail lights had been working, Boucher might have seen the white car stop sooner. Also, the inclement weather interfered with Boucher's view.

14. Mr. Gray objected to my sudden emergency argument. Judge Evans overruled the objection.

15. Sergeant Coleman, who had worked for the Georgia State Patrol for twenty-two years when this case was tried, is the officer who charged Boucher with vehicular homicide and driving on the wrong side of the road. He said that Boucher should have kept his rig at least 168 feet behind the white car. Boucher said that he had been about 70 feet behind the white car.

16. As I stated, Boucher's guilty plea was a difficult problem. It was important to give the jury a plausible explanation for it.

17. It was important to point out that the plaintiff had brought in all kinds of evidence, some of it expensive. Yet the plaintiff did not bring in Mr. Holcomb, the driver of the white car. If Holcomb had merely pulled off the road, as plaintiff contended, the plaintiff would have called him as a witness. I harped on this throughout the case. I wanted the jury to know, in clear terms, that plaintiff's counsel had overinflated the claim.

18. The decedent's son had filed suit against Boucher for funeral expenses only, but he denied this when he testified on cross-examination. That slightly damaged his credibility, I believe. Also, I was trying to get the jury to wonder about the decedent's health, since the plaintiff presented so many witnesses but only the son testified on that issue.

19. I tried to plant a seed of doubt about John Brown's credibility. I felt that he was very aggressive in his figures and in his presentation. Eighty percent of his work had been done for plaintiffs. I felt that he had been arguing with me from the moment I started questioning him. I decided to let him argue so that during closing, I could paint a picture of him as an advocate for the plaintiff. Also, I had asked Dr. Brown during his deposition to furnish me with certain information regarding his testimony. He neither produced it nor brought it to trial. When the court commented that he was "a little late" supplying the information, the jury may have perceived him as less than candid. Certainly, this helped me persuade the jury that Dr. Brown was not simply an unbiased economist from Georgia State University.

20. By my remarks I was trying to drive home the fact that if Sergeant Coleman had really believed that Boucher was driving improperly, he would have charged him with one of the offenses I mentioned.

21. The economist's present cash value figure for the economic value of Mr. Luck's life was between $904,000 and $935,000.

Zachery v. Schneider National Carriers
Nos. 1:87-CV-2104-ODE; 1:88-CV-185-ODE (N.D.Ga)

Result: $23.2 million verdict
Plaintiffs' Counsel: W. Carl Reynolds and Katherine L. McArthur of Reynolds & McArthur (Macon)
Defense Counsel: Robert E. Corry Jr. and R. Clay Porter of Dennis, Corry, Porter & Gray (Atlanta)
Judge: Orinda D. Evans
Date of Verdict: October 3, 1990

Chapter III

Mother and Daughter

Introduction
By W. Carl Reynolds*

In the predawn darkness on a cold winter morning, January 24, 1986, twenty-eight-year-old Laverne N. Zachery set out for work with her two little girls, five-year-old Allyson and three-year-old Kayla. Ms. Zachery secured the children in their seat belts and car seats in the back seat of the car.

At 6:15 A.M., Ms. Zachery made a right turn onto Roosevelt Highway in Fulton County, less than half a mile from where a tractor-trailer was stuck across the road, completely blocking it. The rig's driver, Albert W. Blow, placed no flares, reflectors, or any other type of warning device to alert oncoming vehicles of the hazardous situation. Ms. Zachery apparently did not see the trailer in time to avoid it, and her car slammed into the rig. The force of the impact sheared off the top of the car, killing Ms. Zachery instantly and crushing Allyson's head. Allyson survived but sustained crippling injuries. Kayla survived with only minor injuries because the trailer passed over her head.

Roderick Zachery, Laverne's husband and Allyson's father,

brought a negligence action on Allyson's behalf and individually to recover compensatory and punitive damages as a result of the injuries she sustained in the accident. Mr. Zachery also brought suit individually as next of kin and surviving spouse of Laverne Zachery and as administrator of her estate for her wrongful death.

Albert Blow was the agent and employee of Schneider National Carriers, Inc., and was acting within the scope of that employment at the time of the accident. Schneider National Carriers, Inc., is an ICC carrier and was covered by an insurance policy issued by Truck Insurance Exchange. (Insurers of ICC carriers can be sued directly.) Originally, two separate causes of action were filed, but they were consolidated for trial.

The evidence showed that Albert Blow had tried to make an illegal U-turn on Roosevelt Highway. The two-lane road was too narrow, and the front wheels of the tractor went off the side of the road, leaving the rig perpendicular across the road. At that point, the landing gear, which attached the trailer to the tractor, became impaled in the pavement. Although he had gotten his rig stuck, Blow took no steps to warn oncoming traffic. For five or ten minutes, he completely blocked both lanes of travel while trying to rock the truck loose. The tractor's headlights were at approximately a forty-five-degree angle to the road, facing back toward the direction from which Laverne Zachery was coming. At trial, a bystander, The Rev. R. D. Williams, testified that he told Blow to set out reflective devices to warn oncoming traffic. Williams testified that Blow told him to mind his own business.

Negligence and Damages

Plaintiffs contended that Albert Blow was negligent per se in attempting to make an illegal U-turn, that he was negligent in failing to have proper illumination or to set out warning devices such as flares or reflectors, and that he was grossly negligent in failing to place flares and reflectors after a bystander instructed him to do so.

Defendants contended that Laverne Zachery was contributorily negligent in failing to avoid the collision, and that this contributory negligence was greater than 50 percent of the cause of the accident, precluding recovery for her death. The defendants admitted liability for Allyson Zachery's injuries since they were responsible for her claims if they were found even 1 percent responsible for her injuries.

Plaintiffs sought damages for the full value of Laverne Zachery's life. She had been a factory worker in a canvas sewing company and was being trained to become a supervisor. She was a very active worker in her church. She had a beautiful singing voice and was the lead singer in her family's gospel singing group, which performed regularly at religious events and weddings. She was a loving wife and wonderful mother to her two children. Plaintiffs sought $3 million to $5 million for the value of her life. Because Laverne Zachery was killed instantly, plaintiffs did not seek damages for pain and suffering or loss of consortium. Her funeral and burial expenses were $4,393.10. The jury awarded $10 million in compensatory damages for the full value of her life.

Allyson Zachery suffered a severe, crushing brain injury and crippling leg injuries. Dr. Dale Richardson, her treating neurosurgeon, testified that Allyson would have a permanent mental age of four to five years old and an I.Q. of 47, which is in the mild to moderately retarded range. Allyson will be totally dependent on others for the rest of her life and will require group home care. She does not, however, have a diminished life expectancy.

Plaintiffs sought recovery for past medical bills totalling $130,821 and future medical bills in the amount of $35,000 because of two anticipated surgeries to Allyson's legs and two to her eyes. Past and future child care sought totaled $72,500. After being reduced to present value, her future group home care cost was estimated at $1,517,418 and her future lost income was estimated at $510,484. Total special damages sought for Allyson were $2,266,223. The jury awarded her $8.2 million in compensatory damages and $5 million in punitive damages.

The Result

The defendants moved for a new trial. Judge Evans granted the motion as to damages on the wrongful death claim, ruling that the award of more than ten times Ms. Zachery's future lost earnings was excessive.

Judge Evans also ruled that the court's charge to the jury on the wrongful death claim erroneously permitted the plaintiff to recover for the "intangible elements" of Ms. Zachery's life. This is an opinion which is contrary to the Georgia wrongful death statute, O.C.G.A. § 51-4-1 *et seq.*, and Georgia caselaw—see, e.g., *Consolidated Freightways Corp. of Delaware v. Futrell*, 201 Ga.App. 233 (410 SE2d 751) (1991). It is an opinion, to my knowledge, held only by Judge Evans. The "intangible elements" referenced certainly embody what is meant by the "full value" of the life of the decedent. To exclude intangible elements, meaning the enjoyment of life, would reduce the meaning of the statute to a recovery for only the economic value of the decedent, rather than as it is intended, which is for the full value of the life lost. There is no right of appeal from the grant of a new trial by the trial judge, but obviously this opinion held by Judge Evans would affect our decision concerning settlement at a later time.

Next, the court held that the compensatory damages awarded to Allyson were excessive. Subtracting out the special damages, the court determined that the jury had awarded Allyson $6 million for pain and suffering. Considering that Allyson was in a coma for two months after the wreck, the court stated, she was unaware of the pain associated with her surgeries. Thus, the court also granted a new trial as to damages on Allyson's personal injury claim.

The court's ruling ignores the fact that Allyson sustained a crushing brain injury that left her significantly and permanently impaired mentally and physically. The undisputed evidence was that she would never function mentally or emotionally at more than five years of age. She was blinded in her right eye, permanently disfigured, lost her depth perception, and also had crippling injuries to her right leg, foot, and ankle, which left her unable to walk without dragging her right foot some three years post-accident. This is still the case as of March 1994, when this chapter was completed. Her physical and mental pain, past, present, and future, is self-evident and readily observable.

Additionally, her fight to recover from these devastating injuries and the great pain associated with them from a physical, mental, and emotional perspective were testified to by treating physicians, school teachers, rehabilitation workers, and family. The further evidence was that Allyson would never be able to live independently, would never be able to have a husband or family, and would only be able to "work" in a sheltered workshop environment. She has a 90 percent chance of developing epilepsy.

Next, the court ruled that a new trial was warranted on the punitive damages claim due to newly discovered evidence. After the trial, the defendants located Selby Johnson, a coworker of Mr. Williams who apparently was prepared to testify that he and Mr. Williams witnessed the wreck together and that Mr. Williams did not speak to Albert Blow beforehand.

Finally, the court ruled that certain comments I made in closing were improper. Although Mr. Corry did not object contemporaneously to my remarks, the court stated that the "stonewalling" portion (see p. 53) was prejudicial and entitled the defendants to a new trial on damages.

The cases were settled after the second day of retrial for lump sums and structured settlements for Roderick Zachery, Allyson Zachery, and Kayla Zachery, which paid out in excess of $17 million and had a present value of $7.5 million.

Trial Strategy

It was particularly important to make the jury focus on the fact that two suits were involved—the mother's and the child's. The standard of proof and the amount of damages sought were different for each case. Liability was admitted in Allyson's case, so the only issue was damages—general, special, and punitive. The defendants contested liability for Laverne Zachery's death. Thus, we had to make the jury understand that in order for her family to recover for the full value of her life, the jury had to find that the trucking company was at least 51 percent negligent in causing the accident, and then reduce the damages by any percentage that Laverne Zachery was negligent. However, we had to make it clear that since liability was not an issue in Allyson's case, her damages should not be affected by any negligence on her mother's part. These factors made the *Zachery* argument especially challenging.

We approached the case in a three-pronged manner. First, we put up evidence on liability. Second, we established the value of the loss of Laverne Zachery's life. To create a portrait of her life, we called as witnesses her family, friends, co-workers, and other acquaintances. Third, we proved Allyson's damages by having her testify and demonstrate some of her physical disabilities. We showed several films of her that cataloged her recovery from the accident through trial.

Allyson's treating physicians, school teachers, and rehabilitation workers testified on her behalf. Moreover, her younger sister, Kayla, who was seven years old when this case was tried, was called as a witness. The comparison between the sisters' testimony dramatically showed how much Allyson had fallen behind. The jury saw that it was heartbreaking for Allyson, who was nine years old at trial, to be surpassed, physically and intellectually, by her little sister. Undisputed testimony indicated that Allyson would remain at the mental age of five for the rest of her life.

No specific amount of damages was requested until closing argument. During voir dire, we did let the jurors know that we would be seeking a tremendous amount of money, and we asked them to let us know if they felt unable to consider awarding sums over a million dollars if the evidence warranted it. In dealing with damages in the opening statement, we do not get into the general damages which ultimately will be requested in the closing argument. However, we do set forth in great detail special damages which the evidence will support, both as to past and future medical bills, as well as past and future wages, so that they will serve as a foundation at a later point in the trial to argue general damages. We waited until the jury saw and heard all the evidence and testimony before we asked for a particular amount. Even then, as illustrated by the closing argument, we suggested a range of possible awards rather than tell the jury what we thought was an adequate verdict. This avoided offending the jury, which otherwise might have presumed that we were trying to usurp its decision-making role.

The Defendants' Evidence

The defense had very little to offer on the damages issues and chose instead to cross-examine the plaintiffs' witnesses. Concerning liability, the defense was limited to the testimony of one witness, who said that he had been able to see the truck and avoid it. However, it was established that this witness was probably standing in front of the only light on the trailer that would have been visible to Ms. Zachery.

Albert Blow, the driver, could not be located and therefore was not a defendant at trial. The statement he gave to the insurer within forty-eight hours after the accident was ruled inadmissible.

Other defense witnesses testified about lighting conditions, distances from certain points, and visibility, but they had nothing to say about damages or exactly what Ms. Zachery saw.

Opening Argument

MR. REYNOLDS: May it please the court, Mr. Corry, Mr. Porter, Mr. Lester [Schneider National Carriers, Inc.'s representative], and ladies and gentlemen of the jury, good morning to you.

We are now almost at the end of what has been a long trial. I am going to summarize plaintiffs' case in approximately forty-five minutes. I will address you initially, and then Mr. Porter or Mr. Corry will have the opportunity to respond, and then I will respond to their response.

Now, I guess the best place for me to start is to tell you what closing argument is all about. To the extent that I can, I would like to help you put this case or these two cases in some focus or perspective. I don't presume to supplant your judgment with my judgment, your response or reaction to what you have seen and heard with mine, but merely to try to bring it into focus and to comment on some of the evidence and some of the issues that you will have to decide.

Now, ours is an adversarial form of justice. Everybody has a role in the trial of this case and in the administration of justice for these people. Our role is adversarial in nature. We represent Mr. Zachery, and we represent Allyson, and we represent Laverne, although she is not here.

Mr. Corry and Mr. Porter represent Schneider National Truck Carriers, Inc., and National Truck Insurance Exchange, and they present their side of the case.

Her honor, Judge Evans, is here to make sure that what we say and do for you all is within the confines of the evidentiary laws of this state.

Your role is to hear the evidence, to determine what the facts have been, and then to make a verdict after you have heard the entire case, the arguments of counsel, and instructions as to the law from the court.

Now, to open, we begin this case with a complaint, a complaint filed in this court by Allyson Zachery for her personal injuries and by Laverne Zachery through Mr. Zachery for her wrongful death. And they allege that the defendant Schneider National Carriers, Inc., was negligent in the operation of their business, and that negligence caused them to be injured on the one hand and to be killed on the other. As a result of that, [plaintiffs] claim they are entitled to damages, damages for the wrongful death and damages for the personal injuries.

Schneider National Carriers, Inc., denied [liability] originally, and then more recently, after we got here to court, and within, I guess, a year ago in the pretrial order, they have admitted liability as to Allyson Zachery. So, as to her, your only concern is a question of damages. They still deny liability as to Laverne Zachery. So that places upon us a burden of proving to you Laverne's case as to liability.

Now, we have certain bases for offering this proposition to you; that is, that they are responsible for Laverne's death. One, they were negligent in the operation of their tractor-trailer. That negligence can be seen by exactly what they did—they being the trucking company of which Mr. Blow [the truck driver] is no longer a part.

Schneider National Carriers, Inc., is responsible for anything and everything Mr. Blow did or didn't do. On that morning of January 24, 1986, he attempted to make an illegal U turn at a point where he couldn't make a U-turn. That's negligence in the attempt to do something that anybody who is a truck driver ought to have known couldn't have been done to start with. It's also negligence per se in that it is against the law to turn around like that as testified to by the police officer [O.C.G.A. § 40-6-121].

That negligence was further compounded by the fact that the law requires that upon a truck being disabled on the traveled portion of a roadway, the driver not "may" but "shall" turn on his emergency flashers [ICC Reg. 392.22 and O.C.G.A. § 40-8-28 (b)]. I don't recall any testimony about his emergency flashers being on. "He shall as soon as is practicable and as soon as possible, but in no event more than 10 minutes, put out reflectors." Her honor will charge you as to where those reflectors have to be put.

Now, that's the basis for this claim as to the damages for the wrongful death of Laverne Zachery, that is, the negligence, common law negligence. What does that mean? In its simplest form, it means carelessness. The carelessness of that truck operator and/or his company in the operation of the truck set a scene out there that morning that was designed to lead to the death of this lady.

There is one additional claim made by the plaintiffs, and that is that that conduct that morning went beyond just ordinary negligence, just ordinary carelessness. Her honor will charge you about that. That's a duty that we all have to each other to conduct ourselves so as not to do harm to anybody. We all have that. Sometimes we fail in it, and that basically is what negligence is, carelessness. When it causes an injury, then you have to be responsible for that injury, and the responsibility portion is liability.

"Mind Your Own Business"

Now, there is an additional theory under which the plaintiffs are seeking to recover, and that is that the conduct that morning by the driver was so utterly lacking in any care or concern or regard for the safety of other people on the highway that it amounted to all but willful and wanton conduct, that it was so lacking in care for the other motorists on the roadway that it rose to the level of a conscious disregard. And it was that conscious disregard for the safety of other people on the roadway, i.e., Laverne Zachery and Allyson Zachery, that led to this tragic death and the tragic and catastrophic injury to this dear child. That negligence was aggravated to the point that it authorizes you to return a verdict of punitive damages, punitive damages to deter this company from lax conduct in the future.

Now, the punitive damages aspect of this case applies only to Allyson Zachery. It does not apply to Laverne Zachery.

Laverne Zachery's claim is for the full value of her life, and we will talk about that in a minute. [The defendants] contest that, as to whether they are responsible or whether they were negligent and their negligence caused the death of Laverne Zachery.

They admit liability, or they admit responsibility, for everything that Allyson Zachery has had happen to her and that she will have to go through in the future—that is, as to the negligence and the liability and the damages that are authorized for Allyson Zachery. But they certainly do not admit the punitive damages that would be authorized in Allyson Zachery's case.

In order for you to make an award of punitive damages, you have to find that the conduct was aggravated, that what the driver did—or more importantly in this case, what he failed to do—was egregious, that it was an utter disregard for the safety of others. What facts do we look to to establish that? We all come down squarely upon the shoulders of Reverend Williams [the witness who was working near the scene of the accident].

We start off with the police officer, Officer David Reed. He came up, and what was the first thing he said he asked Mr. Blow? Where are your reflectors? Everybody knows that if you have a disabled vehicle and it is on the traveled portion of the roadway, or even if it is off the traveled portion of the roadway, you put out reflectorized warning signals to keep people from hitting you.

Officer Reed never got a satisfactory answer.

Then we heard from Reverend Williams—who came up before anything happened that morning. He got to work at what, 5:30 or 6:00 o'clock. Selby Johnson [Williams's co-worker] was there. They heard the motor revving up, and they went over to investigate.

Reverend Williams said he walked up to the tractor-trailer—and here is a man who drives tractor-trailers for a living, he trains truck drivers—and the very first thing [Williams] said to [Blow] was, "You need to get out and put reflectors out. You need to get out and protect this vehicle, and secure it, and protect the public. Somebody is going to have an awful accident."

Then the driver for whatever reason—and we don't know, he is not here to testify before you, and neither has whoever was out there that same morning investigating for Schneider been here—he says, "Mind your own business."

Reverend Williams persisted in talking to him, and said, "What you are doing you can't do. You can't get that truck unstuck. There's going to be a bad accident out here if you don't go get some reflectors and put them out."

Well, it escalated according to Reverend Williams. They finally got into an argument. [Williams] said, "I will call you a wrecker. You need to get out and put the reflectors out." And finally what did the driver say to him? "You go mind your own damn business. You go mind your own damn business. I'm handling this situation."

And Reverend Williams and Mr. Selby Johnson walked off scratching their heads in consternation as to why somebody who held himself out to be a professional truck driver would take such a totally nonunderstandable position. They walked up on this hill and they stood there, and they looked back, and they were talking with each other about it, wondering why in the world wouldn't he do that? Something bad is going to happen.

Reverend Williams said as they were walking off, he heard a car or maybe two cars, tires squealing as they swerved to the right to miss the truck, and he got up there and stopped. And then in a little while he said he saw what turned out to be the Zachery vehicle come along. And what did he say spontaneously standing there on the bank? He said, "Oh my God, it's going to hit." He said, "I saw it because of the speed, lights, proximity to the truck. I knew it was going to hit." And it did hit, and he saw it come out the other side.

He went running down there to see what had happened. Ms.

Zachery was dead. He put his coat over one of the children, and you recall Reverend Williams—I mean he was a pretty intense man about what he was doing. He was mad about the fact they wouldn't put out the reflectors. He was mad about the fact of what he had predicted happening coming true. But he went running down there, and he saw what the situation was. He obviously could do nothing but put a coat around the little girl [Allyson] and go running off to call an ambulance.

Now, [the defendants] said earlier in this trial they were going to bring a witness in here to refute all that, and that witness was going to be Mr. Lawrence Lamar [a passerby who stopped and was standing at the center line helping Mr. Blow rock the truck]. Mr. Lamar came in, and he started out and sounded pretty good for the defense. [He said] that he could see the truck over a mile away, that he was there for what—four or five minutes—that they talked, and they did this and they did that, and then the Zachery vehicle hit.

And he was standing right there, and he never saw any reflection of light?

Now, that was after nearly four years and after he talked at length with the representatives of Schneider National Trucking Company. But you can make Mr. Lawrence Lamar's testimony and Reverend Williams's testimony reconcile and fit if you look at the big picture and disregard what Mr. Lamar's memory tells him four years later.[1]

You look back at what his sworn testimony was within three weeks of when this tragedy occurred. What was it he said? He said as he approached there, he didn't see the truck until he was but three hundred feet away from it—whether it was this [showing a picture of the accident scene] with headlights and flashbulbs shining on it, or whether it was this [showing a re-enactment trying to depict light conditions at the scene], and this picture was made in January of 1990. I've got no idea whether it represents what it looked like in 1986, but it's still pretty dark.

And it ties in exactly with what Mr. [John] Cerny [plaintiff's engineer] said about the fact that it's just a known phenomenon that in the nighttime your vision is degraded, your perception is degraded, and you don't expect to see something there, and you just simply don't see it; and that there were six hundred traffic deaths in the last year from underride collisions at night with vehicles with headlights on running up and under tractor-trailer trucks, six hundred deaths. That doesn't count the ones that were near misses or only injuries, and there are zero—zero—in the daytime. Do you remember that testimony?

Now, that tells you exactly why the law requires that the driver as soon as possible get out and place reflectors out to warn the motoring public. And in this case, this man—I presume he was well trained. I presume that Schneider has some kind of training program for their drivers, and I presume that Schneider gives them the proper equipment to put in their trucks. I have to presume that he had the flares, the reflectors in the truck. I don't know that. Nobody has been here to testify about it. He simply refused even in the face of somebody's urging. It wasn't just that the law required it. In the face of somebody urging him to do what was needed to protect the public, he made a conscious decision and said no!

Now, why would he say no? Either he didn't have reflectors in there, which would fall back on Schneider National Carriers, Inc.—and again, we know, don't we, from Mr. Lamar, that they [Mr. Corry and an investigator/adjuster from Schneider and Truck Insurance Exchange] were out there within four hours of this tragedy. Before this woman was cold in her grave, they were out there investigating this wreck. We know that, don't we, because that's when they started talking to Mr. Lawrence Lamar about what he could say about it.

And they have introduced the bill of lading showing Mr. Blow should be over at someplace called Surefine Drive by 7:00 A.M. This wreck happened at what, 6:20 or 6:30. Maybe he felt it was more important to do whatever he needed to do to get unstuck to get his load delivered than to protect the motoring public who might be maimed and injured and killed by his failure to get out and do what the law told him to do and what a man [Williams] with God-given common sense who trains truck drivers walked up and also told him to do. That's the basis for the claim for punitive damages. And those damages, the law will tell you and her honor will tell you, are designed to deter this company from that kind of conduct.

Stonewalling

What have we heard here in terms of what Schneider did or didn't do with regard to the training of their drivers, or the hiring of their drivers, or the equipment they placed in the truck? You know what we have heard. We have heard zero! We have heard absolutely zero! It's what is called stonewalling.

It reminds me back during the days of Dick Nixon. I can hear it now: "Boys, they have caught us. They have caught us breaking in Watergate, and they have caught us lying about it."

"What are we going to do, Chief?"

"We will stonewall them. We just won't say anything because no matter what they think, it won't be as bad as what they would think if they knew what we did."

That's a stonewall defense, and that's the only justification for a stonewall defense. I submit to you that's what you have seen here today.[2]

I wouldn't draw that inference, and I wouldn't presume to suggest that but for the fact that we learned from Mr. Lawrence Lamar that these people were on that scene within four hours of the event. And don't you know they were examining the truck and the equipment in it, and talking to the driver, and measuring and looking at the distances and the sight views. And I submit they were probably out there on an evening or a morning a lot earlier than January 1990, too, but that's what you have got. You've got a disabled truck creating a roadblock that constitutes a dangerous hazard to the motoring public on a busily traveled highway, and a man who refuses—even when he is asked to do so—to put out a warning to the public.

Now, what about reconciling Mr. Lamar's testimony with Reverend Williams's? Mr. Lamar didn't realize quite that he was doing it when he came up here, but remember what he said? This is the best that they could do in 1990 at eight o'clock at night to show you existing light. But even taking it as that dark, what have you got that Ms. Zachery was looking at? [Displaying another reenactment photo to demonstrate available lighting conditions,] way down here a truck across the road with the tractor turned at a forty-five-degree angle back this way. So, she has got lights over here from the tractor on the one hand. Mr. Lawrence Lamar is standing here. He put himself right squarely over the only light on the body of the truck. He had only seen it himself from three hundred feet away according to his sworn testimony. He had only been there a scant forty-five seconds when this thing happened.

As he stood there, he said, cars came up from the other side, and [he said] that the undercarriage of this truck is about right here [higher than the height of the headlight beams]. Well, you know how high a car's headlights are. If there were automobiles coming up from the other side, their lights would have been shining under that truck straight in the direction from which Ms. Zachery was coming. So, you've got oncoming headlights that are lower than the carriage of the truck. You've got the truck's headlights. You've got the sign over here, and there are two other signs that are billboard signs right here.

So, what did she perceive? We don't know. She may have seen the truck and perceived it as another billboard sign. She may not have seen it at all. One thing is for certain. You have heard described that she wasn't the type of woman headed down there for suicide. So, for whatever reason, she didn't see it. But she would have seen it if they had put out the triangle reflectors that are required by the law. And that's why punitive damages are applicable in this case and [why] you need to make an award of punitive damages that will get their attention and make them understand that that simply will not be tolerated, that kind of conduct.

A Wonderful, Beautiful Woman

Now, we have heard from Ms. Zachery's friends, pastor, and family. They have all described her as a wonderful and beautiful woman, and your role here is to decide what was the value of her life. You heard from an economist. You've heard that she would have earned over the course of her life, giving her the benefit of the doubt to age sixty-five, $719,000. That's only one component part of the value of her life, and it's not by any stretch of the imagination the full value of her life.

You have two things to remember about that. One is when you project lost future income, the law says you reduce it to present cash value. That's why we went through that process with Dr. [Bruce] Seaman [plaintiff's economist], and that's only a small component part of the value of her life.

The value of her life is derived from what was the quality of her life and enjoyment of her life to her. She was a friend, a mother, a wife, a Christian, a gifted singer. She brought joy to other people, she brought happiness to other people, and she lost those things you need in life. She enjoyed giving comfort to her daughters, seeing her daughters grow up, seeing them get married. All those things are elements of the value of her life.

We projected her earnings out to the rest of her life and reduce them to their present cash value of $719,790. As to the value of the lady, you don't reduce that. You put a number there that will reflect the value of her life. You use your own judgment and your own evaluation process for what you put in there.

We have got her leisure hours. That's meaningless other than to give you some idea of the fact that this is how many hours nonworking and nonsleeping she would have had. Any number you write in there should reflect what you evaluate her life to be. I would submit to you that it's in multiples of a million dollars. Whether you evaluate her life at three times what she might have earned, or whether you fix a figure in the range of three to five to seven million dollars, that's entirely up to you. You've read about race horses that are sold every day for more than that. I submit her life is more valuable than the finest blooded racehorse that ever ran around the track, but you have to decide that.

Damages for Allyson

You also will consider the matter of damages as to Allyson Zachery. As a starting point, Allyson Zachery will have these numbers, and they are taken basically from these figures that Dr. Seaman wrote up there [on the blackboard], and they are also taken from some of Ms. [Susan] Bradley's [Allyson's teacher] testimony that she will always have to have care.

She has got $130,821 in past medical expenses. There's $25,000 additional surgery required on her legs or on her ankles. Those are the two surgical procedures that were described, and it may be as much as 50 percent more than that by the time she is twelve. [There's] $10,000 worth of surgery to her eyes. That's in the future. That's for the drooping eyelid and also to alter the muscles so they will both go straight.

Twenty-three thousand nine hundred dollars is what Mr. Zachery has paid out from the date of the wreck until now in child care, $450 a month. Forty-eight thousand six hundred dollars is what he will pay out at the same rate if he keeps it at that from now until the time that [Allyson] goes to where Susan Bradley says she must go for her benefit, and that is into a group home with her peer group.

When she goes into that group home with her peer group, using the figure they gave now, projecting it out nine years and then going out to the total of her life—which is calculated based on mortality tables—is $1,570,418.

Future lost income if you give her the benefit of being a college graduate would be $510,484. If you don't give her the benefit of being a college graduate, it would be $283,602. I say I would give her the benefit of being a college graduate. You heard Mr. Zachery's testimony that they intended to send her and Kayla to college. That was a very important goal for them.

Her total damages—real numbers—are $2,266,223. Ladies and gentlemen, that's the starting point with Allyson. That's the starting point. That's not the finish point because this only takes care of her in the state she has been reduced to. You've got to calculate these things in your heart and your mind and your conscience. What is it worth to her? What is the value of the physical [suffering]—past, present, and future? She has got a crushed brain. She is blind in her right eye. She has no depth perception in her left eye. She is crippled and deformed. She drags her right foot when she walks. She is disfigured.

What about the mental suffering? She is retarded now. She has an I.Q. of 47. She will never enjoy the things that the rest of us enjoy. She is totally dependent. She is permanently trapped in the mind of a four- to five-year-old. She has a 90 percent certainty of being an epileptic. She has got enough intelligence that she wants to have approval from others, and when she sees them laughing at her, she continues to try to get them to [laugh] so she can have that friendship and warmth. But she has enough perception to know at some point that they are laughing at her, and it hurts her feelings.

She has lost the joy of her life. She has suffered pain like we don't even know exists, and you have to put a value on that.

They are going to talk to you in just a minute. I would invite [the defendants] to go over this list and put a number by each one of those things. I submit to you that you can't put too much money on there, and I don't want to offend you. I want you to respond [with] what you think is appropriate. You bring into this jury box your own background and experiences. I will tell you this. If you are looking at the whole value, you can't imagine less than six to eight to ten million dollars on those items because your function is not to determine what she needs or what is fair to the other side as to the damages, but to evaluate the loss. And you take each element and put it on there. As to the general damages within that framework, six to eight to ten million dollars, you decide what you think is the value of the crippling, catastrophic injuries she has sustained.

As to the punitive damages, you write a figure in there that will get the attention of Schneider National Carriers, Inc., and let them know what you think about their stonewall defense. They could have brought anybody in here they wanted to. They could have brought an economist in here to refute these figures if they were wrong. They could have brought an engineer in here to refute Mr. Cerny's statements. They could have brought their investigator that was out there on the morning of the wreck. They didn't bring anybody.

You write that in multiples of millions so they will know what this community thinks about that kind of conduct. And that's all you have got to be concerned about, not just that it speaks the truth, but this is your jury reaction to what they failed to do out there that morning.[3]

That's all we have at this time, your honor.

Concluding Argument

MR. REYNOLDS: I will try to be brief in summarizing, ladies and gentlemen. Let me respond to a couple of things Mr. Corry said. First of all, I didn't compare him to Mr. Nixon. I compared the defense with that. He's a man paid to do what he does, and certainly they have got a right to hire a lawyer to go out there and start investigating as soon as he can. He did his job, and I'm sure he did it well. I meant no personal criticism of him.

Also, as to this business of the future value of money, when I was going to high school, I could go to the movies and get a bag of popcorn and drink a Coca-Cola for twenty cents. I went the other night and it was almost twenty dollars. What he is talking about is present-day dollars thirty years from now and sixty years from now.

One of my bosses in the Army was a colonel. He was tickled to death after his thirty years that he might be able to retire at $1,000 a month, but that was in 1965. What would that $1,000 a month do him in the way of good now in 1990? Very little.

In terms of this child's needs, she is looking at these numbers that we have given you.

Let me just say a word or two about the general principles we are dealing with here. Mr. Corry has very persuasively asked you to consider your verdict and be fair to the defendant. The amount of your verdict in fairness to the defendant doesn't have any real connection or application. You have a responsibility to be fair to this defendant in deciding whether or not they caused the death of this lady and the catastrophic injury to this child, and whether or not the facts justify punitive damages. But in terms of what is the value to be placed on the injury to the child and the death of the woman, fairness has no application in the context of toward the defendant.

What your job is today and what your duty is today is—once you decide the facts warrant a verdict for the plaintiff Laverne Zachery, your role and your legal duty then is to evaluate her life. Once you decide that the facts and the evidence warrant a verdict for that child out there, your legal duty and your legal responsibility is to assess damages, to evaluate the damages and to award the damages based on the loss, not on a misplaced sense of fairness to the defendant. It's simply what is lost by her, and is it compensable in money damages?

You say money won't bring back an eye. And, yes, a brain is a terrible thing to waste, and money won't bring it back, and the enjoyment of life is priceless, but they can't capitalize on that and say because it is a priceless thing you can't make an award, because your job and your responsibility is to price it, to evaluate it, and to evaluate it in the real world, not in the world of Mr. Corry as Mr. Corry would have it. He would even suggest to you that a million dollars would compensate this child to be imprisoned in the mind of a four- to five-year-old person for the rest of her life, who can't even tend to her own bowel habits, to be reduced from bright and quick and energetic and alert to having an I.Q. of 47—a million dollars is what he says.

I say you start here [$2,266,225]. That's the value. The basis of the verdict is the value of what is taken. This is what real dollars are in the context of Allyson Zachery. You can remember them. Medical bills, future medical bills, surgery, crippled ankles, fused ankles, blind eye, half a brain, group home care of $1,517,000. You start at $2,266,225, and then you consider what is the value of these things to have her body altered, her mind altered. What is the value?

I offered a suggestion. I said six million, four million, eight million, ten million. I won't tell you what to put on this. You have to do that. That's your responsibility and your duty, to place a monetary value on it. That's the atonement for the wrong that was done, for the negligence that caused it. They say they admit their responsibility for it, but they don't tell you what it is they want to pay for it. This is what they are bound and legally obliged to pay once they admit that responsibility, these things right here.

Now, as to Laverne Zachery, again he would suggest to you that that dear lady's life has a value of $200,000. Ladies and gentlemen, we are not talking about need here. That has no more place in the value of this case than fairness to this defendant that caused the death. It's the value of her life. She would have made $721,000 even given the "racial discount."[4]

Where do you begin to value a life? I can't make it easy for you. I can't give you a formula. All I can say is that life is precious, and her life was precious to her, and the rights and the things that she lost were precious to her, and that's how you value her life. She wasn't a tramp walking down the railroad track. She could earn that money, and she could do something else. She could sing. She could be a friend, a mother. She could create love and happiness. That has a monetary value, and I can't make your job easy, and I may be wrong. You may not agree with me that three or five million dollars is an appropriate number for that life. But I'll tell you this: Go from what you heard about her in this courtroom. I didn't know her, but I will go with what your value is. I will put my faith in this jury as to what value you place on her.

If you want to discount it [attribute some percentage of negligence to Laverne Zachery and thereby reduce the damages]—I don't know what Laverne did out there. Maybe she had to correct Allyson. "Leave your sister alone." Maybe that's what put her in that statistical category that is going to have an underride collision if you don't protect the people by putting out reflectors and making sure people don't run into your truck. I don't know why she didn't see it, but if you want to give some discount, figure the full value of the woman's inestimable worth, and discount it 10 percent for what her own contribution might have been, which has not been proven by anybody.

Priceless is a Copout

Now, that's your function, ladies and gentlemen. Mr. Zachery is not here looking for sympathy, and neither is Allyson. They are not here with their hands out looking for sympathy, and they are not entitled to it. They are here looking for just and fair compensation for what has been taken away, and your job, difficult as it may be, is to evaluate those losses. And it's simply a copout for the defense to say, it's priceless; therefore, let's be reasonable, and figure 9 percent—because $90,000 by the time this child is seventy-nine years old will be worthless.

Punitive damages—I'm suggesting the numbers to put some idea in your mind. In terms of Allyson, we have got $2.2 million, and then you've got the value of the losses, and you take each of these component parts. They don't have anything to do with her needs. They have a value. What is a mind worth? What is health and mobility and coordination worth? You decide that. I suggest it's six to eight to ten million dollars. That's my reaction to it. You use your judgment, but the basis is not her need or some sense of fairness to them. The basis is the dollar value of this catastrophic injury. What did [Allyson's neurosurgeon] Dr. [Dale] Richardson say? The worst injury a human brain could sustain and still live. And, yes, she does appear happy sometimes because what was done to her was the same as a frontal lobotomy. Mr. Corry says it's worth a million dollars. I reject that.

You put a value on that. Give her what it will cost to maintain and sustain her in her crippled state, mind and body, the rest of her life, which is $2.2 million plus the number you place as a value on the injuries.

On Laverne Zachery, give her the benefit of having worked to the tune of $720,000 real money projected out and brought back for the duration of her life. And that would be plus the value you put on her life as a human being, a dollar value.

It's not easy, but it's your task. It's your legal duty to do that. Don't let one case be diminished by the fact that you are deciding two cases. This court and these parties have consolidated these cases so that we won't have to have two trials to decide two separate cases, but don't you let the fact that you have got to evaluate a wrongful death, on the one hand, interfere with or affect your deliberating on the value of the catastrophic injuries and the severe disabilities to Allyson, on the other.

THE COURT: Your time is up, Mr. Reynolds.

MR. REYNOLDS: Thank you.

And you can use those to help you determine what would be an appropriate amount of punitive damages.

THE COURT: Thank you.

MR. REYNOLDS: Thank you, Ma'am.

Endnotes

* W. Carl Reynolds was born in Atlanta on September 13, 1940. He attended the University of Georgia and received an A.B. in 1964 from Mercer University. In 1966 Mr. Reynolds earned a J.D. from Mercer University's Walter F. George Law School, and in 1976 he was granted an M.B.A. from Georgia College. He is a member of the State Bars of Florida and Georgia.

1. Mr. Williams said the truck was difficult to see; Lawrence Lamar said he had no difficulty seeing it.

2. Page 26 of Judge Evans's July 9, 1991, order granting a new trial states:

> Plaintiff's counsel's argument concerning the "stonewall" defense [was] highly improper, inflammatory, and prejudicial to the defendants. In the first place, defendants' failure to produce certain evidence at trial had absolutely nothing to do with the punitive damages issue before the jury. Punitive damages had been reserved for the jury's consideration, over defendants' objections, solely on account of the testimony of R. D. Williams, who had testified about the driver's allegedly callous reaction to Williams' suggestion that flares should be put out. The training of defendants' drivers had nothing to do with this matter, as neither plaintiffs nor defendants had introduced any evidence whatsoever on the issue of training or the lack thereof. Similarly, the defendants' failure to produce the testimony of an engineer or an economist was patently irrelevant to the punitive damages issue. Plaintiffs' counsel's suggestion that the jury should punish the defendants because of their alleged indifference to these matters was considerably outside the bounds of proper conduct.

Regrettably, we had no right of direct appeal with which to refute this mistake, but the text of the argument adequately shows that Judge Evans completely misread the transcript. Perhaps mitigating the court's error, the transcript lacks inflections and pauses which reflect changes of subject. It is our opinion that it took a quantum leap for Judge Evans to overturn this verdict. Nothing in the closing argument was objected to by defense counsel, nor was any part of the closing argument interrupted or commented on by the court during the time it was taking place. Still, the transcript in this case and the text, when read objectively and straightforwardly, show that the driver's conduct that morning formed the basis for punitive damages. That conduct is summarized in the argument preceding this endnote, which concludes with the declaration, "That's the basis for punitive damages." As shown in this text, I was changing the subject from the basis for punitive damages to a comment on what was not shown by the evidence, which is always proper in a civil lawsuit. Nothing in the text suggests that the jury should award punitive damages for the defendants' failure to produce evidence, though it is always proper in a civil case to argue the inferences from a failure to produce evidence.

It is also our opinion that it took quite a stretch to call Selby Johnson a "newly discovered witness," inasmuch as he was listed on the accident report and he remained employed at Williams Brothers Concrete Company for several years following the accident. Additionally, after he was introduced in the posttrial motions as a "newly discovered witness," we asked an independent lawyer, who had no connection to the case or any information other than Mr. Johnson's employment application at Williams Brothers, to try to locate him. It took that lawyer three days to find Mr. Johnson. His home address, shown on the employment application, was still the residence of his sister, who directed the lawyer straight to Mr. Johnson. It is also noteworthy that defense counsel located and took an ex parte deposition from Mr. Johnson within a week of the verdict in the original trial.

3. See endnote 2. In the text accompanying endnote 3, the cold transcript lacks the gestures, inflections, and pauses which would have made clear that I was arguing two points simultaneously. First, I argued that the punitive damages award should get the defendants' attention. Then, while the jury is getting their attention, the jury should also make unfavorable inferences from the defendants' failure to produce evidence it had obtained on the morning of the wreck. Since the two arguments are related, I verbally connected the two statements with the word "and." I then returned to the punitive damages award, which was to be based on "that kind of conduct,...what they failed to do out there that morning," not what they failed to produce at trial.

It was clear at the time of the argument that I sought punitive damages based upon the driver's omissions, not on the defensive strategy, so that defense counsel did not find it necessary to object to what otherwise would be improper.

4. This phrase was sarcastic. Plaintiffs were African-American, and the economist used a "racial discount" when projecting lost future earnings.

Newton v. Gray

No. 89-v-446 (Fannin County Super. Ct.)

Result: Defense verdict
Plaintiffs' Counsel: E. Marcus Davis of Davis, Zipperman, Kirschenbaum & Lotito (Atlanta)
Defense Counsel: W. Wray Eckl of Drew, Eckl & Farnham (Atlanta) and Weymon H. Forrester of Forrester & Brim (Gainesville)
Judge: Robert Milam
Date of Verdict: May 16, 1991

Chapter IV

A Tree Falls in the Forest

Introduction
By W. Wray Eckl*

On a cold Saturday morning in February 1988 in Blue Ridge, a small town at the foothills of the Blue Ridge Mountains in north Georgia, the two defendants, Homer Gray, seventy-nine, and Dennis "Toby" Rhodes, in his fifties, went into the woods to cut a dead tree for firewood. It was raining lightly, and later the rain turned to sleet.

The woods were part of a city park. Homer and Toby had received permission from the mayor to cut dead trees in the park for firewood. Homer and Toby cut one tree. After the tree was on the ground, Homer cut a measuring stick with his pocket knife, and began to mark lengths of the tree for Toby to cut. Toby cut the tree while his friend Homer waited at a safe distance. Toby cut three lengths from the big end of the tree. The two men stopped to rest, sitting on the trunk of the tree at the small end. About twenty minutes had passed since the tree was felled.

The plaintiff, Shad Newton, a ten-year-old boy who lived in

a trailer at the edge of the woods, came upon the scene with his brother, Jack, and another boy, John Glassen. Shad walked close to where the men were sitting on the small end of the tree and asked what the men were doing. Homer replied that they were cutting firewood. Toby stood up and walked toward the big end of the tree to resume cutting. After a few seconds, he heard Homer yell.

A heavy oak limb had fallen from a nearby tree and struck Shad and Jack. Toby turned around and saw Homer sitting on the ground near the middle of the tree they had been cutting, holding Jack in his arms. Neither man had heard the tree limb fall. Homer had noticed Jack on the ground. After Homer picked Jack up, Jack asked, "Is he dead?" Homer then noticed Shad lying nearby, bleeding from the head. Homer laid Jack on the ground and turned to pick up Shad. Homer took out his handkerchief and began wiping blood off Shad's face.

Toby ran to the Newtons' trailer and called 911. The county coroner, Richard Vollrath, M.D., who was less than a mile away, was monitoring emergency calls on his police radio when he heard the call. The coroner hastened to the scene, where he found Shad suffering from a serious head injury. There were no visible signs of life. The coroner performed an emergency tracheotomy and restored Shad's breathing and heartbeat.

Shad was taken to a local hospital where he was treated and prepared to be transported by ambulance to Scottish Rite Children's Hospital in Atlanta. At Scottish Rite, Shad underwent surgery for twelve hours to repair a depressed comminuted skull fracture and other injuries.

Shad lived with his mother, his brothers and sisters, and several other people. Earlier that week, Homer had told Shad's mother that he and Toby planned to cut trees in the woods on Saturday. Shad's mother testified that she had told Shad many times not to go into the woods when men were cutting firewood. That Saturday, Shad, his brother, and a friend were inside the trailer. Shad and his mother heard the sound of a chain saw in the woods. Shad told his mother that he was going outside to ride his bike. Shad's mother told him not to go into the woods where the men were cutting trees. Shad said, "Momma, I won't." But he did anyway. Shad admitted his mother had forbidden him to go into the woods.

Shad had an I.Q. of 81 before the accident. He had been diagnosed as learning disabled and was attending special classes at school.

Shad's injuries were severe. There was evidence that portions of Shad's brain had been permanently damaged. Shad slowly recovered most of his speech and motor skills, and was released from the hospital in early April. He returned to school in late April or early May.

Shad's teacher, Catherine Tow, testified that after Shad returned to class, he seemed sleepy and lethargic, his attention span had decreased, and the progress he had made during the past year in his special education classes seemed to have disappeared. However, Ms. Tow admitted that she only taught Shad for the remaining month of that school year. Ms. Tow also admitted she had no personal knowledge as to whether or to what extent Shad had recovered from his injury.

Shad had different teachers during the two years preceding the trial, and neither was called to testify. Moreover, the plaintiffs' attorney did not place into evidence the intelligence tests that were performed on Shad the summer after the injury. The results of those tests indicated that Shad's learning abilities substantially lessened after the accident. The defendants' attorneys placed into evidence test results which showed that one year after the injury, Shad's I.Q. had returned to 81.

Shad's mother testified that Shad's personality had changed since the accident. He no longer enjoyed games he used to enjoy. He could no longer read books he had been able to read before he was injured. He became easily frustrated and picked fights with other children. Plaintiffs' counsel did not call any witnesses other than Shad's mother to testify about Shad's mental and intellectual condition at the time of trial.

During the fall of 1989, Dr. Mary Johnson, the pediatric neurosurgeon who operated on Shad at Scottish Rite Children's Hospital, diagnosed Shad as suffering from hydrocephalus, or "water on the brain." Dr. Johnson opined that Shad's accident caused this condition. She inserted a permanent shunt into Shad's skull to drain the water. Dr. Johnson admitted that hydrocephalus causes symptoms such as lethargy, sleepiness, and decreased attention span. She also testified that she expected Shad to return to the level of intelligence he had before the injury.

Shad was friendly and articulate on the witness stand. He made an impression that somewhat rebutted the claim that he was suffering from severe, permanent brain damage.

Neither defendant had been in any serious trouble until now, though Homer testified at deposition that he was arrested for public drunkenness twice, once on the day he went into the Army during World War II, and again on the day he got out of the Army.

Homer made a very favorable impression at trial. Despite his age, somewhat poor health at the time of trial, and diminished hearing ability, Homer had a clear recollection of the event. He stood up well under the opposing attorney's skillful cross-examination. Both he and Toby adamantly maintained that they had exercised reasonable care under the circumstances and had perceived no danger to themselves or to the boys.

Toby was nervous when subjected to a thorough cross-examination during the plaintiffs' case. He was not very articulate and, therefore, not as "likable" as Homer. However, when it was time for Toby to testify on his own behalf, he had lost most of his nervousness and made a favorable impression.

The trial had gotten off to a somewhat bumpy start when prior to the calendar call on Monday, the plaintiffs' attorney's paralegal overheard the mayor on the courthouse steps advising members of the jury pool that the defendants were not at fault. Judge Milam held a hearing and determined that the mayor had acted on his own, not at the request of the defendants or their counsel. Also, the judge called and questioned a panel of jurors, none of whom had been present when the mayor made his remarks. Apparently, it initially had been suggested that the city was somehow at fault for Shad's injuries.

After deliberating three quarters of an hour, the jury returned a verdict in favor of the defendants. The jurors later explained that if they had been in the defendants' positions, they would not have done anything differently. On voir dire it had been established that nearly every juror's family owned one or more chain saws. Would the same verdict have been reached in Atlanta?

Closing Argument

MR. ECKL: I'm Wray Eckl and I represent Toby Rhodes. One of the last things plaintiffs' attorney said to you before he sat down was, "I'd like to hear what these lawyers have to say about this injury and damages." If neither of us say anything about the injuries and the claim for damages, then when he comes back he'll say, "See, they're admitting everything I've said to you about damages."

The judge is going to charge you on the law of damages just as he does in every case in which there is a claim for damages. Before he does, he's going to tell you that the fact that he charges you on damages is not to be taken to mean he thinks you should award damages. Damages are one of two issues in this case.

I'm going to discuss damages first because my mother brought me up to eat my rutabagas first. Let's get damages out of the way so we then can discuss the issue of liability, which is the basis upon which this case should be decided.[1]

You have taken an oath to decide the case on the issue of liability solely on the relevant evidence and not on the basis of

Shad being hurt. I know that each of you sincerely is going to do his very best to do that. I also know you're sympathetic human beings, and I noticed the concern in your faces when you heard the testimony about the injuries Shad received.

Shad received a very serious injury, and that engages the sympathy of all of us. If it didn't, something would be wrong with us. I will talk to you about what we can call the hopeful aspect of his injuries. When plaintiffs' attorney gives his final closing argument, he'll probably say that the defendants' lawyer is so hard-hearted that he tried to tell you Shad was not seriously injured.

Shad received a serious injury when the limb fell and struck him on the left side of the skull. It fractured the skull and drove some of the bone of the skull into the left frontal portion of his brain and destroyed some brain tissue. That is the undisputed evidence in this case. That's a serious injury and that's a really sad thing to have occurred. There is no argument in this case about that. It's not what this trial is about.

There's another important aspect to this case that is not disputed but needs to be recognized. Shad's still alive in spite of his injury, and Dr. [Richard] Vollrath gets the credit for that. Dr. Vollrath is not here and I don't know if anyone thanked him, but someone needs to say that the quality of medical care Shad received from the time this happened until he left Scottish Rite Hospital was really incredible.[2]

I was tremendously impressed by the attitude of all the physicians here in this area, but Dr. Vollrath deserves the prize. You remember he was a mile away when he heard about it. If he hadn't been that close, frankly, Shad probably would be dead. Instead, Shad received excellent medical care here and at Scottish Rite Hospital for Children.

You heard Shad testify yesterday. His recovery shows what remarkable care can do. That's because medicine has advanced so far, but also because children have wonderful recovery powers.

You decide damages, not me—if you get to that issue. I want

to frankly say to you it was clear when Shad testified that he's making a very good recovery, as children can, and therefore, as heartrending as his injuries were, they were not so heartrending that this verdict should not speak the truth on the issue of liability and be decided on sympathy.

Shad had a terrible injury, a terrible course in the hospital, and I'm sure that was a terrible ordeal for everybody. You heard that Toby had been there at the hospital all that day. It was sleeting, one of the worst days in his life. Homer went home, showered, and went to the hospital and offered to take Shad's mother back and forth to the hospital as needed while Shad was there. The defendants are not indifferent people. They are nice folks, and the day Shad got hurt was the worst day in Shad's life and also the worst day in theirs.[3]

But the course of events after that, ladies and gentlemen, is that Shad has done very well. He got out of the hospital in early April and returned to school, and since then he's continued in school. He's now in the seventh grade. It's true he is in the learning disability class, the special education class; but it is also true he had a learning disability before this accident happened, and he was in those same classes.

Now I've introduced into evidence three documents which are exhibit numbers 12, 13, and 14.[4] One is from 1986 signed by Shad's mother, and the other two were filled out by her. These obviously deal with the period of time before the injury. These exhibits will allow you to get the true perspective on Shad's learning disability in school, set out in his mother's own writing and describing some behavioral problems and a lack of interest in learning. The documents were not created for the purpose of litigation. They are documents that came about in 1986. They were prepared in connection with his schooling, not for any lawsuit.

Shad's attorney presented Catherine Tow as a witness who told you about Shad after he returned to school after the injury. Was not Ms. Tow clearly a caring teacher, a very impressive witness? Ms. Tow obviously liked Shad a lot. She was sympathetic with his injuries and she told it exactly like it is.

First, she described what Shad was like in the acute stages just after he got out of the hospital. Shad was suffering from hydrocephalus, water on the brain, and taking phenobarbital, which some of you know from your training[5] has an effect on his alertness and ability to learn. All of that, by the way, occurred when he was under the care of Dr. Mary Johnson. You remember that it was in September of 1989 when Dr. Johnson put in the shunt and solved the problem of the hydrocephalus. Shad has had many teachers since then, including now, which is May of 1991.[6]

Shad had Mrs. Lowery the first semester and Mr. Young this semester. Neither one of those school teachers were called here to tell you where [Shad] stands at the present time. I respectfully submit to you the reason for that is because of what you saw for yourself when Shad came to the courtroom and testified. He's doing remarkably well and making an excellent recovery. He's a very articulate young man. He answered all the questions and was not buffaloed by the court process at all. He told you he'd rather be here than at school. Shad, thankfully, is doing well.

What the ultimate end of all this will be, we don't know. Mary Johnson, a surgeon who is a great doctor, has dedicated her life to pediatric neurosurgery. Her testimony was that, in time, you may not be able to tell he had this injury. That's a possibility. In fact, that was the last thing she wrote in Shad's medical records.[7]

Shad's mother said on the stand when I questioned her that Shad's I.Q. had been 81 and it's now returned to 81 and her words were, "He's about back where he was."

Although she said that, that may be a little optimistic—as a mother glad her son is making such a good recovery. All I say to you is, yes, he had a serious injury. Yes, he is making a very good recovery. He hasn't been to the doctor in a year and a half and is on no medication.

Accidents Happen

Shad probably will always have some residual effects from this and that's unfortunate, but the point is that it was not Toby's fault and it wasn't Homer's fault. Accidents happen. As humans we resent the fact that accidents happen, that disease happens, that death happens, all kinds of bad things happen, and we bring that resentment with us to the courtroom. In trials such as this, we are reminded of all the terrible things that can happen to us at any time, but that's life and we can't change that. Toby and Homer are not responsible for the way life is.[8]

Now, let's discuss the facts. What kind of people the defendants are and whether Toby and Homer would be the sort of people who were careful with a saw is something you have to decide. You heard Mr. Weymon Forrester [Homer's lawyer] speak about Homer's long experience in doing this type work. Actually Homer said he started between the age of twelve and fourteen, and he's now seventy-nine, so we are talking about sixty-five years' experience in felling trees.

Toby has been cutting trees thirty years on a regular basis. That's ninety-five years of combined experience. I'm sure some people are careless with chain saws, and probably some of you may have known some of them. Shad's mother testified that at some point in time—a reasonably close period of time before this accident happened—both Homer and Toby alerted her to the fact they were going to be cutting down dead trees in the woods near the park where the kids play. Toby and Homer were going to cut the trees for heater wood, and they agreed to share the heater wood. They are, for that reason, joint adventurers, working together, and they agreed to share the heater wood.

Joint adventurers means, so you won't be confused by the charge of the court, that if either one was negligent, both are liable because they were like partners. But more to the point, the fact that they warned Shad's mother tells you about their approach to all this. They were not doing anything wrong.

They had permission to take dead trees out of this area.⁹

Every tree at some point falls down, and every limb on that tree falls off. You've never seen a tree last forever. I never heard of anybody being hurt by a fallen limb like this. I doubt you have either. It's not something that usually happens, although this is an area where a lot of logging goes on and folks know a lot about the woods. It was a good idea to remove the standing dead trees.

Were Toby and Homer careless people, or were they responsible citizens? You know the answer. Both Toby and Homer knocked on her door and told Shad's mother, "Ma'am, we're going to cut dead trees." That alone answers the question. You've heard Toby and Homer testify. Some of you know them. They are not careless people. They are both reasonably prudent and careful people. The law doesn't require perfect prevision or knowledge of events before they happen from anyone because none of us can meet that standard. We just can't predict the future. Things happen that we don't foresee happening. That will never change.¹⁰

It's true that Toby and Homer didn't know that limb was going to fall twenty minutes or more after they felled the tree. But that does not mean that under the law they are liable. I'm not going to go through all the facts in detail as Mr. Forrester just did, but I want to talk about some aspects that Mr. Forrester didn't discuss. We have only so much time, and you only have so much patience. Toby talked about the zone of danger once the tree was down. Why did Toby admit that? He admitted that because that's true. You don't have to be a lawyer from Atlanta to know that as a tree falls, it may brush other tree limbs and even dislodge limbs. There could be a danger from falling limbs. Toby knows that, but he also knows that danger doesn't last forever.

The zone of danger exists immediately after you fell the tree. It really was very unfair of plaintiffs' attorney to try to convince you that Toby never looked as the tree fell. You remember the testimony and you know human nature. You get back out of the way when you fell a tree. You watch it go down. Everybody does that. I've never known a person to fell a tree and not watch it go down. They watch it go down; it hits; it's down. All right. Toby and Homer then talked for a while. They knew it was a dead tree, and they walked it over, deciding whether it was worth keeping, and where to make the cuts. You heard the testimony on this.

Toby and Homer have been friends since Toby worked down at the Supply Company when he was a sixteen-year-old boy. Now when you get older these friendships mean a lot more to you. They've been great friends for more than forty years. Homer Gray says he doesn't know what he would do without Toby.

Homer was in the area of the fallen tree throughout this period of time before the boys arrived. Now if Toby thought that there was any danger, do you think he would let an elderly person who means so much to him stand there? No way.

Homer has been doing this for sixty-five years. Do you think he would have been where he was if either of them perceived any danger to anybody? The answer is no.

It's not fair to say that, nevertheless, the limb did come down and that, therefore, Homer and Toby should have known beforehand that it was going to happen. Who knows that? What proof is there of that?[11]

The Police Reports

Plaintiffs' attorney then argues that there is some confusion in these statements taken by Officers Chastain and Darryl Payne. When did these officers get to the scene? Whenever someone is killed in an accident there has to be an investigation and the coroner has to be involved. The concern at the time was that Shad might die and indeed, frankly, but for the prompt medical care, he might have.

They even took blood alcohol tests from Toby and Homer

because the law requires that. As much as I compliment this community on the quality of medical care that was provided, I will tell you that the investigation by the officers was not very thorough. Maybe there was a reason for that. The officers' admissions about not making measurements and about not being more careful about accurately putting down what Homer and Toby told them, [are] troubling.

Plaintiffs' attorney is trying to convince you that Toby and Homer are not being honest with you about what happened. He claims they were utterly indifferent to the safety of the boys and that's why this accident happened. Remember, I don't get a chance to ask you questions and find out what is and what isn't a concern to you, so I have to cover things I know he's going to try to use to convince you that this injury was their responsibility.

Officer Chastain took the first statement. The most important point is that this statement confirms that twenty minutes passed between the time the tree was down and when the accident happened. Twenty minutes is a long, long time to pass before the limb fell and hit Shad. Certainly, it's possible that when the tree fell it dislodged a limb that was not visible to someone on the ground. It's possible that the falling tree did play some role in the fact that the limb came down twenty minutes later. That's a reasonable hypothesis. We don't really know that, frankly, but we don't deny it's a reasonable possibility.

You will have Officer Chastain's report out in the jury room with you. It starts out by confirming [Toby and Homer] had already cut a tree down and were measuring the bottom end of the tree to be cut up. The tree was lying on the ground for at least fifteen to twenty minutes. Two boys [Jack and Shad] came up to where they were. Toby and Homer talked to the boys for a little bit. Then they started back to working on the felled tree, Homer measuring the tree where it needed to be cut, and Toby using a chain saw. After two or three cuts Toby cut the chain saw off and looked around Homer and saw the boys—one lying on each side of the fallen tree—and ran for help. I do appreciate Mr. Chastain taking this signed statement. You understand, first of all, folks, Toby and Homer were incredibly upset. Now here's Toby's statement taken by [Officer] Chastain and it says, "He cut the tree down, turned the saw off, and checked around. No one was around but the man with me, so I started back to work when kids come up and asked, 'What are you up to?' Cutting heater wood. . . . And I looked around to see the two on the ground. I saw blood on one so I ran to the house for help."

Homer says, on the one he signed, "I was standing there with my back towards the kids and heard one holler. I picked [up] the first kid I come to, and the kid started hollering, 'Is he dead?' I turned loose and picked up the other one and seen blood coming from his mouth and nose."

Then plaintiffs' attorney will say to you that [Officer] Darryl Payne talked with them and then he wrote up a little summary. This is Mr. Payne's and it's not signed by anybody. -Darryl Payne's summary says, "Toby stated he had felled the tree with the power saw and it had been on the ground approximately fifteen to twenty minutes when two children walked up. And he talked to the children and then went back to sawing up the tree. He had cut three chunks out of the tree when Homer, the other witness, yelled at him. Homer ran to the first child, who was conscious and alert, and he helped him up. Then he went to the second child laying on the ground. Homer stated the child was bleeding from his nose and mouth and would not respond, and he attempted to clean the child's mouth. Toby went to the trailer to call for help."

Plaintiffs' attorney just suggested to you in his argument that it was fifteen to twenty minutes after the tree was down that the boys first arrived. He suggested that Mr. Rhodes cut the three sticks out of the big end of the tree after the boys arrived. He suggested that then this accident happened. Is that likely the correct sequence? What would Mr. Rhodes and Mr. Gray have been doing in the twenty minutes until the boys came up?

Also, under this version where Toby cuts up the tree after the boys arrive, then it's forty minutes roughly from the felling of the tree to the time of the accident. We don't know the exact time to cut through the large end of the tree three times, but it would take about twenty minutes. Look at these photos of the size of the dead tree. If it was roughly forty minutes after the tree was felled before the limb fell out of a standing tree and hit Shad, that's even more of a problem for the plaintiffs.

If you believe plaintiffs' new version, it is roughly forty minutes after cutting the tree that the limb fell and hurt Shad. Toby and Homer's recollection is that they had finished the three cuts when the boys first arrived. Plaintiffs' attorney now argues that they did the three cuts after the boys arrived. Under either version I don't think Toby and Homer are responsible for the accident. Actually, I think the only issue is whether Toby and Homer have to foresee when a limb is going to fall out of a tree twenty minutes later? If they are not required to foresee that, they are not liable and this is an accident. The same is true for forty minutes.[12]

It's undisputed that nobody did any more cutting after Shad got hurt until the man from the city park asked Mr. Rhodes to cut the standing pine tree nearby, but nobody cut on the fallen tree. Dr. Vollrath told you the old man [Homer] was holding Shad when he arrived. Toby ran to the trailer as fast as he could to get somebody to call for help. Nobody cut on that tree after this happened.

The Officer's Photographs

Let's look at the Polaroid photos Darryl Payne took when he arrived. You see you've got three complete cuts through the thick end of the fallen tree. Doesn't this show that three complete slices were made through this large fallen tree before the boys arrived? There is no partial cut which was begun and not finished. That's consistent with Toby's testimony that he took a break after the third cut.

So that means that this happened after Toby finished that third cut. This fact, along with these photographs, shows that nobody was doing any cutting on that tree when this accident happened. Note where the chain saw is in this photograph. I show you that, in this picture, it is way over next to the stump, a long way from where it would be if Toby was in the act of cutting on the tree when the accident happened. So the physical evidence, frankly, as well as common sense, tells you that what plaintiffs claim is not what happened.

Mr. Weymon Forrester is exactly right when he said that when Shad testified, Shad looked at the defendants when he was asked what they were doing, and Shad said that Homer was "standing almost at us." Homer was between them and Toby. The limb could have just as easily hit [Homer] as Shad.

The Polaroid pictures are important, and I request you study them carefully. Some of them show you the general location and show the limb that hit Shad. It's common sense the limb was moved, at least to some degree, to get Shad out from under it. It's very difficult even with all the evidence we have and all the photographs to reconstruct exactly what happened.

However, these photographs are very helpful. [Officer] Payne has made a mark on this photograph where he says the notch was on a nearby oak tree from which he thinks the limb fell that hit Shad.

If you study the photographs carefully, you see where [Officer] Payne found the notch. It's way up in the standing oak tree where the limb came from that struck Shad. I think that's entirely possible. We don't know that, but that's entirely possible.

These photographs show how high up off the ground that

notch is in the live oak tree. If he's right, then take a look at these photographs here. These are close-up photographs. The problem with these is they don't give the perspective of how high up in the tree the notch is. The notch is way up, as you will be able to see when you match it up with the Polaroid photographs. Now this is the limb there on the ground. These are the three cuts complete through the fallen tree. Toby had a sixteen-inch McCollough power saw and made three complete cuts through this tree. That takes quite some time.

Those of you who have used a power saw know after you used it for a while, you have to stop and take a break. Now notice how rotten the limbs are on the fallen tree. Now look at the limb that fell. I'm not an expert and no great woodsman, and don't claim to be, but if you look at the limb that fell and hit Shad, it appears that Darryl Payne may be right, that this limb probably came from the live oak tree.

Obviously it fell, but it's not dead the way the limbs are on the felled tree. Look at this and see if you think I'm right. I may not be. You folks know more about this than I do.

Plaintiffs' attorney claims that this oak tree limb landed in the pine tree limbs and was suspended there. He claims it later fell and hit Shad, and that Homer and Toby should have seen it.

The Polaroid pictures show you that if this is the limb which hit Shad, as big and heavy as it is, [if it] fell way out of that tree where that notch is, do you think any of the little pine branches you see in this pine tree below would have caught it and held it? Not likely. The likelihood is this oak limb broke off of that oak tree, fell, and hit Shad. That was twenty minutes after Toby had felled the dead tree. The pine tree limbs you see in the photographs are not going to hold this oak limb up for two minutes, much less twenty.

If this is, in fact, the limb that hit Shad, then the most reasonable explanation for this event is that limb broke off the oak tree and fell and hit Shad at the same time. Look at the size of the limb. It's between eight and twelve inches [thick]. That's a heavy limb, and it was wet. Wet wood is heavier than dry wood. If in fact Toby was using the power saw, then why is it located where it is in the photos? If that power saw was on, how could Homer, who has such bad hearing, how could he have heard the boy holler? How could he hear the conversation between Toby and the boys? The power saw was not on. The accident happened the way Homer and Toby say. The boys came up and were reasonably close to Homer. There was no obvious danger.

These defendants are not indifferent to the safety of children, but that's what you're going to tell them if you find a verdict against them. If you return a verdict based on sympathy, they won't know that you really didn't find them at fault. All they'll know is the jury told them they were indifferent to the safety of children and their carelessness caused this injury. Let me tell you if that's what you find the evidence to be, then that's what your verdict has to be, but if you don't find that it was Toby and Homer's fault, then you violate your oath if you find against them.

You heard Shad's mother testify that Shad was told, "Don't go near people operating a chain saw." She told Shad on that morning when she heard the saw. She told Shad not to go around it, and he told her, "No, Momma, I'm not going." Told her he was going to ride his bicycle. In fact, he disobeyed his mother. Children do that. That's life, too. Perfection isn't expected from anybody.

The accident would not have happened if he obeyed his mother. The accident would not have happened if, having heard the chain saw, Shad's mother had made sure the children stayed in the trailer. The first thing plaintiffs' attorney said earlier was they [Homer and Toby] cut a tree, and then later this limb fell on Shad. He argues that maybe a physical connection between the fallen tree and the much later fallen limb means that the defendants are liable. Well you can go on forever with that kind of reasoning. If Shad had obeyed, it wouldn't have happened; if Shad had not gotten up that morning, it wouldn't have happened. There's no human event you can't go back and find that it would not have happened if a lot of things leading up to it hadn't happened. That does not create liability on each person involved in what happened before the injury.

This was an accident. It was not anybody's fault. It was tragic that it occurred, but the law says there can be no recovery for an accident because nobody is really at fault.[13]

Where Are the Other Plaintiffs' Witnesses?

Let me tell you, ladies and gentlemen, if this didn't happen the way Toby and Homer Gray told you it did, then why didn't plaintiffs call as a witness John Glassen, who was twelve years old and the oldest witness of the children at the scene? Why hasn't he testified? It's been suggested that it's inconvenient for him to come; he's in school. How many videotaped depositions did we have in this case? Five or six. Wouldn't a videotaped deposition have been taken if the eyewitness would dispute what Toby and Homer say? What plaintiffs' attorney claims is not really what Shad said on the stand. John Glassen was not called for the same reason that no current teacher or physician was called: plaintiffs thought that it would be bad for their case to call them.

Plaintiffs have the burden of proof. The law says if they fall short of that burden of proof, that the plaintiffs lose. If you decide you really don't know what happened and you can't reconstruct it, then the judge is going to charge you if the evidence is equally balanced as to whether or not this was the defendants' fault, then your oath is that the verdict must be for the defendants.

That's the reason why the law says that the plaintiffs' attorney gets to argue first and then he gets to argue last. It seems to be unfair that he gets to talk to you twice and we get only one chance. The law permits this because the plaintiff has the burden of proof. If he doesn't call the eyewitnesses to prove his liability claim and doesn't call Shad's current teachers to prove his damages, then he fails to carry the burden of proof.

I don't know exactly what plaintiffs' attorney is going to argue after I'm finished. He may tell you that if this verdict is less than a million dollars the defendants will consider that to be a victory. He'll try to suggest to you that [amount] is based on something other than his statement. I can't anticipate all these tricks.

Let me make it clear that Homer and Toby have always said that this was the most terrible day in their lives, but it was not their fault. They didn't know the limb was going to fall then and don't know when a limb will fall now.

Use Photographs, Not Hindsight

Someone may say all we have now is what everybody remembers years later. You have something more than that. Darryl Payne did take twenty photographs. Payne said when he arrived on the scene that the ambulance was taking Shad away. Darryl Payne testified he began taking the photographs about fifteen minutes after that, so we have the photographs taken very shortly after this happened. You look at the photographs very carefully and you will see absolutely no evidence in those trees of any dangerous condition.

You don't see in any photograph pine limbs that could have held the oak limb of this size. What I'm respectfully suggesting to you is that we're not sure we've accurately reconstructed this event after four days of trial. How could Toby and Homer have foreseen this happening twenty minutes after they felled the tree? Toby didn't see any danger to his best friend, his treasured friend for over forty years, nor to himself, nor to anyone else.

The judge will charge you that you can't decide this case on hindsight. It is human nature to use hindsight in these situations. We have spent four days in court exploring a tragic event, but the truth is that what happened is not something that happens very often. Weymon Forrester told you verdict means the truth, but it means more than just the true facts. It means the facts applied to the law that the judge will give you in his charge. In other words, you find the facts, then you listen to his charge. Then, whether you like the law or not, you have to apply it because that's your oath, and our system of justice depends on jurors honoring their oaths.

If Toby and Homer are held to the absolute standard of knowing that twenty or forty minutes later a limb was going to fall from a tree in the immediate vicinity of where Homer was standing, then they can't meet that standard. The law doesn't require that. The law uses a standard of reasonable foreseeability. Listen to the charge carefully. The judge is going to explain the meaning of reasonably foreseeable. It means that to charge these defendants with legal responsibility for any harm that happens, the event must be the natural, reasonable, and probable result of their behavior.

This limb falling down twenty minutes or more after the dead tree was felled was not the natural, reasonable, and probable result of their actions. It's a fluke. It's an accident. It happened and nothing can change that. If your verdict doesn't speak the truth of this case then the tragedy is compounded. Such a verdict would cause harm that wouldn't be an accident.

I have enjoyed being here this week. You have listened very intently during the trial, and we all thank you for that. We're confident you are going to do your very best to render a true verdict based only on the evidence and the law. We respectfully request that the verdict should be for the defendants.

Endnotes

*Born in Florence, Alabama, in 1936, W. Wray Eckl received a B.A. in 1959 from the University of Notre Dame and earned an LL.B. in 1962 from the University of Virginia. After clerking for the chief justice of the Alabama Supreme Court, Mr. Eckl entered the U.S. Army Judge Advocate General Corps, serving as a Captain from 1962 to 1965. Mr. Eckl then entered private practice, and in 1982 he helped to found Drew, Eckl & Farnham. He is a member of the State Bars of Alabama, Virginia, and Georgia.

1. I discussed damages first to remind the jury that Shad had made a good recovery. As stated above, Dr. Johnson had testified that Shad likely would return to the same intelligence level that he had before he was injured. I mentioned this early in the closing argument because I wanted the jury to decide the issue of liability based on the evidence, rather than out of sympathy for Shad's injuries.

2. By praising a local doctor on the excellent medical care he rendered I hoped to ingratiate the defense with the jury. Also, my remark suggested that Dr. Vollrath had not been thanked before this time.

3. It was important for the jury to understand that the defendants were nice people who were very concerned about Shad's injuries. A defense lawyer who fails to make these comments risks losing the case for the sole reason that the defendants seem heartless.

4. The documents are questionnaires that Shad's mother had filled out years before the accident to help in evaluating Shad and in placing him in a learning-disabled class. Mrs. Newton's responses showed that many of Shad's problems, which she attributed to his head injury, in fact predated the accident.

5. One juror taught children with special problems, including epilepsy.

6. Dr. Mary Johnson had testified that the condition from which Shad was suffering, hydrocephalus, together with his medication, including phenobarbital, would affect his alertness, concentration, attention span, and the like.

7. I complimented Dr. Johnson's testimony because it was basically favorable to the defense. Her testimony helped negate the possibility that the jury would return a plaintiffs' verdict based on sympathy.

8. Jurors have a natural tendency to want to ascribe blame, and it was important to point out that this was a terrible accident which occurred through no fault of the defendants.

9. It was important to point out that if Toby was liable, so was Homer. Homer was elderly and the more likable defendant. I knew the jury did not want to find him liable. Also, I did not want the jury to misunderstand

the court's charge on joint adventurers.

10. Morality—or who was right and who was wrong—is frequently an issue in a negligence case in a small town.

11. The plaintiffs claimed that the defendants created a "zone of danger" within which it could reasonably be anticipated that a tree limb would fall. Plaintiffs contended that as the tree the defendants were cutting down fell, it broke a limb off a nearby oak tree, causing that limb to become entangled in the branches of adjacent pine trees. Plaintiffs wanted the jury to believe that if the defendants had looked up, they would have noticed the limb. Plaintiffs asserted that the defendants were negligent in letting the boys remain in the area, in failing to observe the entangled tree limb, and in failing to warn the boys of the hazard. Defense counsel spent a lot of time showing that the children had been in the area just a few moments before the limb fell, so that there was no time to warn them. Also, we continuously pointed out that the evidence did not support the plaintiffs' claim that the limb had become entangled in pine branches before it fell. Common sense and the photographs taken by the police after the incident supported the defendants' claim that the pine branches were too small to support the heavy oak limb. The more likely scenario was that the oak tree felled by the defendants damaged and weakened a limb from a nearby oak tree. The limb probably broke off and fell suddenly, approximately twenty minutes after the tree had been felled.

12. It was possible to construe Officer Payne's testimony about what the defendants told him to support the plaintiffs' theory that the defendants began cutting the felled tree into sections after the boys arrived. The plaintiffs were trying to show that the defendants were so unconcerned about the boys' safety that they operated a dangerous chain saw in the boys' presence. I spent a lot of time rebutting this theory.

13. Although I did not stick closely to the language the court would use in its charge, it is a good idea to do so if time permits. It should also be noted that the Georgia Supreme Court recently disapproved of the accident charge in civil cases. See *Tolbert v. Duckworth*, 262 Ga. 622 (423 SE2d 229) (1992).

Skipper v. Georgia Power Co.
No. 88-CV-0336 (Cherokee County Super. Ct.)

Result: $28.9 million verdict
Plaintiffs' Counsel: Philip C. Smith and H. Christopher Keown (Canton)
Defense Counsel: J. Clinton Sumner Jr. of Rogers, Magruder, Sumner & Brinson (Rome)
Judge: Frank C. Mills III
Date of Verdict: September 27, 1990

Chapter V

Touching a Power Line, Striking a Chord

Introduction
By Philip C. Smith*

S*kipper v. Georgia Power Co.* was a personal injury case brought by J. William Skipper and a loss-of-consortium case brought by his wife, Janice. Skipper suffered massive electrical burns when he touched an uninsulated guy wire that was placed too close to a live wire on a Georgia Power pole. Plaintiffs sought $5 million in compensatory damages and $25 million in punitive damages based on Georgia Power's negligent placement of the wires and its subsequent failure to inspect and correct the hazard.

The Accident

On May 7, 1986, in Canton, Georgia, while plowing a garden with a tractor, forty-year-old Bill Skipper touched a guy wire that extended from a Georgia Power pole to a stake in the center of the garden at roughly a forty-five-degree angle. A "hot" wire carrying 7,200 volts of current was anchored to the end of the pole's cross arm, less than an inch from the guy wire. A ceramic insulator was located on the guy wire above the point where it intersected with the hot wire. If the insulator had been placed below that intersection, Mr. Skipper would not have been injured.

Instead, when Mr. Skipper touched the guy wire it became energized, sending 7,200 volts into his body through his arm and out the small of his back where it touched the metal edge of the tractor seat. He lost consciousness, and the tractor rolled away from the guy wire. Mr. Skipper was dead at this point; his heart had stopped and he was not breathing. A bystander, John Whitmire, performed CPR and revived him. Mr. Skipper was taken to Kennestone Hospital where doctors found fourth-degree burns on his right arm and lower back.

The Injuries

Electrical burns start small and expand. Over time more and more skin dies off and must be cut away in a painful procedure called "debridement." The skin must then be replaced. Initially, skin grafts were taken from Mr. Skipper's hip. However, the area that had to be covered was so big that this was not a viable long-term solution. Dr. Anthony Musarra, a plastic and reconstructive surgeon in Marietta, created more skin by placing balloonlike tissue expanders under Mr. Skipper's skin next to the grafts on his arm and back and gradually, over a period of weeks, inflating the tissue expanders with injections of saline solution. The tissue expanders were grossly disfiguring for the three months that they were in place, making Mr. Skipper look like he had large balloons under his skin.

The procedures took three years but were ultimately successful, leaving Mr. Skipper with a 3 percent to 5 percent range-of-motion disability. His employment benefits were excellent, and he lost no wages. As a matter of fact, he was earning more when the case was tried than when the accident happened. Therefore, Mr. Skipper's damages consisted almost solely of medical expenses, roughly $10,000, and substantial pain and suffering.

The Plaintiffs' Theories

Guy wires, which run from the pole to the ground to hold the pole in place, are not supposed to become charged. The guy wire that electrocuted Bill Skipper had been negligently placed, plaintiffs alleged. Beyond that, the power company knew of the hazardous condition and chose to ignore it, making the company susceptible to punitive damages. The linemen knew that they had set up a guy wire less than an inch from a hot wire, and that knowledge was imputable to the corporation. Secondly, the power company was under a duty to inspect the wiring, and any inspection would have revealed the hazard. Georgia has a legal doctrine called "negligent ignorance," such that a party who is ignorant of a fact through his own negligence will be charged with knowledge of that fact. Judge Mills charged the jury on this theory, which is codified at O.C.G.A. § 23-1-17.

The Trial

The presentation of evidence was brief. The entire trial took only two and one-half days. The parties stipulated to the introduction of photographs of the scene and a schematic diagram of the pole and equipment. Graphic photographs taken by Jan Skipper, a professional photographer, were introduced, depicting each stage of Mr. Skipper's injuries, beginning from his large, open wounds a few days after the accident and continuing through the closing of those wounds three years later. The other evidence consisted of the testimony of the bystander (Mr. Whitmire); the ambulance personnel who took Mr. Skipper to Kennestone; electrical engineer Roy Martin, who pointed out the many National Electrical Code violations; Bill and Jan Skipper; the treating plastic surgeon who described Mr. Skipper's three years of medical treatment (Dr. Musarra); and the electrical company's linemen (T. A. Johnson and James Walton Haley) and its district director, Robert Logan.

The defense rested without presenting any evidence.

The Closing Argument Structure

The defense, even in closing argument, did not present an alternative version of the facts establishing liability. Thus, plaintiffs' closing argument focused almost exclusively on compensatory damages for mental and physical pain and suffering and punitive damages.

The argument itself is couched in familiar and colloquial terms. I presented it from a sheath of five or six handwritten pages of notes which highlighted points that I did not want to omit. The content of the argument and the tone I used in presenting it depended to some extent on the reaction of the jurors. If their attention was rapt, I would continue for some time on a subject. If their attention flagged, I would move on to something else. My fundamental goal was to instruct the jurors how to fill out the verdict form and to give them abundant justification for filling out the form as I requested.

The fact that the plaintiffs had delivered on all that we promised in opening statement and the defense's failure to impeach or even attempt to contradict the essential facts of the plaintiffs' case gave me great credibility as we came to the closing argument. The evidence of gross negligence was clear: the power company did not introduce any evidence concerning its safety standards or an inspection program. The testimony of the eyewitness, the engineering expert, the power company's district director, and the plaintiff himself all established an overwhelming case for liability. Similarly, the graphic photographs of Mr. Skipper's injuries depicting all stages of his three years of medical treatment, the treating physician's testimony, and Mr. Skipper's testimony made out a clear case of almost unbelievable suffering on his part.

Pain and Suffering: One Dollar Per Second

The biggest task in closing argument was to show the jury how to translate the pain and suffering into dollars and how and why the power company's acts warranted a punitive damage award. In order to get the jury used to thinking in large numbers, I first discussed damages through the per diem pain and suffering argument. This is an old but effective argument, so effective that it is prohibited in a number of jurisdictions (Delaware, Kansas, Missouri, North Dakota, Pennsylvania, South Carolina, Virginia, West Virginia, and Wisconsin; see 5 *Am Jur Trials* p. 1,011)

As I began the argument, I asked the jurors to look at their watches for five seconds. They all looked at their watches. At that point, I knew that I had them on my side and that it was up to me not to lose them. That would have happened if I had suddenly presented them with huge demands for damages without sufficiently preparing them.

Once I decided to argue the pain and suffering at the rate of one dollar per second, I had to determine what period of time to break down into seconds. I was tempted to use Mr. Skipper's entire life expectancy, but this yielded an unreasonably large figure. Ultimately, at co-counsel H. Christopher Keown's suggestion, I decided to use the twenty-six-day period that Mr. Skipper was hospitalized: it yielded a reasonable figure ($2.5 million), and the pain he suffered in the hospital was well documented. I made similar per diem arguments for the pain he suffered while recuperating at home and for the loss of consortium Mrs. Skipper suffered. This allowed me to cover the courtroom blackboard with large, though credible, numbers that gradually grew in size with each new item of damages. Once the jurors accepted the reasonableness of those figures, they were psychologically ready to consider a punitive damage award in the tens of millions of dollars.

Economic Realities: Tens of Millions of Dollars

The punitive damage argument bypassed the ideas of punishment, moral outrage, and evil. Instead, it concentrated on economic realities. I argued that Georgia Power was an economic entity that made decisions based on economic facts, so that by changing the economic realities of the situation, the jury could change the underlying safety inspection policies of one of the largest corporations in the state. In short, by returning a sufficiently large punitive damage award, the jury could make it so expensive for the power company to pay claims that it would be cheaper for the company to implement a system of effective inspection.

I stressed the jury's duty to return a verdict sufficient to deter the defendant from repeating its conduct. I demonstrated to the jury that its authority, as the sole branch of government charged with addressing the problem, could best be exercised by issuing a large verdict that would speak loudly and clearly to the defendant. The focus was on the effect that the verdict would have upon the defendant; obviously, I said nothing about the effect of such an award on the Skippers. Thus, when I asked the jury to return a punitive damage verdict in the amount of $25 million, not one juror blinked. In fact, it appeared that a collective realization swept over the jury that to return such a verdict was exactly the right thing to do. And after deliberating for one hour and forty-five minutes, the jury returned the following verdict:

Compensatory Damages for the Plaintiff	$ 3,500,000
Compensatory Damages for Loss of Consortium to Plaintiff's Wife	400,000
Punitive Damages	25,000,000
TOTAL:	$28,900,000

I had argued that Mr. Skipper had experienced death itself during the accident. The jury apparently awarded $1 million for that experience in addition to the $2.5 million I had requested. I later settled the case for $11.2 million.

Years of Preparation

My co-counsel Chris Keown and I began planning and discussing the closing argument years before trial. Almost every idea I used in the closing argument had been prepared ahead of time. We tried and discarded innumerable ideas. We spent months reading the considerable literature on damage arguments and per diem arguments. (Especially useful in this regard is Jack H. Olender's lengthy treatise *Showing Pain and Suffering* at 5 *Am Jur Trials* 921. Other useful ideas were derived from Gen. Heinz Guderian's *Panzer Tactics* and Sun Tzu's *Art of War*.)

All of that preparation was invisible to the defense. They had no way of knowing that we were capable of the argument that we made. Also, factually the defendant had nothing to offer. So we had the luxury of being able to disregard the defendant, and we spent almost no time in answering its arguments. Finally, we never pleaded damages in a dollar amount. Thus, when we raised the stakes into the range of tens of millions of dollars in closing argument, the defense was caught wholly flat-footed.

Closing Argument

MR. SMITH: Ladies and gentlemen of the jury, this is the last opportunity I'm going to have to address you about some salient facts in this case and some of the points of law that I think are relevant to this case.

In the beginning, I'd like to point out that [defense counsel] Mr. [J. Clinton] Sumner [Jr.]'s theories and speculations are all very nice, but I would point out to you that if there was anything to support them, he would have brought witnesses in to testify, as there are in this world accident reconstruction experts. There are engineers, such as Mr. [Roy] Martin [plaintiffs' engineering expert].

Georgia Power has well within its means to bring in every single expert they would need to support their case; and if there were anything in Mr. Sumner's theories, he would have brought these folks in to say, "We did this measurement; we did that measurement. This is how it happened." What do we get from Georgia Power in this case? Stony silence.

Y'all may have missed it; but what the defense, that is, Georgia Power, did in this case was close their case without presenting an iota of evidence. They brought in nothing for your consideration today.

The only party to bring you any evidence into this courtroom, to show you this event and the consequences of this event, are the plaintiffs, the Skippers, and Mr. Keown and I on their behalf. The negligence of Georgia Power is so obvious in this case that they haven't even bothered to try to contest it with evidence.

When we first started, I drew a picture of what I expected the evidence would show was the layout of the top of that telephone pole. As the evidence developed, we got a look at Plaintiffs' Exhibit Number 1. Mr. Martin showed it to you and Mr. [Robert] Logan [Georgia Power's district director] showed it to you; and they both agreed it was all wrong. This was no way to set up the top of a pole.

There are such glaring defects. The insulator which should have been below the hot spot in order to protect the people below is set above it, where it serves no purpose whatsoever. It's an obvious mistake that these wires are so close that they present a danger to people below, that when they will come in contact a person, such as Mr. Skipper, will receive a jolt of 7,200 volts, enough to kill a man.

They don't even attempt to defend this. They did not bring in an engineer that said, "Well, I was familiar with the standards back in 1936 and that's how they did it. And since they put it up in 1936, that's good enough for today." They don't have any evidence to support an idea like that. Their obligation is to safely transmit electricity, a dangerous, dangerous force.[1]

Mr. Skipper had no way of knowing whether or not that guy wire was charged until he touched it; and he took every precaution as he approached it.

Mr. Skipper was driving a tractor that he had stripped down to bare metal, rebuilt, and repainted. If someone takes such pride in their possessions it would indicate that he's a careful man, and all of the testimony is he brought that tractor to darn near a dead stop before he touched the wire with the back of his hand. He didn't grab it because he knew from his training that if you grab a wire, your hand will hold on because you can't let go. That's why he touched it with the back of his hand. He did everything in his power to look after his own safety.[2]

A Misplaced Insulator and No Inspection

The negligent party here obviously is Georgia Power. If they had had it within their power, they would have brought in to you evidence to show that this was good engineering—this was good electrical engineering—[and] that these standards were not violated—the National Electric Safety Code, which Mr. Sumner would like to dispute, but which Georgia Power's own documents say are their standards for operating. They violated those standards in many, many instances as outlined by Mr. Martin, an old experienced expert in this area, a man whose qualifications are so good that even Georgia Power uses him.

But the insulator was misplaced, and the gap between the wires was too close. The fact [was] that you had two wires so close together without any insulator around the wire, the fact that they were not using the modern guy string isolator, a section of fiberglass about [two and one-half to three feet long] that you put into a guy wire over eight feet above the ground, but below any possible contact. That way, even if the guy wire is uprooted from the ground by an automobile accident or a tree falling, it won't become charged at ground level because the string insulator will be between the hot wire and the ground. So that way, a child or a passerby who touches that wire won't be electrocuted.

In this case they didn't use that, and that's what's called a safety appliance, which they are required to use. They did not use it.

And lastly, and this is probably most important, they have brought you not one iota of evidence that Georgia Power inspected its installations. There is no evidence at all that there was any serious effort to go out and inspect their installations.

We heard that as these fellows are on service calls and such, they're supposed to look up and see if there is a problem. We know from Mr. Martin that due to the different ages of the equipment on the pole—the original pole being 1936, and then some of the equipment that joins up on the pole as being equipment that wasn't even made before twenty years ago—we know that some of this stuff was installed within the last fifteen or twenty years.

And the person who was up there is the lineman. He's the only person charged with inspecting. He went up there. There were all these obvious defects. Nothing happened. We didn't hear anything about a serious inspection program. None of the witnesses from Georgia Power testified that there was any sort of a serious inspection training program.

What do you look for when you inspect a pole? What's the problem? How do we prioritize problems that you spot? If you spot a problem, do you fill out a form 100 or form 101?

We didn't hear about any of the paperwork that would back up a meaningful inspection procedure. I didn't hear anybody say, "Oh, yeah, when we see something like that, we fill out this form; and it gets routed to so and so, through such and such." We didn't hear anything about it, because they don't have a procedure for that.

Safety is more of a slogan than anything else there. We didn't hear anything about how many hours of safety training or inspection training these fellows got, nothing about safety, because inspections simply don't occur, because they don't want to go out and replace all of this old equipment, because they've got a lot of it out there. And the next thing, too, it'll be too expensive.

Now I notice that Mr. Sumner was saying "we," as if Georgia Power were the folks you see here, Mr. Logan and Mr. Sumner and the other folks. These people are the paid employees of Georgia Power. Georgia Power, itself, is a purely economic being, and the only thing that motivates Georgia Power to do one thing or another is the bottom line. And Georgia Power has made an economic decision that they're not going to inspect this old equipment. They're not going to update this old equipment because it's cheaper to leave it in place and then pay claims as they arise, such as this. But I will get back to that later.

Now, back to the question of inspection. They didn't bring you any record showing any type of inspection ever occurred anywhere in this power grid. They didn't bring you one document to show that we have an inspection program, and this is how it works. Nothing. And with a company like Georgia Power, something like that is going to generate a tremendous amount of paperwork. There was no paperwork because there was no inspection program that really is intended to do that. Safety inspections are simply not a priority. As a matter of fact, they're such a low priority that they don't exist.

Now, there's no question that this pole violated the National Safety Code. There's no question that the setup of this pole violated their own regulations. Mr. Logan told you that; Mr. Martin told you that. They didn't bring in an expert to say that it does comply; and if they could have found one to say it, they certainly would have brought him. If Roy Martin was wrong, where is their engineer? That's all I have to tell you. That is a man who has long experience and long studies in the field. I don't think there's a more qualified man in this state.

Now, something you ought to also keep in mind is this. Is Georgia Power's inspection program, which doesn't exist apparently, is it the only inspection program for power transmission and household power distribution? There's no government agency out there looking at these lines. That's supposed to be Georgia Power's duty as a utility company. They don't do it. There's no backup government agency that's going to step in behind them. Their inspection is the only thing that guarantees your safety. It's failed utterly.

Now, it's very clear from the evidence that due to the fact that Georgia Power had this pole out there set up in such a fashion that its guy wire could become electrified at ground level by someone in the garden using what Georgia Power should have anticipated would happen, a tractor—they're coming by plowing, and they touch the wire. There's nothing surprising there. Georgia Power knew that was a garden from the beginning of time, as far as we can tell. This is not an unusual event.

And the question is established beyond a doubt and it's uncontradicted that they were negligent. So, the question then becomes what damages have Bill Skipper and his wife suffered?

Damages: Disfigurement and Humiliation

Now, you can look at the obvious things. The medical bills are in evidence. Dr. [Anthony] Musarra [Mr. Skipper's plastic and reconstructive surgeon] testified, I believe, that his bill for all of his treatment is $9,310. You can add all of those up, but there's a lot of intangibles to be taken into account. And you should keep in mind that these are all injuries inflicted on Bill Skipper by the Georgia Power Company, and the Georgia Power Company had no right to inflict these injuries on him.

There's the obvious disfigurement, the humiliation of these various procedures you have to go through. Mr. Sumner complains that we didn't have Mr. Skipper show you his scars during the course of the trial. I'll point out to you that Mr. Sumner had an equal chance to ask Mr. Skipper for a look at his scars.[3]

Mr. Skipper, I believe, has been through enough humiliation. The disability, he says it's not so bad, 3 or 5 percent. Look what's left. Well, look at what has been taken from him.

You heard testimony that Bill Skipper was a tremendously energetic, driven man, that he was one of these folks that gets more done in a day than most people get done in a week. He would go to work, do his job, get home at five o'clock. And he's got his welding shop in his basement, his woodworking shop in his basement, and he was just getting started when he got home.

He built the trailer that this tractor got hauled around on, and he completely rebuilt this tractor to the point of repainting every part with original paint from the manufacturer. He built furniture. He built a house, almost single-handedly with his friends, all the while teaching himself out of a college textbook how to do it. He was a tremendously driven, tremendously energetic person, and [he was] rated a highly energetic person at work. And now? That was changed in a flash, in a flash.

At the time that Bill Skipper touched that wire—there was some debate here earlier. I believe Mr. Sumner and Mr. Martin got into some differences of a definition over electrical burns versus electrocution. I think it could be safely said that Mr. Skipper was electrocuted, that he went mentally and physically through everything it would take to kill you by electricity.

Now when John Whitmire pulled Bill off of that tractor, [Bill] was dead, and if John Whitmire hadn't been a highly trained CPR tech, he'd still be dead. Mr. Skipper has experienced everything that it takes to die. But for the intervention of John Whitmire, he would not be here with us today. When Bill Skipper was in contact with that hot wire, he died. There was no difference between what he experienced, and what the person who is actually deceased experienced.

The judge will charge you that mental pain and suffering are an element of damage to go along with physical pain and suffering in an injury case. I don't know how you would value that. What is it worth to die?

Now, Mr. Sumner, in his closing, said that these lawyers, they get up here and they ask you to value things by the day, and such like that. How else would you value it? How can we value it? In our society, everything's got a dollar sign on it. We cannot come here and bring a legal action against Georgia Power to make Mr. Skipper whole and have any relief other than money damages. That's the only relief we can get from them. We can't restore Mr. Skipper to what he was before. We can't restore [to] his wife the husband she had before. We can't do that.

Georgia Power is answerable for its wrong in money damages, and this leads into very serious questions. But in the first instance, I want to point out to you that essentially Mr. Skipper was killed by Georgia Power and then saved by the intervention of John Whitmire.

So, insofar as the debate between "Is this an electrocution versus an electrical injury," it doesn't matter. It was enough to kill him.

And then once Bill was revived and taken to the hospital, and the first thing he hears when he's in the [emergency room] at Kennestone is a doctor speaking to him in terms of, "If you live the night, we'll do such and such in the morning," which presents him with a situation where he's going to go to sleep that night, or lose consciousness due to pain killers or due to his injuries and not know if he's going to wake up in the morning. That's almost beyond the imagination.

Wounds that Started Small and Grew

Now, another part of this case and a part of this injury that makes it more complicated than your average case is the fact that Bill sustained injuries that started small and grew. You've seen the photographs—they have been explained to you by the doctor—of how large, say, the injury on his back became. And in order to get an idea of where the injury began, look at his coveralls.[4]

This is the belt line in the back. See how small—[indicating three holes, each the size of a silver dollar]. And then to lay there in bed for days with these terrible injuries growing and growing every day and not knowing where it's going to stop. The same is true for his arm, his right arm. Laying there not knowing how large that burn is ultimately going to become. As a matter of fact, there was some uncertainty, and they told him and Bill had to contemplate this, that the burn on his arm almost wrapped around his arm. As a matter of fact, he came very close to losing that arm, and he lost part of his biceps.

And keep in mind, ladies and gentlemen, these are very unpleasant facts. People fear sickness; they fear injury. But I want you to please empathize, if you can, with my client and understand what he went through. Most people don't like to think about these things. These are unpleasant subjects. It's my duty to my client and to this court to bring out the truth here, and I know of no other way to bring out the truth other than to show you directly what occurred to Bill Skipper in these photographs. You've seen them. I'm not going to show them to you again. You'll have them with you in the jury room.[5]

But I want you to understand the truth of what he went through. I don't want you to tiptoe around it. It's not very pleasant; and if any of this material has offended you, I ask you, don't hold it against Mr. Skipper. You should instead hold it against the Georgia Power Company, the wrongdoer that inflicted these injuries on him in the first place.

Now, once Mr. Skipper got over the initial uncertainty about whether he was going to die, and then had to get over the additional uncertainty of whether or not he was ever going to have the use of his arm or perhaps even lose the arm, then he ends up in the hospital with what Dr. Musarra calls the ultimate injury that may be sustained by the human body; and it can only be cured with aggressive treatments. He says it's the most painful form of injury that one can sustain. They have to change the dressing. They have to guard vigilantly against infection because the body's protection, the skin, is gone. These are what is classified as fourth-degree burns. When it comes to skin, fourth-degree burns means you don't have any. You have had a complete area of your skin taken from your body.

Now, Mr. Skipper spent twenty-six days in the hospital, all of them in intense pain. All of it heavily sedated with narcotics, everything they could bring to bear. It still didn't alleviate the pain. Eventually, at the end of three years, they finally got his wounds to close. Three years of back and forth to the doctor, uncertainty as to the future.

And parts of that treatment involved three months of what we saw as the tissue expander therapy. Where day and night for three months, Mr. Skipper was, what we can only call, grossly disfigured. He couldn't even go out in public because he would just draw stares. It's hard to imagine that unless you've been through it. But that was almost the least of his problems.

But keeping this in mind, Georgia Power had no right to inflict this pain and these damages on Mr. Skipper; and the wrong that they have done him can never be repaid. However, we can begin to do so in dollars.

Now, I'm sure that Mr. Sumner—well, he's already argued this, and I'm sure he'll come back to it. He's going to tell you that Mr. Skipper is fine and he's recovered, that his job is okay, that he's making more money.

Well, essentially what's happened in Mr. Skipper's life is this. Due to his injury and his disability and his loss of memory, he has had to make adjustments in his work. Whereas before he could keep it all in his head, now he has to make lists constantly. And Mr. Sumner would hold it against Mr. Skipper that he's a fighter and he's come back with the best of his ability. He'll never be back 100 percent.

And essentially what's happened is this. He now has to devote so much energy just to do his job, [whereas] in the old days when he'd come home, his day was beginning; and he could get on with his various projects, making things that gave him satisfaction and pride to manufacture with his own hands in his basement. Now he'll just be ready for bed. He's tired. He has put first things first. He has put his job first, but the rest of his life is not the same. He's struggled back.

And Mr. Sumner would have you believe that he's 97 percent back. Well, he used to be able to run a mile. Now he can't. He can't run 97 percent of a mile. He can't run. He used to be able to do thirty push-ups in thirty seconds. Now he can't. To use Mr. Sumner's theory, he ought to be able to do twenty-nine.

You can't put a number on things like that. He went from being a man in the prime of his life. He and his wife for many years have finally—the children have left home, and they've built their vacation cabin, getting ready to enjoy the fruits of their labors. And building this cabin was just the beginning. This was the first project of how he was going to get to the point where he could really enjoy his life, and this happens.

And Georgia Power takes from him the best years of his life. He went directly from his prime to essentially—there's no other way to put it—he's older, much older. I think he probably—well, it's sad to say—but this probably put ten years on him overnight.

Ladies and gentlemen, when you think about all of these changes in Mr. Skipper and the ordeal he went through and the pain—the court is going to charge you that pain and suffering is a legal item of damages. But the measure is the enlightened conscience of fair and impartial jurors. The questions of whether, how much, and how long the plaintiff has suffered or will suffer are for you to decide. It's in your hands.

The Measure of Pain

Now, pain and suffering also includes mental suffering, but mental suffering is not a legal item of damage unless there's physical suffering also. Now, there's no question about physical suffering in this case, and, therefore, you are, in considering this verdict, to also consider mental pain and suffering. And under that would fall the uncertainty of impending death [and] the certain fact that he did die. You can include those in that calculation.

Now, if you find that Mr. Skipper's pain and suffering will continue into the future, you can award damages for the future pain and suffering. And, again, your standard will be your enlightened conscience as impartial jurors, and you'll be entitled to take into consideration the fact that the plaintiff is receiving a present cash award for damages not yet suffered.

Now, Mr. Sumner said that we're going to talk to you about the future, the unknown. We don't know how long Mr. Skipper will remain the way he is. Well, it looks like he'll be that way indefinitely, and what he's suffering now is more of a lessening. He's not himself. He has lost his energy and his stamina.

But look at something that is certain. Let's look at something that we know has occurred, and this is just a "for instance." My suggestion to you on how to look at valuing these things that we don't usually assign dollar value to—well, let's look at it this way: assume—we know for a fact that Mr. Skipper has spent twenty-six days in the hospital. We know for a fact from Dr. Musarra that he endured the worst pain that you can endure. Let's break it down. Look at your watch for five seconds. It's longer than you think. Would you endure the pain that Mr. Skipper endured for five seconds in exchange for $5?

MR. SUMNER: Your Honor, we hate to object, but I don't think it's proper for counsel to ask the jury to put themselves in a position of one of the parties. That's called the golden rule argument, and we object to it [as] being improper.

THE COURT: Do you want to respond?

MR. SMITH: Your Honor, I didn't realize that I was making it that way. I'll put the argument in the third person.

THE COURT: All right. I'll sustain the objection. Go ahead.

MR. SMITH: All right. Let's look at it this way. Would a person endure five minutes of the pain that he endured for $5? Probably not. You're going to say you have undervalued that pain. Not for $5 would a person—a person's going to say not for $5 would I endure five seconds of that pain. So we already know that the value we've assigned is too low, but that value we've assigned is a dollar a second. And we know it's too low.

If you do some quick math, and you think about how long Mr. Skipper suffered, this is not the speculation about the future. This is what we know now. We know that this suffering, from the doctor—and doctors always tend to minimize pain—we know that from him. There are 3,600 seconds an hour, twenty-four hours in a day, which leaves you 86,400 seconds in a day.

Now assign a value of one dollar per second to that, and then you multiply that out, times twenty-six days, which we know Mr. Skipper was in the hospital. What you get is a figure of $2,246,400. That's assigning a value of one dollar per second to endure the worst pain that Dr. Musaiia knows about.

Now, we can take another tack, and that's just for the twenty-six days in the hospital. This is not counting his loss of enjoyment of life—which he'll have the rest of his life—that loss of stamina, that loss of drive, the loss of enjoyment of so many things. This is just to look at that, and look at what he's lost.

Now, if you take that same number of seconds per day—86,400—and you look at, say, the ninety days he was home out of the hospital and unable to go to work: his pain is less; however, he's disabled, he cannot work, and he has bandages that need to be changed. And you, for instance, can say there is less pain than there was in the hospital. So you assign a value of half of that to the same figure.

Well, you're going to end up with—over a period of ninety

days convalescence at home in pain, taking pain pills—with a figure of 7,776,000 seconds. That's ninety days in seconds. Multiply that times fifty cents a second, and you will end up with a figure of $3,888,000.

Now this is all up to you. These are just some suggestions. But this is—when you start adding—and something that y'all should keep in mind is this. When you're in pain, time takes forever to pass. Time never passes so slow as when you're sick or you're in pain. But think of the time that Mr. Skipper has endured in deep pain.

Now these are just some suggestions for you, but I would suggest to you that if you're going to be fair and adequate in your award that these are the ways you ought to look at it. Mr. Sumner has been doing this for many years, but this is the fairest way to do it. How can you give someone back what they have taken from them in terms of time and agony?

Loss of Consortium

Now, how much of what I have said about Bill also applies to Jan. She and her husband were just ready to start enjoying the prime of their life together. The kids were grown, and [they had] a cabin in the mountains, and everything else. Instead of that, instead of being married to a strong, vigorous man with a drive to achieve so much, suddenly she's got to care for him. He's slowing down, and he doesn't have the energy. His memory is slipping. He doesn't hear as well, and it's a loss to her.

Now, loss of consortium is defined like this, and you'll be charged as this. A married person has a right to recover for the loss of consortium, sometimes called loss of services, of her spouse. You should be careful to remember that services the law refers to in this are not only household labor but also society, companionship, affection, and all matters of value arising from the marriage. There does not have to be any direct evidence of their value, but the measure of damages is their reasonable value as determined again by the enlightened conscience of the jury.

Now, if we apply similar mathematics to this, to Jan's claim, and we just look at the twenty-six days in the hospital, and since Jan is not—she is basically in a position where she doesn't know if she's going to lose her husband or not, and she certainly doesn't have his services. She certainly doesn't have him whole there and regular. She has him flat on his back, undergoing the health struggle of his life, trying to overcome these terrible wounds. And if you take her time or the time that he was in the hospital for twenty-six days and, say, you discount her time and her anxiety and worry. Constant trouble with Bill's injuries is only worth twenty-five cents a second. Again, you end up with a figure of 2,246,400 seconds.

But assume we discount that. I hope we don't offend anybody, but we assign only twenty-five cents a second to it. If you agree with that reason[ing] for that short period of time, disregarding the rest of their life—I'm just talking about one month here—you end up with a figure of $551,600.

It's similar if you take the time that he's out of the hospital, not at work for ninety days laying home disabled, and you assign a value of her loss to him of twenty-five cents a second. At that point you're going to come up with $1,944,000, and if you add that together, just assigning a value of twenty-five cents a second to it, you end up with a value of roughly $2.5 million.

Now those are high figures, but you should think of—the only way I think, to think of money in that degree of suffering and that degree of loss, is to break it down. Think about the unit of the second of pain or five seconds, and if you think about that five seconds of pain, also think about this and add this to your consideration: Imagine undergoing that five seconds of pain not knowing when it's going to end, or what the next medical problem is going to be, or if you're going to lose a limb from it. Add that together, in addition to the pure physical suffering.

Now, I know Mr. Sumner disagrees with that approach, but I haven't seen him assign an alternative. He's not giving you any basis upon which to value these things, and they certainly have value, both in real life and in the law.

A Financial Incentive For Safety

Now, the court is going to charge you that you may find that Georgia Power is liable for punitive damages. Now, punitive damages are damages awarded when the situation or the circumstances are so aggravated that the jury finds that it's necessary to make an award in order to deter the actions of the wrongdoer—in this case, Georgia Power.

Now, punitive damages can be found if a wrongdoer, such as Georgia Power, knowingly subjects others to a risk in disregard of the consequences; that is, if they set up a situation that they know will probably cause someone an injury and do nothing about it, and recklessly disregard the safety of others, [then] they are liable for punitive damages, which is exactly what happened in this case.

At some point in the past they erected this pole in this fashion. Had their linemen been trained—and they are under a duty to be trained—they would never have put it up this way. In addition, in the passing years, other linemen were on that pole, and they never even made a meaningful inspection of the pole. They totally disregarded their duty to inspect. Now, as I said earlier, the reason that they don't inspect the poles and they don't upgrade this equipment is they consider it too expensive.

Now, Georgia Power, for all of Mr. Sumner's reference to "we," is a purely financial being. It's not a group of people. It is capital, operating expenses. It is a bottom line. And Georgia Power's behavior is directed purely by economics. If you make it too expensive for Georgia Power to maintain unsafe installations, they will quit. They will appropriate the necessary amount of money to make their installations safe.

Now, if they have claims made against them based on the lack of safety, but those claims can be paid off for a very small amount of money, then there's no incentive for them to bring safety into their system.

Send a Message to Georgia Power

So what this means is, that you, as the jury, you are the wisdom and the conscience of this community. This is the only place that Georgia Power is going to be called into account for this accident and for the policies that led to this accident—the fact that they do not inspect their lines. They have no meaningful program of taking care of dangerous situations. You have the power to change that, and it's pure economics.

If you make such a punitive damage award—and the measure of a punitive damage award is an amount of damages which is sufficient to deter the wrongdoer from repeating the wrongdoing. That is, a punitive damage award is only effective if it sends a message, and it's enough to deter them from their wrongdoing, that is, in this case not maintaining a safe electrical system. Then, the question becomes, what do you mean by deter? How do we change their behavior?

Well, the definition of deter is going to be charged as this. It's to discourage, to stop by fear or prevent from acting by danger, difficulty, or other consideration which disheartens or countervails the motive for the act. In other words, enough money to make them stop, to make them stop and reconsider their safety policies from top to bottom, because right now, the economics are such that they think they can't afford to make the system safer.

You can change that. You can make it such that Georgia Power cannot *not* afford to make their system safe. You can send them a message; and if you're making a punitive damage award, if you want to deter somebody, you better send them a loud message, because this is Georgia Power, and it's up to you in your enlightened conscience to decide how much it's going to [take to] change their policies, to change their behavior. They're a purely financial institution.

What would it take to get Georgia Power to pay attention? Five million dollars? Is that just their operating expenses? Ten million dollars? Would twenty million dollars get them to sit up and reevaluate these policies? Twenty-five million dollars? It's up to you.

And I will tell you that this is one situation that, from the evidence and all of the facts, cries out for a remedy. Everyone assumes that guy wires are safe. Children swing on them. Why, that was some of Mr. Sumner's testimony about how safe the situation is, that we have children swinging on guy wires; therefore, they must be okay. Probably, folks wouldn't be so free with letting their children swing on guy wires if they knew how inadequately inspected these systems were and what a danger there was.

I'm going to ask you, ladies and gentlemen, to send them a message, send them a loud message, to get their attention and cause them to make safety more than their slogan and make an actual policy out of it. If safety had been a priority to them, they would have inspected these things, and they would have seen the obvious dangers on the pole, and they would have actually seen it while they were working. Their linemen said they drove by that place hundreds of times.

Well, the theory of their inspection now is that they're supposed to notice the stuff as they're going up and down the system. They drove by it hundreds of times, and I can't think of a more obvious defect than having the insulator up above the hot wire, especially to a trained person. They should have spotted that. Ladies and gentlemen, according to the evidence that we have, they didn't spot it in fifty-four years, because no one ever looked.

Now, they're going to argue to you that it's too expensive to inspect, [that] annual inspections are too much. Well, maybe they are. But maybe if they had a meaningful system of periodic inspections where they actually did look at the materials on the poles when they were out there doing other work, instead of simply saying they did, this wouldn't have happened. And maybe an award from you would motivate them to properly train their people to spot problems like this and prevent this from ever happening again. It's up to you, ladies and gentlemen.

And, as I said, in the eyes of the law, they knew that danger was there because it was their duty to know. You're going to hear a concept from the judge called negligent ignorance, which means that if by law you are supposed to know something and you don't know it because of your own negligence, the law will presume that you know it anyway. That is the equivalent of knowledge.

So by their actions, Georgia Power has placed themselves in a position where, in the eyes of the law, they knew of these defects and did nothing about them. They consciously disregarded an obvious danger. That, ladies and gentlemen, is the legal test for the appropriateness of punitive damages. This case meets that on all fours.

Now, ladies and gentlemen, Bill and Jan are two people whose lives are now divided very clearly. There's their lives before the accident and after the accident—cut like a knife. Their lives are completely different now from what they had been before. It would only be appropriate for you, as a jury, in sending a message in the form of punitive damages, [to] make life for Georgia Power very different before and after this verdict: Before this verdict, where safety is given lip service, to after the verdict, where perhaps they will make some meaningful changes, and they will make these installations for the transmission of power, which are so dangerous, safe.[6]

Now, I believe, ladies and gentlemen, that by sending such a verdict you'll do something constructive. You'll do something that you can be proud of. You will get their attention and send a message they cannot ignore. And you can change the way they do business. Believe me, you can, if you simply make it too expensive for them to carry on the way they do now.

I haven't heard anything about stepped-up safety policies. You heard no evidence at all from Georgia Power, because Georgia Power has made an economic decision; but they don't think you're going to send them a message. They don't believe you'll do it.

Ladies and gentlemen, you've sworn an oath. You've heard the evidence, and you'll hear the law from the judge. And under that law and that evidence, I believe that you will find that it's clearly authorized that Bill and Jan have been damaged by the negligence of Georgia Power and are entitled to a large compensatory damage award, that is, for the disability, the medical bills, the pain and suffering; [and] on Jan's part, for her loss of services, love of the husband she used to have, as opposed to the new person that Bill is now. Every time you take away from a person they become a different person. He's not 97 percent of what he was. He's a different person.

And I think that if there was ever a case that justified an award of generous compensatory damages, this case is it. And if there was ever a case that cried out for a verdict, a large verdict, of punitive damages sufficient to where Georgia Power is going to hear it loud and clear [and] change the way they do business, this is it.

Ladies and gentlemen, I'm going to tell you that you can take these calculations—these are just "for instances." The bottom line is that I believe that if you come back with a punitive damage award less than $20 million, you have not gotten Georgia Power's attention. But it's in your enlightened conscience.

Ladies and gentlemen, I believe that if you take the facts, the figures, the effect on the life of Bill and Jan, and compensate him for everything that he's lost in his life and will lose in the future, and all that could have been and will not be now [you will return] a compensatory award of $2.5 million for Bill. For Jan, in a like amount for all that she has lost. Those are not exaggerated. Those are called for by these facts, and they are called for by this law.

And, ladies and gentlemen, I think once you will examine your consciences, you'll agree with me. We can't make them whole again. We can't undo this. We can't go back and have Georgia Power find this [problem] through some miracle before [the injury] happened. That pole could still be standing there if this hadn't happened.

The only way you can prevent this from happening in the future is to speak loud. A verdict is derived from a Latin word meaning "speak the truth." Ladies and gentlemen, if you want to speak the truth and you want to speak in a fashion such as to deter this from happening again, I ask you to, please, return a verdict as I've outlined to you.

Now, ladies and gentlemen of the jury, this is the only resort that Bill and Jan Skipper have. You are that branch of government that we come to in order to get compensation. Their lives, the safety of the community, all of these other larger considerations are all delivered into your hands and your collective wisdom. Thank you.

Endnotes

*Philip C. Smith currently serves as Municipal Court Judge for the City of Canton and Associate Juvenile Court Judge for the Blue Ridge Judicial Circuit. He was born in Atlanta in 1955. He graduated from Vanderbilt University in 1976 and from the University of Georgia School of Law in 1979. He was admitted to the State Bar of Georgia the same year. Mr. Smith practiced law with numerous small firms until 1985, when he opened a solo practice. *Skipper v. Georgia Power Co.* was his second personal injury trial.

1. I made much of Georgia Power's failure to present evidence in order to imply that the defendant's whole system was as unsafe as the pole in question. Also, the defendant's resting without presenting evidence insulted the jury.

2. Here, I was trying to anticipate and rebut a contributory negligence argument that the defense might raise. As the defense had not put on evidence, it had the right to open and conclude the closing arguments.

3. The defense commented in its opening argument that I did not have Mr. Skipper remove his shirt and display his scars to the jury. I did not want to humiliate my client.

4. I displayed to the jury the coveralls that Mr. Skipper was wearing when he touched the guy wire.

5. The pictures showed large, open, oozing burns. I wanted to draw attention to them without waving them in the jurors' faces, which would have been exploitive. It was a backdoor way of getting the jury to blame the power company.

6. Jan Skipper contributed this "before and after" argument.

Yearwood v. Crosland

No. 90-CV-609S (Stephens County Super. Ct.)

Result: $720,000 verdict

Plaintiffs' Counsel: Charles W. Stephens of Stephens & Shuler (Gainesville) and Janney E. Sanders of Adams, Clifton & Sanders (Toccoa)

Defense Counsel: Weymon H. Forrester of Forrester & Brim (Gainesville)

Judge: Robert B. Struble

Date of Verdict: August 6, 1992

Chapter VI

Soft Tissue, Solid Recovery

Introduction
Reprinted from the Daily Report, *Opinions Weekly, August 14, 1992 (revised)*

A Stephens County jury awarded $620,000 damages for soft-tissue injuries Danny Yearwood sustained in a car wreck and another $100,000 loss-of-consortium damages to his wife.

On August 25, 1989, as Mr. Yearwood slowed to make a left turn off Highway 123 in Stephens County near Toccoa, Ben Crosland started to pass on the left and hit Yearwood's truck on the left rear wheel. Yearwood, who was thirty-one years old at the time, sued Crosland for negligence, and Yearwood's wife, Susan, sued for loss of consortium. Crosland denied liability, claiming that Yearwood did not signal before he turned and appeared to be turning right instead of left. Crosland also claimed that the collision did not proximately cause Yearwood's injuries.

Yearwood testified that the morning after the wreck he awoke with severe pain in his neck and upper back, so he went to the Stephens County Hospital emergency room. The physician on call prescribed a soft cervical collar and pain medication. Yearwood explained that his back and neck pain worsened, and he saw many physicians seeking relief for his pain. No one diagnosed an objective injury and he began taking more and more pain medication, at one point taking up to eight Dilaudid daily. Dilaudid is a powerful synthetic morphine.

Yearwood's counsel introduced deposition testimony from eight physicians and live testimony from a ninth physician Yearwood saw searching for relief from his back and neck pain. While not all the doctors' testimony was entirely favorable to Yearwood, his counsel Janney E. Sanders explained that he and Mr. Stephens thought it was important for the jury to understand Yearwood's entire medical history, which documented his attempts to find relief for his continuing pain.

Emergency room physician Donald Ruesink testified that Yearwood came to the emergency room on numerous occasions seeking pain medication, and Ruesink testified he believed Yearwood really was in pain. Emergency room physician John C. Lawrence also saw Yearwood many times, although he believed Yearwood only wanted drugs and that his complaints were exaggerated. Treating physician Irving Hellenga, orthopedist Raj Bohle, and neurosurgeon Steven Gardner testified that all of Yearwood's X rays, neurological exams, CT scans, MRIs, EMGs, and thermograms were negative. While Hellenga and Bohle testified they believed Yearwood was actually in pain, Gardner thought Yearwood was exaggerating his symptoms.

Pain management specialist and anesthesiologist Robert Pilon, director of the anesthesiology department at Athens Regional Medical Center, testified that Yearwood finally obtained some relief from his pain after Pilon inserted into Yearwood's abdomen a computerized pump that releases a preprogrammed amount of Dilaudid. The pump is refilled by a nurse and Yearwood has no control over its dosage.

In March 1990, seven months after the wreck, Yearwood was

severely burned while he was trying to put a new wick into a kerosene heater. He spent thirty-five days in the hospital. Plastic surgeon Herman Orlet testified that, while Yearwood underwent skin grafts and had permanent scars on his arms, he had no residual disability due to the burns. Urologist Robert Cowles subsequently treated Yearwood for impotency, and Cowles concluded the condition was caused by neurological damage attributable to the wreck.

Finally, pain specialist Robert Gerwin from Baltimore testified via video deposition that as of the time of trial, he was treating Yearwood for myofascial pain syndrome and had isolated trigger points, or focused muscle spasms, in more than twenty-five muscles in Yearwood's body. In his opinion the injuries were caused by the wreck and only aggravated by Yearwood's inactivity resulting from his burn treatment. He further testified that Yearwood had made some improvement with treatment, which includes massage and other passive muscle manipulation, and had some hope for the future. Pilon thought it would be years before Yearwood would regain some semblance of a normal life.

Susan Yearwood testified that at the time of the wreck, she and Danny had been married for two years and were expecting their first child, who was born in January 1990. Yearwood had just started a heavy-equipment business and thus did not seek lost wages or profits, although he did introduce evidence of $150,000 in medical special damages.

Defense counsel noted that the investigating police officer described the damage to the vehicles as "slight." Further, Yearwood made no complaints of injury to the officer and went out that evening as he had planned. Two of Yearwood's doctors, neurologist Gardner and emergency room specialist Lawrence, thought Yearwood was dependent on narcotics and was exaggerating his complaints in order to get more pain medication. At most, Yearwood experienced a soft-tissue injury, as no testing revealed objective evidence of injury, the defense argued.

Radiologist Louis Spear confirmed that X rays of Yearwood's neck revealed no fracture. Finally, defense counsel argued that Yearwood's serious kerosene burn caused or contributed to his condition.

Judge Robert B. Struble presided over the four-day trial, and the jury deliberated for two hours. Defense counsel indicated that he ran out of strikes and had to leave several of the Yearwoods' acquaintances on the jury, one whose daughter had attended the Yearwoods' wedding and another whose employer, a bank, was a client of one of the Yearwoods' attorneys. However, plaintiffs' counsel noted that Crosland had lived in the area for seventeen years, and had only moved away a year before the wreck. The juror who worked for the bank also knew Crosland's family well, counsel said. Finally, the one juror plaintiffs' counsel spoke with reported that the women on the jury wanted to award Yearwood the $1.5 million he asked for, but the men, including the one whose daughter attended the plaintiffs' wedding, "held it down" to $720,000. Crosland was insured by Aetna Insurance Co.

Commentary on the Trial Strategy
By Charles W. Stephens*

Danny and Susan Yearwood's case is typical of soft-tissue injury cases and the problems they present. Always, the overriding problem is credibility. Jurors are exposed to lawyers advertising heavily on television, hawking cases. They are exposed to huge campaigns designed to convince the general public that many automobile injury cases are fake, fraudulent, exaggerated, or imagined. The fact that Mr. Yearwood's injuries were indeed quite real, and quite devastating, was the key to his success.

Nevertheless, although Danny Yearwood's injuries were more severe than in many soft-tissue injury cases, he still had to overcome the credibility hurdle. Several factors could have destroyed the credibility of the Yearwoods' claim. This case, like many, began with what appeared to be a relatively insignificant impact. Indeed, following the collision itself, Danny Yearwood felt that he was not injured. The next afternoon, after nursing a severe headache continuously since the wreck, he went to the emergency room for evaluation and treatment. As is typical for soft-tissue injuries, all tests and X rays were negative, and despite the fact that over the next several years Mr. Yearwood's pain became increasingly unbearable, all X rays, MRIs, CT scans, EMGs, and other standard tests were negative.

Numerous physicians examined Mr. Yearwood, and nine of them testified, either live or via deposition. As stated above in the verdict report, two of the physicians disbelieved Mr. Yearwood's complaints of pain. One of them, Dr. Steven Gardner, testified: "To have pain with every single movement that one performs is really not normal. It usually reflects some exaggeration...."

Another barrier to recovery was Mr. Yearwood's preexisting exposure to radiation. He had become temporarily contaminated while employed with a power authority several months before this wreck occurred. Moreover, seven months following the wreck, Mr. Yearwood's back was burned in a kerosene stove flash fire. These burns were severe and life threatening, and Mr. Yearwood spent a considerable period of time in the Augusta Burn Unit recovering. The defense contended that his burns caused his neck and back pain.

Still another problem was that the defendant Crosland was a private defendant. While he had insurance coverage of $300,000, co-counsel Mr. Janney E. Sanders and I were concerned that a jury in Toccoa, Georgia, would not award a substantial verdict against a noncorporate defendant.

Finally, while Mr. Yearwood had earned approximately $40,000 during the year preceding the accident, he had gone into business for himself just a few weeks before the wreck.

Accordingly, it was difficult to establish the amount of Mr. Yearwood's lost wages during the next several years.

In keeping with our intent to do absolutely nothing which could distract from the credibility of the Yearwoods' claim, Mr. Sanders and I decided to address in our opening statement virtually every unfavorable contention that we knew the defense would argue. We also outlined to the jury all facts and issues which would arise during the trial. Moreover, the tone of the opening was not grandiose, but humble and beleaguered; we made a conscious effort to avoid overstating anything. For example, the jury was told that at the conclusion of the testimony they would have an opportunity to evaluate Mr. and Mrs. Yearwood's damages, but no specific figure was mentioned.

One of our goals during opening statement was to be sure that nothing arose during the trial that could cause the jury to feel we had failed to mention some very important point. Thus, every controversial issue the defense was expected to raise was carefully laid before the jury as a matter of fact and, as such, to prime the jury to draw its own conclusion after hearing the evidence. For example, we told the jury that Danny Yearwood had been burned in a fire. Then, anticipating the defense's argument that the burns to Mr. Yearwood's back caused his neck and back pain, we told the jury that before the fire he had been to the doctor eighty-six times complaining of back and neck pain.

Also, we told the jury that Mr. Yearwood would not seek recovery of any lost wages for the almost three years he had been unable to work. We jettisoned the lost-profits claim because we believed that if we struggled to convince the jury on that issue, we would likely weaken our credibility on the crucial issues.

Most importantly, we wanted the jury to view the medical evidence with a preconceived understanding of what kind of injury Mr. Yearwood experienced. The jury needed to be able to visualize and understand why Danny Yearwood continued to hurt and why many of his tests were negative. To that end, we told the jury that Mr. Yearwood went from one doctor to the next until, finally, Dr. Robert Gerwin was able to touch damaged fibers called "trigger points" in approximately twenty-six different muscles in Mr. Yearwood's body. The jurors were told that if Dr. Gerwin could guide their fingers to these trigger points, the jurors would feel tense, taut bands of muscle fibers with a hard nodule in the middle and that these areas were extremely painful and tender.

Setting the Stage

With respect to the medical testimony presented on behalf of the plaintiffs, we decided to introduce Dr. Gerwin's testimony first so that the jury could keep it in mind when they heard all the other medical testimony, including the opinions of the two doctors who thought Mr. Yearwood was not injured. Moreover, as Dr. Gerwin was Mr. Yearwood's most recent treating physician and accurately explained the cause of his pain, we hoped to persuade the jury that, unfortunately, some of Mr. Yearwood's earlier treating doctors simply did not understand soft-tissue injuries.

As for Mr. Yearwood, we decided to leave him at home during the nearly week-long trial. He was called to the courtroom solely for the purpose of presenting his direct testimony, and following cross-examination he returned home and remained there. We felt that it would be difficult for Mr. Yearwood to remain in the courtroom during the long trial. We also felt that many jurors might be distracted by continually watching Mr. Yearwood. Accordingly, only Mrs. Yearwood was present during the trial, and at no time did anyone make any comment whatsoever about Mr. Yearwood's absence. Incidentally, we believe that defense counsel was quite correct in not making an issue of Mr. Yearwood's absence. We believe it would have been a serious mistake to have opened this issue.

In this case, as is so often true in soft-tissue injury cases, much of the final argument time had to be spent on liability. We tried liability expecting a strong defense; to have assumed otherwise would have made our position on damages less credible. Mr. Sanders argued liability and used thirty-five minutes of the allotted one hour for final argument.

Having provided the jury early on with a framework for understanding why Mr. Yearwood continued to hurt, and why most standard tests were understandably negative, the stage was then set for the concluding argument on damages.

Concluding Argument on Damages

MR. STEPHENS: Ladies and gentlemen, I sat here and watched defense counsel and Mr. [Janney E.] Sanders almost in a battle to convince you which one of them was more credible with respect to why the wreck happened. I cannot help but suggest that there is a good backdrop against which you can measure the sincerity of the defenses that have been raised.

You will remember what the defense did. You remember that when Mrs. Yearwood was on the stand and defense counsel asked her if she had testified that her husband, Danny, had always earned a good income before this wreck, and she said yes. Then he took their joint income tax returns for the year before and, while waving them in the air, asked if it wasn't true that it showed only $84 as her husband's income; and the defense made this big point of that fact, all the while knowing that Mr. Yearwood's income that year was reported through Danken's Store, the business corporation of the Yearwoods. The evidence shows that we had provided the defense with a copy of that corporate tax return and a copy of Danny Yearwood's W-2 forms showing earnings over $40,000 that year, and yet the defense chose to make it appear that Danny did not earn an income for his family before this wreck.

This is the backdrop against which you can judge the sincerity of the defendant's defenses in this case. Keep in mind they chose to take this tack knowing that we had stated to you in opening statement that Mr. and Mrs. Yearwood would not seek recovery for lost wages since Danny Yearwood had started a new business only three or four weeks before this wreck. And we honestly told you we were seeking no recovery for lost wages because we could not establish what earnings he would have made in this new business had it not been for this wreck.

I submit this is the backdrop against which you can judge all of their defenses in this case. They come in here at the start of this trial and they tell you that the evidence will show that the neck pain and back pain of which Danny is complaining were caused by an explosion and fire which occurred months after this wreck. We told you that the doctor at the Augusta Burn Unit who treated Danny for his burns would tell you that the fire and burns in no way caused Danny's neck and back pain. And that is what Dr. [Herman] Orlet [Mr. Yearwood's plastic surgeon] testified to on deposition, and the defense knew that [about the testimony] when they told you at the beginning of this trial that this fire caused Danny's pain.

You will have out with you a summary showing the dates that Danny Yearwood went to the doctor complaining of neck and back pain following this wreck, and you can see that Danny had eighty-six visits to doctors with this neck and back pain before this fire ever took place. Many of these were emergency room visits begging for pain relief. Yet they stood here telling you in opening statement that the fire caused his problems. The truth of the fact is that the fire itself was caused by these injuries; he had been in so much pain and was on so much pain medication that he couldn't possibly have known what he was doing when this fire took place. But this suit seeks no damages for the fire. You have a summary of all medical expenses, and you can see that not a single medical bill relating to that fire is included in those expenses.

This is the kind of evidence you can judge [the defense's] sincerity upon. They come in here today and they argue to you that his neck and back pain was caused by some radiation exposure he had on his job in New York. Let's look at the sincerity of that defense. Did they bring you any medical evidence on that contention? All told there have been nine or ten doctors testify in this case, and not a single time did [the defense] ever ask a single one of them whether [Mr. Yearwood's] radiation contamination in any way contributed to his neck and back pain. Not a single question about it—nine doctors. They brought you a radiologist to tell you his X rays were negative. This was a man who deals with radiation every day, but they never asked him within your hearing whether exposure to radiation could have been the source of his symptoms. They knew what the answer would be. They would rather suggest and insinuate and hope that one of you might be influenced by this argument, which was unsupported by any evidence. This is how you judge the sincerity of their defenses in this case.

And so, just in case you see through those defenses, they tell you that Danny Yearwood was not hurt; he didn't go to the emergency room until the next day. They tell you that all these visits to the doctor and emergency room were because he was seeking drugs. Indeed, one of the emergency room physicians [Dr. John C. Lawrence] testified he felt Danny was seeking drugs. You should keep in mind that we took that deposition, we brought that evidence to you, not because we believed the doctor was right, but because we wanted you to know all the evidence which you would need in order to fairly and honestly reach the truth in this case.

And what did that doctor say when I asked him: "Doctor, could you be wrong about that?" His answer was: "Certainly, I have been wrong before." More importantly, I asked him if he knew anything about the later treatment of Mr. Yearwood, and the doctor said no. I asked him if he knew whether there had now been a diagnosis made of the cause and source of Danny's pain, and he said no, he did not know.

But the defense in this case knew about [pain specialist] Dr.

[Robert] Gerwin's testimony; the defense knew all the time they were suggesting to you that Danny Yearwood was not having the pain and was only seeking drugs; they knew that Dr. Gerwin was one of only a few doctors in the world with his degree of knowledge and training relating to this myofascial pain, and they knew he had already examined Mr. Yearwood. They knew that Dr. Gerwin had found around twenty-six muscles in Danny Yearwood's body in which Dr. Gerwin could actually feel and palpate trigger points with his hands, and yet they chose to tell you in opening statement that Danny Yearwood wasn't hurt in this wreck and that he was a drug-seeking person.

Ladies and gentlemen, Danny Yearwood could have purchased drugs off the street corner in Gainesville a whole lot cheaper than they were costing him and his family at the emergency room. But still, [the defense] holds out these insinuations to you with the hope that one of you might believe them.

This much I will agree with: Danny Yearwood is today addicted to narcotic drugs; he is addicted to drugs which have been prescribed for him because no one could put his finger on why he was having such severe pain, and this addiction is something that Danny Yearwood and his family are going to have to deal with. You will decide his case today based on the evidence, not insinuation, and not the kind of evidence the defendant has held up to you.

A Window into Hell

Ladies and gentlemen, you are going to go out to that jury room and you are going to decide what amount of money should be awarded for the damages and pain and suffering that these two people have suffered through—and it is not over. If there is one thing that I can do to justify my fees in handling this case, it will be to cause you to look at each element of these damages separately and independently.

First, let's look at Danny Yearwood's past, present, and future pain and suffering. You will have out with you the summary showing the date of each trip to the doctor and the charges for that treatment. Just look at them—over 150 trips to the doctor, many of them in the middle of the night. You see him going into the emergency room crying with pain, and on every one of those visits except one his wife was with him. You know from the evidence that Mrs. Yearwood was pregnant when this wreck took place, and so in the middle of the night Danny Yearwood is down at the emergency room begging for pain relief and his wife being eight months pregnant is driving him to the emergency room. You see them 12:30 at night on Christmas [Day] in the emergency room begging for pain relief, and every time that he went to the emergency room he called his doctor and told him about it. And then you see them again only two hours later on Christmas [Day] back in the emergency room pleading that the earlier shots didn't work.

This has been their life for years now. Ladies and gentlemen, I think you have seen a glimpse of the pain he has had, and it's not over. For almost three years now, Danny Yearwood has been in a deep, dark hole, and his family has been desperately trying to reach out to him and pull him out. At times, they have almost been sucked into that hole themselves, and it has truly been a window into hell.

Danny Yearwood has a chance to get out of that hole, and so you say, how much should be awarded? I will tell you that I don't like to suggest an amount; if the amount I suggest is too high, then I am afraid you might blame the Yearwoods, but I am going to suggest an amount anyway and if I am wrong, then you can just chalk it up to the fellow being from Gainesville—what does he know?

Pain and Suffering: $1 Million

I submit that $1 million is an appropriate amount to award for his mental and physical pain and suffering. Now, remember that we told you in the beginning that although Mr. Yearwood had earned over $40,000 the year before, that he had changed jobs and started a new business only three or four weeks before this wreck; we told you we were not seeking any lost wages or profits because we could not show you with certainty what this new business would have earned. And so, we said to you we are not going to seek recovery for that. The court will charge you that as a part of the claim for pain and suffering you may consider the loss of the ability to work and earn wages, and we ask that you consider that as a part of the claim for mental pain and suffering.

You have seen and will have out with you the list of medical expenses. We have brought to you the evidence of what those expenses have been, and you will remember that, although Danny is finally better today than he has been, he still may have years ahead of him of medical treatment; he still has to find a way to deal with the fact that he is now chemically dependent on pain medications. We would ask you to award $300,000 for past, present, and future medical expenses.

I am sorry that I have almost run out of time and I only have a short time to talk to you about Mrs. Yearwood's loss-of-consortium claim. You know, some people snicker about this kind of claim, but the law recognizes that when one spouse goes through agonizing injuries the other spouse is pulled through a terrible ordeal also. And as I said to you before, at times Mrs. Yearwood was almost sucked into that deep, dark hole—all the while desperately somehow trying to find a way to help her husband survive. I would suggest a verdict of $200,000 for loss of consortium would be appropriate. You know, even if you accept the view that Mr. Yearwood's sexual problems relate to something else, the fact is, Danny Yearwood is not the same man she married, and under this evidence I doubt that he will ever be the same.

Ladies and gentlemen, I am out of time. We told you what the evidence was going to be in this case in opening and I believe you know we stated it to you accurately. It would be wrong for your verdict to be based on sympathy for the Yearwoods, and it would be wrong for you to reduce your verdict based on any concern about the defendant's ability to pay. You speak the truth in this case and when you have done that, I assure you that neither Mr. and Mrs. Yearwood nor their attorneys will complain, and no one else has any right to complain.

Epilogue: The Credibility Battle
The Lawyer's Post Mortem of His Argument

When Mr. Sanders and I tried the *Yearwood* case, we assumed that jurors in rural north Georgia would have certain preconceived notions and doubts about the credibility of a "whiplash" case. Thus, to a large extent our goal in the concluding argument, as in the whole case, was to win the credibility battle. We had to convince the jurors in final argument that the defendant's positions were not credible. We also had to convince them that any preconceived doubts that they had concerning the plaintiffs' case were in fact wrong.

To accomplish our goal, we reminded the jury of a number of things that illustrated very clearly that the defendant's position in this case was not credible and that the plaintiffs had been open, honest, and forthright concerning each aspect of the case. For instance, we reminded the jury that the defense argued the burns Mr. Yearwood sustained in the fire caused his neck and back pain. On the contrary, we pointed out, the physician who treated him for his burns said that was not the case. Also, we noted that the defense introduced no expert testimony to support its claim that Mr. Yearwood's pain was due to radiation contamination. Moreover, we reminded the jury that *we* had introduced the deposition of Dr. John C. Lawrence, who said he felt that Mr. Yearwood was exaggerating his pain in order to obtain drugs.

We wanted to draw a striking contrast between the defense's and the plaintiffs' credibility. Also, we wanted to remind the jury that we had been very careful to present to them all relevant evidence, which was in no measure exaggerated.

My concluding argument on damages is a good example of how to argue damages in a soft-tissue injury case when little time remains. In that situation, detailed summaries of medical visits and medical expenses are invaluable because counsel may refer to them without going into detail. Such was the case here because the jury had seen the summaries and would have a copy of them during deliberations.

The evidence during the trial itself was certainly adequate to allow the jury to deliberate on damages virtually without any final argument. If we had won the credibility battle, there could be little doubt in the jurors' minds that the Yearwoods had been terribly damaged by this automobile wreck. The number of medical visits in the summaries that went out with the jury was alone sufficiently impressive to warrant a substantial verdict.

Because of the time limitation, I used analogies that would graphically portray the Yearwoods' predicament. I compared the Yearwoods' ordeal to a deep, dark hole. At least indirectly, I set up the argument on loss of consortium by noting that Mrs. Yearwood had desperately tried to help her husband get out of that hole and, on numerous occasions, she was nearly "sucked" into the hole with him. I subtly suggested to the jury that if Danny Yearwood was going to get out of that deep, dark hole, and if his family was to avoid being sucked into that hole with him, only this jury could do the job.

While considerable evidence of Mr. Yearwood's devastating pain had been presented during the trial, I selected one example that highlighted the impact of his injury on his family. That example was Christmas Day, when pregnant Mrs. Yearwood had to get up in the middle of the night and take her husband to the emergency room twice for pain relief. During what should have been a joyous Christmas, the Yearwoods' lives were dominated by Danny's pain. This example certainly presented to the jury the concept of loss of consortium and pain and suffering.

I also wanted to emphasize to this jury that Danny Yearwood had a chance to recover and that he would never give up that chance. I wanted them to realize he was better than he had been at any time since the wreck occurred. I wanted the jury to know that, finally, Danny Yearwood's treatment was indeed working and that there was hope. We did not want to dwell on the negative aspects of what the future held for Danny Yearwood. We wanted to emphasize the positive aspects and to at least indirectly say to the jury, "You can help him get the rest of the way out of this hole."

Less Can Be More

I believe that if a plaintiff has passed the credibility test a jury will make an award for loss of consortium, provided that the subject is handled with dignity and subtlety. Explicit discussion of the claimants' sexual activity is generally counterproductive. In this case, the goal was to get across to the jury in a very short amount of time the hell that one spouse goes through when the other spouse is sick and injured. I believe I saw in the faces of the jurors an appreciation for the dignity with which this issue was treated.

During voir dire, we did not inquire into the jury's willingness to award substantial damages and made no references to the amount of damages being sought. We felt that discussing large sums of money before the jury had the necessary evidence to understand the unique aspects of the case would damage our credibility.

Since juries in Toccoa were typically conservative in soft-tissue injury cases, I broached the dollar amount issue with some hesitation even in final argument. The amounts I requested were subjective, based on our assessment of the strength of our case and what we knew our clients had suffered. I used no magic formula, nor did I try to convince the jury of any particular logic to the sums requested. I told the jury that if the figures I suggested seemed too high, they should simply ignore them because I was from Gainesville and what did I know? Indirectly, I hoped to convey a subtle message to the jury that the injuries of one of their fellow citizens were worth at least as much as those of a Gainesville resident.

Letting the jury know that we were not making a claim for lost wages or profits because we could not prove them in a specific amount was a strategic move, fairly rare for a plaintiff, that paid off. We put great confidence in the belief that it is better to score credibility points with the jury than to strain to collect damages that will become a central controversy during the trial. Our philosophy was literally less can be more, and I believe this concept should be applied in all soft-tissue injury cases. Moreover, a claim for lost wages or profits might have increased the likelihood of a successful appeal in the event that the jury returned a substantial verdict.

Also as part of my brief argument on damages, I wanted subtly to remind the jury that the plaintiffs in this case would have to pay attorney's fees. ("If there is one thing that I can do to justify my fees in handling this case it will be to cause you to look at each element of these damages separately and independently.") I wanted the jurors to know that they would have to add money to their verdict to cover attorney's fees if they wanted the plaintiffs to receive a specific sum of money.

I have agonized for years over how to obtain a substantial verdict against a private individual. Plaintiffs lawyers have from time to time expressed the view that juries return substantial verdicts against corporations simply because they are corporations. Indeed, frequently, in trucking accident cases, we try to join the insurance carrier as a defendant with the view that the verdict will likely be more substantial. In doing so, I believe that to some extent we bring on ourselves a tendency for juries to be more conservative in cases against private individuals.

My approach to this issue in recent years has simply been to be honest with the jury. I am honest in the sense that I say to the jury, "We don't want your verdict based on sympathy. We want a full appraisal of the damages, and it would be wrong to award a verdict based on sympathy, just as it would be wrong to reduce the verdict based on your belief of what the defendant could afford to pay." I believe that this argument is appropriate, and no judge I've tried cases before has ever sustained an objection to it. Once the jurors know that they are not supposed to base their verdict on sympathy or to reduce their verdict out of concern over the defendant's ability to pay, most of them will struggle to abide by these ideals.

I believe that most lawyers defending soft-tissue injury cases feel that a jury in rural north Georgia is not likely to award anything substantial. If this is not the view of most defense lawyers, then I am convinced that it is the view of most claims people. To my knowledge, until the *Yearwood* verdict, the largest jury verdict in Toccoa for a soft-tissue injury case was approximately $60,000. Danny Yearwood's case certainly shatters the image of conservative north Georgia juries.

–CWS

Endnote

*Charles W. Stephens is a partner in the law firm of Stephens & Shuler in Gainesville, Georgia. He received his L.L.B. degree from Tulane University Law School in 1967 and was admitted to the State Bar of Georgia in 1968. He served as an assistant district attorney (then called solicitor general) of the Northeastern Judicial Circuit in 1968–69, and as a special prosecutor during the next several years. From 1969 to 1981, he was a partner in Telford, Stewart & Stephens. In 1981 he formed Stephens & Shuler; the firm's practice is limited to personal injury cases. Mr. Stephens served as president of the Georgia Trial Lawyers Association in 1992–93, and he is an associate member of the American Board of Trial Advocates.

Pittman v. Saker
No. 926410 (Fulton State Ct.)

Result: $2.5 million verdict
Plaintiff's Counsel: Don C. Keenan and William J. Berg of The Keenan Law Firm (Atlanta)
Defense Counsel: George W. Hart of then Hart & Sullivan (Atlanta), and Robert G. Tanner of Long, Weinberg, Ansley & Wheeler (Atlanta)
Judge: Frank M. Hull
Date of Verdict: June 5, 1986

Chapter VII

Tragedy at Birth

Introduction
By Don C. Keenan*

P*ittman v. Saker* was the first plaintiff's verdict in an obstetrical negligence case in Georgia's history and the first verdict exceeding a million dollars in a Georgia state court. The suit was brought by Cheryl Pittman on behalf of her child, Tawanna Lashann Pittman, who suffered profound brain damage, due to severe asphyxia, during her birth on Saturday, October 24, 1981.

Mrs. Pittman had received regular prenatal care from Dr. Patrick Anders. Initially, he estimated her due date as September 21, but later he changed it to October 21. Despite Mrs. Pittman's obesity (281 lbs. by October 21), Dr. Anders performed no sonograms or other diagnostic tests.

On October 24, at about 5:45 A.M., Mrs. Pittman arrived at South Fulton Hospital in labor. At 7:30 A.M., Dr. Anders called a fellow obstetrician, Dr. Alexander Saker, and asked Saker to attend Mrs. Pittman. The physicians did not discuss Mrs. Pittman's condition. By 10:00 A.M., her cervix was dilated only three to four centimeters, so Dr. Saker told the nurses to give her Pitocin, a drug that increases the strength and frequency of contractions. The dosage of Pitocin was increased throughout the day. Finally, by 5:45 P.M., Mrs. Pittman was fully dilated.

At 8:04 P.M., Tawanna was delivered vaginally. She had aspirated meconium (fetal feces) and had to be suctioned. Within a few hours, Tawanna began to suffer seizures. She was transferred to Egleston Children's Hospital, where she was diagnosed with severe, permanent cerebral and neurological damage. Tawanna remains profoundly retarded, is not likely to increase her intellectual skills, and requires constant maintenance with phenobarbitol.

Plaintiff alleged that her condition was caused by the severe asphyxia she suffered during birth due to the negligence of Drs. Saker and Anders. Specifically, plaintiff alleged that Dr. Saker administered excessive amounts of Pitocin for too long a period of time; failed to perform a cesarean section delivery when one was clearly required; and failed to provide adequate monitoring of the mother and baby's condition. Plaintiff alleged that Dr. Anders failed to perform appropriate prenatal tests and did not properly apprise Dr. Saker of Mrs. Pittman's condition.

Dr. Saker claimed that Mrs. Pittman's obesity did not make electronic fetal monitoring necessary. He also claimed that the amount of Pitocin administered to Mrs. Pittman was proper and did not harm the baby. Further, he contended that the molding of Tawanna's head that occurred during labor was normal; that she was only mildly physically depressed at birth, as her Apgar scores were nine within ten minutes; and that she was in good shape when she was turned over to the nursery. In his defense, Dr. Anders claimed that he monitored Mrs. Pittman's pregnancy properly and left her in the care of a competent physician during childbirth. Both doctors claimed that Mrs. Pittman's pregnancy did not exceed forty-one weeks.

Five physicians testified that Tawanna suffered severe asphyxia, or lack of oxygen, during labor and delivery. I had never used these experts before. On the other hand, the defendants' expert witnesses had a long-standing relationship with defense counsel. I used that relationship to attack the experts' credibility.

Closing Argument: Keeping it Simple

The trial of an obstetrical medical negligence case is enormously complex and exposes jurors to highly technical and often confusing medical terminology and phenomena. The strategy employed on closing argument is the basic KISS principle—Keep It Simple Stupid.

My overall objective in closing argument in *Pittman v. Saker* was to impress upon the jurors the finality of their verdict and how it would affect Tawanna's quality of life, given her normal life expectancy.

During the opening final argument, which consumed less than ten minutes, I stressed the seventy years of future care that Tawanna would require. Also, I discussed the basic jury charges on burden of proof, standard of care, and credibility, which proved quite important given the testimony in the case.

The concluding argument was essentially a point-by-point rebuttal of the defense case. I strongly believed that at the conclusion of the defense arguments the jury was at best confused and at worst convinced that the defense had merit. Thus, I decided to attack and discredit each defense issue, rather than spend precious time reiterating the plaintiff's theories of the case both on standard of care and causation. I believed that a successful attack on the defenses would bring a successful result.

In attacking the defense arguments, I constantly referred to the medical record and the conflict between the defense experts' opinions and the record. Further, I launched a wholesale attack on the credibility of two primary defense experts.

On the matter of damages, the jury had heard extensive testimony through life care planners, economists, and caregivers as to the needs of the child—presently and in the future. The range was a low of $1.2 million and a high of $2.8 million.

I decided to mention neither of these amounts during closing argument, but instead pushed the theme that she would need seventy years of care and had to be fully compensated for her losses.

Once again, the strategy included an attack on defense arguments. During the damages phase of the trial and in argument, defense counsel urged that government services for brain-injured children were sufficient. I countered that argument by contending that no one wants to be a ward of the state.

The jury deliberated approximately one hour and ten minutes and rendered a $2.5 million verdict against both physicians. The defendants appealed, but while the appeal was pending, we settled the case for the full amount of the verdict plus interest. St. Paul Fire and Marine Insurance Co., the defendants' insurance carrier, had made no settlement offers before the appeal.

When interviews were held with all of the jurors after the verdict, it became clear that the defense closing argument had been persuasive and thus, my strategy in mounting a point-by-point attack on all defense issues was correct.

Opening Final Argument

MR. KEENAN: Good morning, ladies and gentlemen.

I don't need to tell you how very, very important this case is. And I know you realize that there will never be another trial in this case and that your decision is for all time. And the "all time" in this case goes some seventy years, the normal life expectancy of Tawanna.

You know, we don't think in the terms of the year 2065, but that is the end of her life, at least as far as the actuaries tell us. So what you do today and the decision you make here in June of 1986 is going to affect her for the rest of her life and well on into the next century.

You've heard the evidence and you've heard the facts. Next, after the lawyers sit down, the judge will tell you the rules, the guidelines that you, as a jury, must apply to the facts.

You are the judges, even though you don't wear a black robe. You are the judges of the facts in the case. You must be guided by the law.

The Burden of Proof

The most important principle in a civil case to remember is that Tawanna has the burden of proof. She brought the action; she must prove her case.

Now, from television and even from the news media we hear about proof beyond a reasonable doubt, that you have to prove your case beyond a reasonable doubt. Well, that's true in a criminal case. If someone was going to jail, then we would have to prove the case beyond a reasonable doubt.

But the court, when it tells you what the law is, it's going to be very clear. And this is very important about the evidence in the case. The court is going to tell you that Tawanna must prove her case, but she must prove it by the greater weight of the evidence. And the words used will be "by a preponderance of the evidence."

Now what does that mean? How do you, if you've got the scales of justice and you're trying to put evidence on one side for one and the other side for another, how do you even it out? How do you do that?

Well, the greater weight of the evidence is simply more than 50 percent out of 100. And that is, if you have the scales of justice and if the evidence for Tawanna that she has presented to you tips the scales however slightly in her favor, then she's carried her burden.

Now, for those of us that maybe are familiar with football, I'll give you a better example. If we have 100 yards on the playing field—of course, we all know in order to score we either have to get in the field goal range and kick a field goal or we actually have to get in the end zone. We have to go the whole way. Not so in a civil case.

A civil case has a 50-yard line. If Tawanna, with her evidence and her testimony and her experts, has pushed the nose of the ball however slightly over the 50-yard line, she has carried her burden. Now, that's an important principle.

The second important principle is this: that Tawanna has alleged and has brought forth evidence of numerous mistakes, breaches of the standard of care that these doctors have made. In fact, there are three as to Dr. Anders, and there are six as to Dr. Saker.

The law of Georgia is very clear that [the plaintiff] is not required to carry her burden on each one of those [mistakes]. It is sufficient that she carry her burden as to [one mistake by] one doctor and one as to another doctor.

So you may look at the various mistakes made and decide that of the six that five simply didn't matter, didn't cause any damage. But if you find that one did, then that is sufficient enough to support your verdict.

The Standard of Care

Now, I submit to you that this case is about responsibility, a doctor's responsibility to Cheryl, the mama, and to Tawanna, the little fetus that then became the little baby.

We hold doctors in our society to perhaps a higher position. We look up to them, we respect them, we pay them more. Why? Because they accept great responsibility, and they get paid for it, and they get paid good money for it. So they will be put to a higher standard, and it will be called a standard of care for all physicians, and you will hear that time and time again. "What is the standard of care?" Well, the standard of care, ladies and gentlemen, as it applies to doctors, is the same anywhere. That is, a person in Vidalia, a person in New York City, a person in Sioux City, Iowa, [are] all entitled to the same standard of care.

Now, that standard, then, is set by experts. Ladies and gentlemen, you're not permitted to decide that a certain standard applies. You have to take that from the witness stand and decide who it is you believe about the standard. It's just that simple.

Now, the court is going to give you the law on another important principle that sometimes doesn't matter in cases, but I think it matters a great deal here. And that's about credibility of the witnesses. What you're going to be faced with here is balancing which doctors you believe, which doctors you find to be the most credible.

And when you look at those doctors you've got to ask yourself, what is their financial stake in this, how much [have] they been paid? You've got to look at their track record of whether or not they have, indeed, been biased or impartial in the past. Have they picked one side as opposed to another, and what is their relationship with the lawyers [who] brought them into the case? Do they have some ongoing relationship with them? And, as well, do they—the experts—have a relationship with the defendants in the case? That all goes to the credibility. That all goes to whether or not you accept what they say as the truth. And we submit to you that that's going to be real important when we get down to the nitty-gritty of who you believe and who you don't.[1]

Damages

Now, I think the last thing that we need to talk about just generally is the most important part of the case, and that's the damages. Because what we must do here today—and your responsibility will soon be to take care of Tawanna for the rest of her life.

You will have to remember that there was testimony about what medical expenses she's going to have, what adaptive necessities she has to have. You heard testimony that she'll never be able to work, she'll never be able to [earn] an income. But if she weren't brain damaged she would have been able to earn a wage, and that's called capacity to work.

And you've also heard and will hear about the pain and suffering. The mental anguish that the little girl has gone through. Those are all elements of damage. And whether you like it or not, you're going to have that burden in this case. It's going to be shifted to you. You're going to have to assess it with your common sense and your wisdom, and it has to be a verdict that speaks for all time.

Now, I'm going to sit down. I'm going to pay careful attention to what the two able defense lawyers are going to say. And then, after that, I'm going to have an opportunity to get back up and talk to you about the specific facts, the allegations, and why we think and why we feel in our heart that we have a very, very strong case. If there ever was a case, this is it.

Thank you.

Final Argument

MR. KEENAN: Ladies and gentlemen, as I indicated earlier this morning, it's now my purpose to get up and respond to each and every thing the defense attorneys had to say. And I hope that you'll pay me as equal attention as you did [them], because I'm going to try to go item by item, step by step, through everything that [they] said and put this case back into perspective.

First of all, you know that if Tawanna had the medical care rendered to her as the doctors in this case have had very able lawyers render to them, there wouldn't even be a lawsuit.

You have seen two of the finest lawyers that this state has. You have heard from prior testimony that [defense counsel] is so good that he's traveled all the way to Texas to represent doctors. So I guess I shouldn't be surprised that things are a little confusing, things are a little out of whack.

But I was surprised that he emphasized that the case must be based on facts. And then he further said the case must be based on medicine. But yet during his entire closing argument he referred to no medical record, he referred to no medical textbook, and he really referred to no concrete medical opinion, the way I have throughout this case.

I'm not a doctor. I bring you what the expert witnesses have said in the case.

Tawanna Pittman Suffered Perinatal Asphyxia

Now, what is the very, very first thing that [defense counsel] said to you? That there's no doubt about it, that there's no asphyxia [lack of oxygen] in this case. No evidence in this case of asphyxia, he says. The plaintiff is just absolutely crazy as a bedbug for suggesting that the mechanism for this damage was asphyxia.

Do you recall the deposition of the two Emory doctors, Dr. [Peter] Ahmann and Dr. [James] Schwartz, who weren't picked by either side? In fact, if you will recall, the deposition of both Dr. Ahmann and Dr. Schwartz was not taken by the plaintiff but [was] taken by [defense counsel]. [Defense counsel is] the one [who] asked the questions.

And what did these two impartial doctors say?

Dr. Ahmann, you'll recall, first saw Tawanna two days after [her] birth. And what does he say? He says it's a 36-hour[-old] female with seizures. "Conclusion: perinatal asphyxia."

And, of course, CAT scans were run, tests were done. He sees her again a year later, May 14, 1982. And what did he tell you from the witness stand?

"Tawanna is now six-and-a-half months old, born with Apgars [scoring of organ functions at birth] of five and seven"—and we'll spend a lot of time on that—"complicated course indicating perinatal asphyxia."

[Dr. Ahmann] then has more CAT scans done, more diagnostic tests before this lawsuit ever came about and before anybody took a position. And what did Dr. Ahmann tell you from the witness stand about 1984?

"Tawanna is now three years old who we have seen and followed in the past."

Why? Why are we caring for this little girl? Because of cerebral hypoplasia? Because of virus? Heck no. We are caring for her because of "perinatal asphyxia."

Do you remember what perinatal was? Every single witness except one defined perinatal as "labor and delivery."

Even the defendants: "What is perinatal?"
"Well, that means labor and delivery."
Labor and delivery asphyxia. Impartial witness.
Is there just one [witness who] says that? No.

Dr. Schwartz—who you'll remember was the head of the [pediatric neurology] department at Emory when Jones, their expert, was a mere medical student—what did Dr. Schwartz say from the witness stand? He first saw Tawanna [in] December 1981. She was six weeks old. What was his impression? "Severe asphyxia." Severe.

He then saw her two years later. Did he change his opinion after looking at the CAT scans, after looking at the tests? Heck no. This impartial, unbiased witness from the witness stand said, "severely asphyxiated at birth." "Perinatal asphyxia."

He was not a witness that was paid a dime by either party in this case. And what did he say? Did he change his opinion in three and a half years?

"Impression: Mental retardation with a seizure disorder caused by perinatal asphyxia."

But, see, [defense counsel] thinks that since that testimony was heard by you on the first day that you've forgotten it. Well, you ain't forgot it because it's right there.

The Bias of the Defense's Experts

Now, do you remember when I stressed in my opening statement about credibility of the witnesses, that you are the judges?

Well, the court is going to tell you some of the things to look out for: the motive of the witness, the bias of the witness, the interest in the outcome, and the witness's memory recall.

Let's take a look at the kind of witnesses that actually came to this court.

We have Dr. Burke. Profession: University of Florida, Georgetown Medical School. He was the national president of the Perinatal Obstetrician Society, the number one guy in the whole country. And what did he say from the witness stand?

This child was severely asphyxiated, and he used the words

"no question about it." And then he went on to tell us about the [need for a] C-section.

Was there a suggestion that I had ever represented Dr. Burke? Was there a suggestion that I paid Dr. Burke $60,000 to $90,000? Was there a suggestion that I ever brought Dr. Burke into another court? No. He is impartial—he has no motive, no bias, no interest.

Dr. Williams, director of Child Neurology at the largest children's hospital in the United States. Author of four textbooks, two hundred journals. What did I ask him?

"What happened to this child?"

"The child suffered severe asphyxia."

"When, doctor?"

"During the perinatal period."

"When is that, doctor?"

"Labor and delivery. The asphyxia caused the mental retardation."

Again, have I ever called him as a witness [before this trial]? Did I even know the man before this case? Have I ever represented him? No.

Dr. Swain. She's been all over the world—Scandinavia, France, Germany—conducted asphyxia research. Do you remember that woman? God bless her, she was so clear. She gave the clearest testimony in this trial about how this case came about. And what did she say? "This child suffered severe asphyxia during the labor and delivery time, much like a stroke." And she explained it with the records. Not with opinions, with the records.

Asphyxia caused the mental retardation.

Now, how can [defense counsel] then get up to you at the end of the case—hopefully thinking you're confused—and tell you that this baby wasn't asphyxiated, when two Emory doctors say it and at least three unbiased, noninterested witnesses have said it also?

But what do they [the defendants] say? Who do they [have who] says there ain't no asphyxia in this case?

Dr. Ivan Backerman. Is he an impartial, nonbiased witness?

Come on, use your common sense, ladies and gentlemen. [Defense counsel] represented him ten years ago. He tried to get out of it right here on the stand.

"I don't know how his name got on the answer to that lawsuit."

But there wasn't any mistake about it. [Defense counsel] started representing this expert before he was asked to be an expert in this case. [Dr. Backerman has] known both the defendants in this case for years.

Now, how unbiased, how impartial is that? I can get my best friend to say darn near anything about me, including I'm a good lawyer. But who's going to believe him? If you're going to get an expert, get one that doesn't have an interest, doesn't have a connection with it.

What about their other expert, Dr. Jones? My goodness sakes, testified at twenty different trials, twenty different trials. He now has another case right now with [defense counsel].

Do you think that [defense counsel] is going to use him again in that other case and pay him $5,000 or $6,000 if he doesn't do a good job? That man's thinking in the back of his mind, "Hey, if I don't do good in this case, then I'm not going to be able to review those other cases and get $5,000 and $6,000 and $7,000."

But it doesn't stop there, ladies and gentlemen. This so-called impartial, unbiased witness is now working with the other lawyer in the case. And that other lawyer happens to represent [Dr. Jones's] hospital. Now, is that impartial? Is that unbiased? Is that a true opinion?

The Wandering Dr. Wander

I submit to you, they couldn't find anybody they didn't have a string on to get on that witness stand and contradict the two Emory doctors and the three nationally acclaimed experts we had. They had to resort to friends. They had to resort to people that they had a hook in by way of representing. And then they finally, finally resorted to "Dr. Wander" [Kenneth Niswander].

I call him "Wandering" because there's hardly a state in this country [where] he's not testified. I mean, were you shocked when he told you? He's not a medical doctor, he's a professional testifier. [He's received] $94,000 testifying on behalf of doctors. He's been so busy that in the last three years—he's an obstetrician, now. His business is delivering babies. And he has been so busy testifying that he's only been able to deliver eight babies. Eight babies.

[Defense counsel] toted him all the way to Texas.

They played this song and dance and road show before. I mean, he hit the witness stand like he was a fair and impartial witness—didn't have any stake in the venture—until cross-examination.

And I'll tell you, if there's one thing [defense counsel] was correct about, it's the crucible of truth. It cuts the case down to where it belongs.

And [defense counsel] asked, "Well, have we ever had any dealings, Dr. Wander?" He didn't say a word.

I was the one that had to pull out that they went to Texas, Brownsville, Texas. The two of them representing another doctor put this road show on. And here he is again, and he's reviewing another case.

Those are the defense witnesses.

Now, is there any doubt that there was asphyxia in this case based on the fair, impartial, unbiased witnesses in this case? Don't believe me. Look at the facts. Look at the facts.

Signs of Fetal Distress: First, Meconium

If it's one thing we've learned this week, [it's that] the most important indicator of fetal distress is meconium.

Did [defense counsel] once during his closing argument address what caused that meconium? Did he whisper to you? Did he say the baby was just taking a rest and enjoying labor so well it just decided to excrete its bowel? He couldn't do anything with that one, so he stayed away from that.

What does [the medical record] say? It says Tawanna was meconium stained at birth. What did we learn about that—meconium stained? [The fetus] just wasn't covered with it, it had been stained. It had been around so long, ladies and gentlemen, that it was stained.

What did we learn about meconium? Not opinions. Medical facts: "Fetal distress may lead to defecation of meconium into the amniotic fluid." There is a relationship between fetal distress and the amniotic fluid and the meconium.

Now, where do we see that? When do we see the meconium? At 8:04 P.M. when the baby's delivered. It was covered with meconium-stained fluid. It was covered so bad that when we brought the nurse from Henrietta Egleston [Children's Hospital] in, who took care of the baby the day afterwards, she said that meconium was so thick that baby was still stained on the second day. That baby still had meconium under its fingernails. Do you remember?

Now, what do we know about the meconium production?

Well, Dr. [Niswander], their expert, wrote in a book that if you see meconium staining at birth, the likely onset is six hours before or perhaps before that. You listened to that deposition. You listened to his testimony.

And you listened when I asked him, "Well, doctor, under that opinion—and you still hold it that way, don't you?"

"Yes."

"The likely time that the meconium was produced was between one and three o'clock in the afternoon, wasn't it?"

He said yes.

And to make absolutely sure what time period we're talking about, I said, "Doctor, Tawanna was still in the tummy of the mama at one o'clock and three o'clock when the fetal distress in the meconium was coming out?"

He said, "Absolutely."

Now, why is that important?

You'll see that between one and roughly five o'clock when the meconium was being produced, that baby wasn't moving.

It was stuck. It wasn't going anywhere. It didn't even move a centimeter. It was stuck in there.

Why was it stuck? Because the head size was thirty-seven centimeters, in the ninety-fifth percentile.

Now, I'm going by Dr. Swain's testimony, and you'll remember. It was Friday, and I know we shouldn't have called her on Friday because you all were tired and we were wanting to get out of here.

But with a big head lodging in the birth canal, just the way it shows here, stuck, stuck.

Well, the question is, why [wouldn't] you see any meconium oozing out during the labor and delivery period? Why [wouldn't] you see it?

I said, "Dr. Swain, why [wouldn't] you see any?"

And you know what she said? She said because the head was stuck. I mean, if you've got something in there pushing down, nothing is going to get around it. That's why you [wouldn't] see any meconium. And you see a stopping of the fetal descent clearly at 1:30.

Now, what was going on at 1:30? Pitocin had been started at 10:00, hadn't it? And what do we know about Pitocin? We know it's a powerful drug that has killed and maimed mothers. It causes hypoxia. That's asphyxia. It causes hypoxia asphyxia [lack of oxygen].

Is that my opinion? Is that [the opinion of] any of the experts in this case? It's a medical fact right here.

It was started at 10:00. That baby was stuck.

What does Pitocin do? It increases contractions, doesn't it? As you increase the Pitocin, you increase the contractions. Boom, boom, boom. Every time there's a contraction, it pushes on the placenta. What does that do? It cuts down on the placenta's ability to feed the fetus. What was going on then between 1:00 and 5:00? What was going on during this period when the baby wasn't moving?

You've got Pitocin running at forty drops a minute—boom, kaboom, kaboom, kaboom—and the head ain't going anywhere for four hours. A big head.

Now, is that all we've got?

I said, "Well, Dr. Swain, that's not too significant."

She said, "Oh, yes it is."

I said, "Why?"

"Because you've got molding. Molding is starting."

Did [defense counsel] mention molding to you in his closing argument? He did not say a whisper about molding, did he?

And what do you know about molding, not from any of the experts but from medical facts in the book [*Williams on Obstetrics*]?

"Under pressure of strong uterine contractions, the bones of the skull overlap one another."

When did that occur? It occurred right during the time when the baby's head was stuck. We've got it noted: caput at 3:40, again at 3:55, 5:45, and then again, again at 6:40 we've got molding. So what? So what if we've got molding? What did that do?

Ladies and gentlemen, Dr. Swain was right on the money with this. If you take your finger and you compress it and you cut off the blood supply and you do it long enough, the top of your finger is going to die. Why? Because it ain't getting any blood. Blood carries the oxygen.

Refuting the Trauma Argument

Now, [defense counsel] would have you have trauma.

"Well, Mr. Witness, was there any trauma in this case?" Well, of course, there was. I mean, you take a hammer and hit your finger, that's compression. Okay. Compression. That's not trauma. That's compression. Compression is molding, and that's exactly what was going on.[2]

Now, do we know that that caused any problem? Do we have any independent proof that it caused any problems? I'm talking about medical facts now.

Do you remember [defense counsel] when he said why didn't

any of the plaintiff's witnesses talk about the CAT scans? Why didn't they do that?

Well, he must have been taking a restroom break, because I remember standing right up here with these [enlargements of the] CAT scans and Dr. Swain coming down. And I said, "Well, doctor, show us where the molding is. Show us. Give us proof."

She says these are the CAT scans that were taken—the first CAT scans in November of 1981 about a week or so after the birth. And every one of you were leaning over, and you looked and you saw the indentations [on the baby's head]. You saw from the frontal portion of the brain the compression, the indentations.

It doesn't take a radiologist to look at those and see that you've got an indentation. And it doesn't take a radiologist to see that you've got hypodense [dark] areas in the front corresponding with those indentations.

And I said, "Well, doctor, are they permanent? Do those little indentations that were seen in November of 1981, are they permanent?"

She said, "Oh, no. They grow out."

I said, "Well, show us."

And she then grabbed the other CAT scans and she said, "See. They then grow out."

I said, "Well, what caused that indenting?"

She said clearly it was the molding. It was the pressure. It was the compression on the head.

Do we have any other evidence of it? Do we have any other evidence of compression of the head?

Again, it's a real disadvantage when you start a case and the jury isn't familiar with the terms and maybe not understanding the importance. We can't stand up and editorialize and say, "Ladies and gentlemen, this is going to be an important witness. Really listen to this one."

But do you remember when the nurse from Henrietta Egleston came over and I said—and this was the day after the child was at Henrietta Egleston—"What are fontanelles?"

And she said, "Well, it's the area up here where the suture line is [where the skull comes together]."

"How do you record that?"

She said, "Well, a normal one is flat."

"Well, what's a full fontanelle?"

She said, "Well, a full fontanelle is when you've got swelling."

"And what did you find the day after the child got to Henrietta Egleston?"

"Oh, I recorded it as a full fontanelle. No question in my mind it was brain swelling at that point."

We didn't pay her a dime to come and say that.

Plus it was Dr. Ahmann—remember now, an Emory doctor. He has no stake in this case one way or another. He was just telling the truth. They measured the head circumference of that baby within a day after the birth. It went from thirty-seven centimeters to thirty-nine. Why?

It's completely consistent with the molding. It's completely consistent with the Pitocin. It's completely consistent straight on down the line.

Seizures

Now, let's get to this seizure business. I thought [defense counsel] was rather eloquent with his categorization that medical science—no question about it, if you don't have seizures starting at twelve hours, if you've got them before that, then you ain't got asphyxia. Just as clear and simply as that.

But again, one of the first witnesses in this trial was Dr. Francine Dykes [pediatric neurologist]. During cross-examination [defense counsel] said, "Well, Dr. Dykes"—at Emory, an impartial witness—"Dr. Dykes, didn't you write back in 1975 that you have to have seizures after three hours in order to have asphyxia as a condition?"

She said, "Yes, I did. I wrote that." And then she said, "But I'd like to explain my answer."

[Defense counsel] didn't want to hear the answer. But she gave it to him anyway. And what did she say?

She said that was eleven years ago. I've been studying the issue. I've seen seizures immediately. I've seen seizures right away. I've seen seizures that there's no question in my mind [were] caused by asphyxia and there ain't no time limit.

In fact, Dr. Swain and the rest of them, they said it's more consistent now with more study that they've done on the issue, it's more consistent to have seizures within three hours [after birth].

You're going to look at the records when you get back there [in the jury room], and they're going to have an average, a mean, and then you're going to see what it was in this case. That little baby was hyperventilating and having respiratory problems from the get-go straight on through.

Every single one of those is proof of asphyxia. It's proof that's in the records. It's proof that came from the witness stand.

False Issues

Now, I wrote down as many of the things that [defense counsel] gave us about the reasons why we don't have asphyxia.

First of all, he says there is no intraventricular bleeding. There's never been any [such] contention. There shouldn't be any [such bleeding] with a stroke. I asked that of Dr. Swain.

I said, "Dr. Swain, if you've got head compression in the birth canal why don't you have a lot of bleeding on these CAT scans?"

She said, "You don't have bleeding. You've got infarctions."

I said, "What's an infarction?"

She said, "It's right there on the CAT scan" [dead tissue caused by blocked circulation].

[Bleeding is] a false issue. Never contended by the plaintiff.

And the pH readings were normal. I saw you all write that down. That's very significant, isn't it? When you have asphyxia, it increases the acid in the blood. If you're not getting enough oxygen it increases the acid. That's why you get a high pH reading.

[Defense counsel] cleverly comes in and says, well, you have normal pH readings, jury, therefore, you don't have asphyxia.

What was going on before the pH readings were taken, ladies and gentlemen? This will show you what kind of lawyer [defense counsel] has been in this case.

The first pH reading was taken at 10:25 in the evening. And at 8:04 P.M. [two hours earlier, when the baby was born], and you're going to see it right in the records. The very second the baby got out, they put a mask on that little thing and rushed oxygen into her body.

What did that do two hours before they took the first pH? It increased the oxygen in the blood so that two hours later, the pH was within normal limits.

Now, then, [defense counsel] says, well, the other pH's were within normal limits. And what happened at 10:25, ladies and gentlemen? They put the baby in an oxygen tent. They were forcing oxygen over this baby. If you're forcing oxygen into someone, you're going to increase the pH.

A false issue. So the pH readings are smoke. The fetal heart tones are smoke. Because, as you know, and I don't want to beat this dead horse, but during the last three hours, which is the critical time of this labor and delivery, there are two forty-five-minute gaps where nobody knows what's going on. Not during the beginning of the day, but two forty-five-minute periods [when there are no nurses' notations in the medical records].

And then [defense counsel] says the baby has normal activity levels.

Good Lord. Take a look at the records. That baby began seizing at three hours and seized and seized and seized. Normal activity. Are you kidding me? Within two hours, the child was on oxygen. Floppy. Nonresponsive. [Defense counsel] says the activity levels are fine.

And the Apgars. The Apgars, ladies and gentlemen, what a false issue. The first Apgar was before oxygen was given. This baby's problem was it didn't have enough oxygen. That's why it's brain damaged. That's why the Emory people say it was asphyxiated.

The one at five, the first Apgar at five, was without oxygen. And then, as you'll see in the records, right here, right here, oxygen was given, and of course the Apgars went up. Of course they went up. That's why they gave the oxygen. Did they give the oxygen because the kid was not asphyxiated? No.

I just want to make a note here that there's a confusion as to the experts. You will note Dr. Backerman, who's never studied the issue, he got up and said, "Well, ladies and gentlemen, I know it's not asphyxia. I think it's chromosomal." "I think it's chromosomal." And not one more peep out of him at that point.

And then, of course, we've got Dr. Jones who [defense counsel] conveniently asked him about one of his opinions, and that is the cerebral white matter hypoplasia.

But then I knew he had another [theory].

Remember he had the hypoplasia up here and he says, well, there's another [theory] that looks pretty good, not quite as good. It's down here. It's the virus, the little bitty bug that parachuted into the fetus a day or two before the birth and then all of a sudden disappeared.

But yet, Dr. Jones—and if you would've seen the expression on [defense counsel's] face when he admitted, he said, after all is said and done, "Mr. Keenan, I still think that there's a 25 percent possibility that this child was asphyxiated."

Ladies and gentlemen, we have Dr. Ahmann, we've got Dr. Schwartz, we've got Dr. Swain, we've got Dr. Burke, and we've got Dr. Williams. Every single one of them say this child was asphyxiated during labor and delivery.

Now, I ask you, have we carried our burden of 51 percent? Have we carried our burden, even when their main expert admits that he puts [the possibility of asphyxiation] up to 25 percent? Under the rules of the civil court there's no question under anybody's construction that we've carried our burden by 51 percent.

Breaching the Standard of Care

We've got clear testimony from the witnesses. Even Dr. [Niswander] said under the facts of this case there is a breach of the standard of care. And even Dr. [Niswander] said that a non-stress test should've been done.

Now, let's get to Dr. Saker. What is the goal of the labor and delivery? Again, out of here, out of the textbook: "The major goal to be constantly strived for during labor is the preservation of the fetal well-being by the early detection of fetal distress."

Is there any question that an [electronic fetal heart] monitor would have greatly assisted this doctor? I mean, he'd known how to use it, ladies and gentlemen, for six years before that. And he didn't use it.

I submit to you that a monitor strip is just like in the military when you post a guard and you have a radar to back it up. And you tell that guard, "Listen, guard, go out there and stand on top of that mountain and you watch for the planes." But you've got sophisticated radar equipment behind you. All you have to do is turn it on. Do you say to yourself, "Well, that soldier is so trained that we're going to shut off the radar and not use it?"

You use whatever you can to protect the fetal well-being. There's no question about it.

And what about Pitocin? Now, I think that goes back to the molding aspect clearly. What does [*Williams on Obstetrics*] say about Pitocin, ladies and gentlemen? It says, "Pitocin is a powerful drug which can cause fetal hypoxia. It should be employed for no more than a few hours."

Ten hours? Is that a few hours?

"If easy vaginal delivery is not imminent after a few hours, cesarean section should be performed."

What did Dr. Burke and the rest of the experts say? They said that Pitocin was started at 10:00 A.M. and it made no difference—that baby stayed the same for all of that period. So, therefore, between 1:00 and 3:00, there should've been a cesarean section.

Now, why is that time period [between] 1:00 and 3:00 so important? It's when the meconium was being produced.

What else does the medical text that [defense counsel] didn't refer to say? It says, "ready resort to cesarean section in cases where the oxytocin fails."

Look at that graph. Look at how the baby was stuck. And the experts clearly say that a cesarean section [was indicated]. I mean, how much more simple can you get?

"Doctor, if they would've done those things, what kind of baby would we have right now?"

Well, ladies and gentlemen of the jury, we wouldn't have a brain-damaged baby. We would have a normal, healthy baby.

Now, you know about the other breaches of the standard of care. The only other one that I really want to tell you is something that came up yesterday, and I thought it was great. Because the doctor indicated that—that is Dr. Saker—I didn't use a laryngoscope and I didn't visualize the [vocal] cords. I didn't look below the cords.

And you remember now, Dr. Saker disagreed with his expert, his own expert hired by his lawyer, twice. But then I showed him this statement.

"Well, doctor, would you agree with me that as soon as possible after delivery all meconium-stained fluid that remains about the cords is aspirated and the vocal cords are visualized? Would you agree with me?"

He didn't disagree with me. He just said he didn't do it. He said, "I didn't do that."

And then I said, "Well, doctor, you didn't get all the meconium, did you?"

He said, "Yes, I did."

You're going to have the records, ladies and gentlemen.

Meconium is bowel movement from the baby that is swallowed while the baby's inside its mother. Is there any other place that this meconium could've come from if it wouldn't have come from the stomach area? But Dr. Saker missed it. Just didn't get it.[3]

Now, there shouldn't be any question at all that asphyxia occurred in this case. Because we've got at least four doctors that have taken the stand and have said there were multiple breaches of the standard of care. Not disagreement in what should be done, but the national standard of care as practiced by all physicians generally was breached.

Causation: Safeguards Make a Difference

But then the doctor says, well, wait. Even if we didn't have a monitor and even if we didn't do a cesarean, it didn't make any difference in this case.

Use your common sense, ladies and gentlemen. Why does the medical profession have standards to begin with? Standards are nothing more than safeguards. It's not 100 percent certain that the safeguard's going to work, but it's here.

Now, [defense counsel] says, well, there's no proof that an electronic fetal heart monitor can stop fetal distress. It sounds good. And then you say, well, that's right, you just shouldn't use it.

Well, ladies and gentlemen, is there any proof that seatbelts stop accidents? Of course not. That's not what it's intended to protect. Seatbelts are to protect us. There is no way that a seatbelt is going to stop somebody from rear-ending us.

That's the same way with an electronic fetal heart monitor. It's a safeguard. If something goes wrong, you're in a position to do something about it.

Let's use some common sense. And this is really what it all comes down to.

Close your eyes for a minute. What is the purpose [of] electronic monitoring? Why do they have it? Because it safeguards against asphyxia. It doesn't prevent it 100 percent of the time. Why do you have proper use of Pitocin? Because it safeguards against asphyxia. Why do they do timely C-sections? Because it safeguards against asphyxia. Straight on down the line. Proper use of suctioning? Why do you look below the cords? To safeguard against asphyxia.

Now, if the Emory doctors and all the experts have established that asphyxia was the cause in this case, which clearly it is, and we know that none of those safeguards were used, can you honestly say, ladies and gentlemen, that the failure to do those things didn't matter in this case? Because the plaintiff's experts, again whom I've never represented, whom I've never used in court before, all clearly said if those safeguards would've been employed, we would've had a normal, healthy baby.

Now, [defense counsel] have one other defense, and that is this child should not get a dime because the State of Georgia is going to take care of [her]. Don't you worry a single bit about this child because taxpayers are going to take care of this child.

Well, ladies and gentlemen, who are the taxpayers? I mean, why do you think governments today are in such a fix? Why do you think social security is going bankrupt? Why do you think that property taxes and sales taxes are going through the roof? Do you know why? Because you and I are paying.

And if you all buy that argument and let these doctors free from their medical mistakes, then you and I, ladies and gentlemen, until the year 2065, are going to be footing the bill.

She's going to be getting the therapy. She's going to be groveling at the door of the state, waiting on a waiting list. And then when she finally does get something, it's going to come out of my pocket and it's going to come out of your pocket. Is that fair?

This child has suffered the worst kind of injury that can befall one. You recall in opening statement I mentioned that the mind is a terrible thing to waste. Well, you have seen an awful lot of that in this case.

Tawanna is a prisoner of her own body. Can you think of a more horrendous injury?

You can talk to blind people and blind people say, "Well, I'm getting along fine. At least I can think. At least I can appreciate the world. At least I can love. And at least I can touch and at least I can feel."

And the deaf person—it's a horrendous injury—but they say "At least I can think. At least I can feel."

[Tawanna] has no brain. And she's not going to get any better.

Now, [defense counsel] suggests to you that, well, don't award any money because you don't know where it's going, [or] who will get the money. Is that any reason not to give this child and her representative money—because you don't know where it's going?

The child has legal rights. The child is in this court bringing this action through a representative. That child will have for the rest of [her] life a representative. The probate court will supervise the money.

It's a heavy burden that I've got. And I'll be honest with you, I've carried this burden for about two and a half years. And I'll tell you, I feel the greatest that I've felt in two and a half years. You know why? Because the burden that I've been carrying is going on your shoulders in just a few minutes and you're going to have the responsibility of this case. And I will have no further involvement with it except this: If I have [made] a mistake in this case, if I have committed malpractice—and professionals can, lawyers can, maybe more often than doctors can—then a representative of that child will come back on my doorstep fifteen, twenty years from now and say, "Mr. Keenan, you didn't protect the interest of that child right. We're suing you."

And I want to be able, if that day should ever come, to look that person dead in the eye and tell that representative, tell the lawyer, tell that court, I did everything I possibly could. Honest to God, I did everything I possibly could.

That's the kind of responsibility our justice system has.

These parents have been loving parents from the very beginning. You're not going to see a better cared for child. They do the best they can. They scrape. They are on a waiting list [for government services]. You saw the car they drive and the house they live in. They don't come from great means. But they can't take care of the child. They cannot provide the special education. They cannot do the therapy that's needed.

And [defense counsel] would have you deny them the right to take care of their child. [Defense counsel] would have you as a jury give no money whatsoever because you don't know how it's spent. Well, I can assure you, ladies and gentlemen, that this court system that we have in this country is such that if the money is not properly accounted for, there will be a lawsuit. There will be accountability, and there will be heads to roll. That's a false issue.

We've proved to you that this child in the average work force [would] have made over a million dollars. Now, if you want to reduce it by the taxes, reduce it by the taxes, which are $151,000. We show the necessary medical expenses from now until age eighteen, together with the necessities, and your notes will properly recount that it was some $899,000. And then from age eighteen on for the rest of her life until age seventy-four it's $1,800,000. That's fair.

Now, that's just what she's lost out of her pocket, ladies and gentlemen. What about the pain and suffering and the mental anguish? Did we try to drag the child in front of you and make you cry and weep and feel sorry? I hope there's none of you that feel like we pulled on your heartstrings and made this an emotional case.[4]

We don't want your sympathy. The child doesn't want your sympathy. Cheryl and Harold don't want your sympathy. The only thing that they want is what Tawanna wants, and they want justice out of this case, a verdict that's going to speak for the rest of Tawanna's life.

Now, in evaluating the pain and suffering in this case, how are you going to do that? You've got seventy-four years worth of mental anguish, loss of life, loss of happiness. And I'm going to tell you this just as nonemotionally as I can. This child's not going to be able to experience a first job. She's not going to be able to experience a high school graduation. She's not going to be able to experience the joy of having that first car, whether it's a clunker or not. She's not going to have the experience of marrying the person that she chooses. She's not going to experience the joy of having a baby. She's not going to be able to experience anything in life. She doesn't have a brain to do it.

What is that worth? You know, the average baseball player makes $319,000—the average one. I'm not talking about the stars. The average baseball player makes $319,000 for going out on the mound and giving us enjoyment. And, you know, we've heard about school teachers that got terminated and got their feelings hurt, and jurors say I guess that's worth $2 million. I don't think that's right. Because if you put it in proportion, if that school teacher whose feelings were hurt received $2 million then this child should receive $10 billion. That's the kind of value that our society puts on hurt feelings. This is a lifetime of hurt feelings.

Now, again, I hope I'm not being emotional about this, but you've got to put the damages in perspective. You've got to be able to put a value on the loss of income, a value on what she's going to need in the future, and a value on the pain and suffering.

Stick by Your Guns

Let me end with a couple of comments. One would be this: Each one of you was chosen for a purpose on this jury. You know, some of you had different educational backgrounds, and some of you are older and maybe wiser. But each and every one of you were chosen for a particular reason because you represent a cross section of this community. Collectively you've got one mind, and it's the mind of the jury. But in coming together you've got to bring each one of your life experiences, each one of your common senses.

Now, although you have to reach a final verdict—your verdict should be unanimous—if you feel down deep about a certain issue in the case, if you feel down deep that we didn't prove our case by 51 percent, or that the standard of care vio-

lations didn't cause any damage—and I mean this sincerely—
if you don't feel that, then you should stick by your guns. You
use your mind, something Tawanna doesn't have. Stick by
your guns. Don't give up your opinion because you want to go
home. Don't give up your opinion because you think the other
person may be smarter than you, because there's nobody any
smarter than you.

So before you give up that gut feeling that you've got about
the case, and before you say "My opinions on the case are
wrong, I'm going to switch," please be sure about it. You know
why? Because just like twenty, thirty years from now when I
may get a knock on my door to justify what I've done here in
May and June of 1986, I want you to be comfortable with this.

It's a terrible, terrible burden that a jury has. I mean, a lot of
jurors say later, "Well I wish we could do two out of three. I
wish there could be a couple of juries to decide to make sure
what we did is right." But that's not the way it's going to go.
Your decision, ladies and gentlemen, based on the facts in this
case, is going to be for the rest of Tawanna's life, period. We're
not going to get another trial. There's not going to be another
jury. So when you knock on that door and come out with your
verdict, you've got to be comfortable with it and you have to
feel good about it.

In five years or ten years down the line, if you see a mentally
retarded child, I want you to feel about this case that you won't
have any problem with that, that you can remember this case
of Tawanna Pittman and not have any problem with it. I don't
want you twenty years from now to be in Central City Park and
see a black female all tattered and torn wandering around and
wonder if that was the Tawanna that you judged and sat in
judgment on back in 1986.

I want you to feel comfortable with whatever your verdict is,
that you can walk right up to her parents and you can walk right
up to me and look me dead in the eye and say, "Listen, I'm
comfortable with my verdict. I'm not going to be ashamed of
it." And that's all we ever ask out of a jury.

But we feel very comfortable, ladies and gentlemen, that you will take all the time it takes and you will blow through the smoke and you will see that, clearly, without any question, that asphyxia was the diagnosis, that it has remained the diagnosis. And it's only the bought-and-paid-for testimony of the defendants' experts and friends and clients that say anything different.

We demand a verdict. We're entitled to a verdict. We ask for it.

Thank you.

Endnotes

*Born in 1951, Don C. Keenan has been a practicing trial lawyer for twenty years. He graduated from Atlanta Law School, and he was admitted to the State Bar of Georgia in 1975. In 1992 he was the national president of the American Board of Trial Advocates. Mr. Keenan was given the Masters in Trial award for 1992 by the American Board of Trial Advocates. He has written three books and seventeen journal articles.

1. It was important to point out that, unlike the plaintiff's experts, the defense's experts had been paid thousands of dollars to testify all around the United States.
2. The defense argued that no brain damage occurred during labor.
3. Aspiration of meconium leads to asphyxia.
4. The jury saw Tawanna on videotape and live for only five minutes.

Roe v. Bousquet

No. X91-1057-C (Chatham County Super. Ct.)

Result: $1.95 million verdict
(defense verdict for co-defendant Heidary)
Plaintiff's Counsel: Thomas W. Malone (Atlanta)
Defense Counsel: William H. Pinson Jr. of Beckmann & Pinson (Savannah), William P. Franklin Jr. of Oliver, Maner & Gray (Savannah), and Paul W. Painter Jr. of Painter, Ratteree, Connolly & Bart (Savannah).
Judge: Frank S. Cheatham Jr.
Date of Verdict: July 9, 1992

Chapter VIII

A Paralyzing Case of Pneumonia

Introduction
By Thomas W. Malone*

T his is the summation from a medical negligence case tried in Savannah, Georgia, against three well-known and respected physicians and their professional corporations. The case was defended by three excellent local law firms whose trial counsel fought valiantly to extricate their respective clients from circumstances which paralyzed a delightful seventy-one-year-old lady.

Mrs. Grace I. Roe, then a very active person, was admitted to St. Joseph's Hospital in Savannah with respiratory problems on November 15, 1989, under the care of Dr. Joseph De Haven. Dr. De Haven left town for the Thanksgiving holidays on Friday, November 24, and arranged for Dr. Douglas Gresham to monitor Mrs. Roe until Dr. De Haven's expected return on Monday, November 27.

On November 24, Mrs. Roe developed acute pain in her left foot due to a blood clot in her left leg. Dr. Albert R. Howard, a member of Anesthesia Associates of Savannah, P.A., placed her under an epidural anesthetic and Dr. Dariush Heidar Heidary surgically removed the blood clot that same day. Dr. Howard administered the anesthesia through an epidural catheter, which he inserted into Mrs. Roe's lower back and left in place following surgery. This is the currently popular method of postoperative pain management. To minimize the formation of additional blood clots, Mrs. Roe was medicated with a blood thinner called Heparin. Unfortunately, blood thinners increase the risk that the patient will bleed into the epidural space when the catheter is removed.

The following morning, November 25, at 11:00 A.M., Dr. Howard's partner, defendant Dr. Franklin Phillip Bousquet III, removed the catheter from Mrs. Roe's epidural space. Dr. Bousquet observed some oozing from the site and attributed it to the blood-thinning medication.

About three hours later, Mrs. Roe began to complain of pain in her back and across her midabdominal area. She was seen by Dr. Heidary at 4:00 P.M. and Dr. Bousquet at 6:45 P.M. Both physicians noted the pain, and Dr. Bousquet noted that an epidural hematoma might be the culprit. An epidural hematoma is a serious complication associated with the removal of an epidural catheter which, if left untreated, will put increasing pressure on the spinal cord and paralyze the patient. Such a condition demands prompt surgical decompression. Despite Mrs. Roe's symptoms, neither Dr. Bousquet nor Dr. Heidary called a neurosurgeon at that time. Dr. Heidary testified that had he been aware Dr. Bousquet even suspected an epidural hematoma, he would have called in a neurosurgeon that afternoon.

The next day, Sunday, November 26, at 10:00 A.M., Dr. Bousquet noted that Mrs. Roe's left leg was weaker and she had little movement in her right leg. He took his first steps toward contacting a neurosurgeon at that time. A critical care nursing entry notes that Dr. Bousquet requested a consultation with Fremont Phillip Wirth, M.D., a neurosurgeon employed by Neurological Institute of Savannah, P.C. At 10:30 A.M. Dr. Heidary noted in the record that Dr. Bousquet had contacted Dr. Wirth, who was going to see Mrs. Roe. At 3:30 P.M. Dr. Heidary wrote an order for a consultation with Dr. Wirth. At 5:00 P.M. Dr. Heidary again noted that Dr. Wirth was scheduled to see Mrs. Roe. Critical care nursing entries note that Dr. Wirth was called at 6:15 P.M. and saw Mrs. Roe at 6:35 P.M. Finally, at 8:45 P.M., Dr. Wirth performed a decompressive laminectomy and evacuated the epidural hematoma.

The surgery was too late. Mrs. Roe is now crippled and does not have the full use of either of her lower extremities. She requires around-the-clock assistance and must be catheterized every four hours for the rest of her life.

Negligence, Damages, and Experts

I contended that Mrs. Roe was paralyzed as the proximate result of the failure of Drs. Heidary, Bousquet, and Wirth, acting within the scope of the business of their respective professional corporations, to exercise that degree of care, skill, and diligence ordinarily employed by physicians under the same or similar conditions and like surrounding circumstances.

Mrs. Roe sought to recover past and future expenses necessarily attendant to her injuries as well as general damages for her pain, suffering, and disability. As executrix of the estate of her husband, Donald S. Roe, Mrs. Roe also sought to recover for his loss of consortium from November 27, 1989, until the date of his death on April 9, 1991. Mr. Roe passed away during the pendency of the litigation.

The trial consumed the better part of two weeks. The plaintiff's witnesses included an anesthesiologist from Jackson Hole, Wyoming, Dr. John Patton; a neurosurgeon, Dr. Gary Lustgarten, of Miami, Florida; a life care planner from Athens, Georgia, Dr. Jack Sink; an economist from Statesboro, Georgia, Dr. Robert Coston; a treating neurologist from Savannah, Dr. J. Michael Hemphill; Mrs. Roe; members of her family;

home health care attendants; and several friends who helped explain the devastation Mrs. Roe suffered. The defendants each had one or more experts from their respective specialties, including several local physicians.

We had to overcome several obstacles at trial, but the thorniest problem was Dr. De Haven, Mrs. Roe's primary care physician. Notwithstanding that the mortality table showed Mrs. Roe had a life expectancy slightly in excess of twelve years, Dr. De Haven insisted that she had no more than seven years remaining to live, due to her preexisting respiratory and cardiovascular problems. Also, Dr. De Haven's opinion concerning the adequacy of Mrs. Roe's caregivers differed greatly from our life care planner's opinion. After the trial, Mrs. Roe advised me that she told Dr. De Haven she would definitely be around longer than seven years, and she expected him to treat her for free after the seventh year.

Another barrier to recovery was the prejudice, which was evident during jury selection, in favor of the local doctors. I dealt with this in closing by reminding the jurors of the commitments they made during voir dire. Other problems included the claim by defendants Heidary and Bousquet that someone else was responsible for Mrs. Roe's care and treatment and defendant Wirth's claim that he was busy performing brain surgery and could not attend to Mrs. Roe.

Interviews with jurors after the trial revealed the majority of the jurors, who deliberated for six hours, wanted to award the $5 million which plaintiff sought. One juror successfully persuaded the jury to award no more than $1.95 million, which plaintiff has collected.

Opening Final Argument

MR. MALONE: If it please the court, you ladies and gentlemen of the jury, and Mrs. Grace Roe, we are, as the judge indicated, now in the final phase of the trial. We're in the summation. In that part of south Georgia where I'm from, back over on the other side of the state, we generally refer to it as the "hootin' and hollerin'." It's the time when the lawyers have an opportunity to tell you what they believe the evidence has shown throughout the trial.

You will recall before we put up any witnesses, the lawyers all told you what they expected the evidence to show. Now that the evidence is all in, you know very well what the evidence has shown in this case. You have been an attentive jury; you've paid close attention to what every witness for everybody had to say.[1]

I know that there are some basic facts that are very clear. Lawyers have different interpretations of what these facts show and you'll hear from probably the three finest lawyers in Savannah, who will tell you why the evidence doesn't show what I suggest it clearly does show.[2]

You will recall that everybody participating in this trial has taken an oath. You didn't see the lawyers take our oaths, but we took our oaths quite some time ago when we were admitted to practice law. The judge has taken an oath. You will remember in the first part of this trial, you ladies and gentlemen took an oath, and you answered questions that all of us had to ask, and you will notice and remember that some of your number were excused. The judge excused some for cause and then the lawyers excused some others, and that was [based] on what the court and the lawyers thought about the ability of those jurors to be fair and impartial to everybody in the case. And so you ladies and gentlemen of the jury should really swell somewhat with pride, because all of us recognized that you were the fairest and the best suited to sit in judgment in this very important case to everybody involved.[3]

I'd like to remind you just about a few of the questions that I asked you, that I thought were very important. I asked you whether or not you had any disagreement with our system of justice, that provides that disputes such as this are brought to a courtroom before jurors for resolution. Every one of you told me under oath that you had no disagreement with our system of justice that provides for a resolution of these disputes in that manner. And, you know, the thing that makes America so very, very different from the former Iron Curtain countries, or places where freedom isn't at least recognized, is that the people make the decisions.[4]

Some among you had questions as to whether or not you would be able to understand the testimony and follow the evidence, and I pointed out that that was the lawyers' jobs, to make things clear to you. I trust that the lawyers on all four sides of this case have really done that job.

Medicine can be complicated if we shut our eyes and shut our minds and say, we don't want to understand, but when it comes to a [spinal] cord compression brought about by bleeding in an epidural space, we all know now that that's a bad condition and it demands emergency, immediate attention. And if you don't give emergency, immediate attention, a person will end up paralyzed.

It's not real complicated to understand that, once we open our minds and we listen to what the experts have to say, and they've told you. And I would suggest that there isn't anybody in this courtroom, or maybe even in this courthouse, that doesn't understand that if you have an epidural anesthetic and you start getting severe back pain, you'd better say, "Hey, doctor, let's call a neurosurgeon in right now, because it might be an epidural hematoma. Well, let's don't wait around until the last minute and find out."[5]

The Conscience of the Community

Anyway, our system of justice is something we all should be proud of, and if we didn't have it and we didn't have jurors such as yourselves, then people would be strapping on their sidearms like they did in the Old West and taking the law into their own hands. So it is very, very important, very important, if our country is to exist and our way of life as we know it is to continue, that jurors do the right thing.

In recent months, we've seen a jury do the wrong thing—or at least, not having seen the evidence, we think they did the wrong thing, and you see what those kind of things lead to. That's not truly America. Jurors must rise above the influences of the locality and truly be the conscience of the community.[6] And I don't believe this community could find a finer group of people to speak out as the conscience of the community, and I'm satisfied that wherever the chips fall, that's exactly what you will do, based upon your oath as jurors to listen to the evidence, to listen to the law, and apply the law to the evidence, regardless of what your personal disagreement might be.[7] That was another one of the questions I asked, could you put your personal disagreements aside.

Were there any of you, who, for any reason, had a problem with placing a dollar value on human suffering? You all said that you could handle that difficult task, because if you said you couldn't do it, then you would have either been excused for cause or someone, probably me, would have excused you with one of our peremptory challenges. But you all rose above the pettiness that sometimes gets involved in matters such as this and said you could do the right thing.

I asked you if any of you felt that physicians or professional people were entitled to any particular place in our system of justice different from truck drivers or lawyers or teachers or ordinary citizens. Not one of you said that you would give them any special treatment. [You said that] you would feed them out of the same spoon that you would feed any other member of our society. And that's how it should be. And [physicians] understand when they undertake these life-and-death circumstances that they have promised [to] be careful, and they understand that when they are careless—unlike lawyers perhaps. When we're careless, folks might lose a case. Our clients don't lose their ability to walk, don't lose their ability to live, to enjoy their lives. [Physicians] understand when they take on their responsibility [that] they are subject to the law, just like anybody else.[8]

I asked you whether or not you recognized that physicians—I might have put it a little bit more delicately—when cornered, would lie like other human beings. And I would suggest to you that there has certainly been some straying or stretching of the truth, or absence of memory, when you know that memory would recall events of a day that led to the paralysis of a patient under your care. You would remember whether or not somebody said they were coming to the hospital right then or whether or not they said, "Well, I might not be able to be there," and then, "Maybe I'll be there later." Dr. Bousquet [defendant anesthesiologist] says that he was frantic, [that it was] the longest day of his life.

The reason he was frantic, he knew when he got there that morning that, "Oh, my God, what I thought about the night before and didn't do anything about has now come to fruition. It's true. It's real. She's paralyzed. My God, I've got to get help." And he summoned the help [Dr. Wirth, defendant neurosurgeon], who forgets about it. At 12:15 [Dr. Wirth] knew he might be eight hours in coming, but he doesn't even have a nurse call and say, "I can't make it." And Dr. Heidary—they're all nice people, you know, and you, by your verdict, don't have to say that they're not nice. You, by your verdict, don't have to say they're incompetent physicians. These gentlemen are very competent. They are very trained. They are very schooled. This complaint is about them not doing that which they knew how to do. That's all this is. They didn't get there in time.[9]

You call the fire department when your house is on fire. I mean, you see somebody strike a match and throw it in the front yard and it's a little bitty fire, I think it might be good to give them a buzz and say, "If I can't put out this fire, I might need you to come on, before it rages and is out of control." But when it rages and [is] out of control, you call the fire department and they say, "Well, you know, I've got somebody on the other line. They may be able to come. I may be able to get there, but I might have another fire I've got to put out, but I'll be there within a couple hours." You say, "Well, you know, it's approaching my house. My babies are inside. Do I need to get the babies out? Do I need to do something else?" "Well, get a few tests done and do a few things, but I'll be there in time."

And you hang up the phone and you count on the fire department to come, and the fire department not only doesn't come, they don't let you know they're not coming, and your house burns down with your babies inside. That's an analogy that helps you understand, if there is any understanding. If there is any understanding.[10]

Are there any of you who consider yourselves someone who wouldn't wish to participate in health care decisions? You know, back in the days when doctors made house calls, drove out in the buggies and tended to folks [in exchange] for a pig or a pot of soup or whatever, times were different. Times were different and folks didn't question and folks didn't know and folks didn't want to be involved. Just, "Doctor, what can you do? Save me." But today, our society has risen above that blind faith. And in medicine, look at the advances they've made. They're treating epidural hematomas today, they've got CAT scans, they've got MRIs, they've got myelograms, which, in five minutes, by the way, could make this diagnosis.[11]

A Red Herring, Sympathy, and Windfalls

All this gray area—red herring, as one of the lawyers mentioned—all this nonsense about MRIs, that everybody knew they couldn't get in that hospital—but they had Dr. [J. C.] Gouse [radiologist at St. Joseph's] there, Harvard-trained, one of the finest doctors that this county could—this area could hope to get, happens to be Dr. Wirth's brother-in-law. He knows he can do a myelogram.

They were wasting time. They knew they had a lady that had gone bad, and they were doing everything but what needed to be done. And that's clear. What are they going to do with an MRI? What are they talking about an MRI for? Can't get it done in the hospital, the thing's closed on Saturday; don't even think about sending her over there where Dr. Wirth is, where they can do one right there in the hospital where he's at. What are they thinking about?[12]

We talked to you about whether or not you could deal with a number like $5 million if you thought the evidence warranted it, and I will have an opportunity to come back and talk to you in summation, the final talk, as the plaintiff. And I'll talk to you about the money in the case and the money we think is just and adequate. And I'll tell you again, this lady wants no handout. She is not looking for a windfall. She is not coming in here with her lottery ticket. But if she were, what a price to pay for a ticket. She's not looking for that. And, quite frankly, she's not looking for sympathy. These doctors are not looking for sympathy or understanding. What we're all looking for is plain, simple justice.[13]

Now, the judge will give you the law in charge, but I would suggest to you that you will hear it from him for about thirty or forty-five minutes. Some of the principles may sound awesome or frightening, just like some of this medicine might have sounded awesome or frightening before we stopped and thought about it a little bit. And there are some words I know that he's going to give you that I want to talk to you about because there are many lawyers who go to law school and practice law that don't have a real good handle on what some of these words mean. And I think that it just takes a little common sense and a little thinking, and then you will come to appreciate them.[14]

One of those principles of law the judge is going to charge you has to do with the skill required of a physician. He is going to charge you that, first, plaintiff must prove the existence of a physician-patient relationship. [The] physician-patient relationship creates the duty on the part of the physician.

Dr. Heidary was the attending surgeon. He had done the surgical procedure. He had talked to Dr. Howard [Dr. Bousquet's partner who administered the anesthesia to Mrs. Roe] about administering Heparin to a patient with an epidural catheter, because he genuinely was concerned about an epidural hematoma. It's rare. The reason it's so rare is because generally [anesthesiologists] care for the patients properly. That's [why it's] rare.

It's rare that somebody has a ruptured appendix in a hospital and dies from peritonitis. It happens. It's rare. The reason it's rare is because usually [doctors] are careful.

Dr. Heidary did a fine thing. He recognized this condition, knew it might happen to a patient like Mrs. Roe, and talked to Dr. Howard about it. And then [Dr. Heidary] did another great thing. At four o'clock in the afternoon when the nurses called him—and it's important to recognize that nurses called him because he had a physician-patient relationship. And for him to act like he wasn't the attending physician—I'm just a fly on the wall—basically is nonsense and it flies in the face of his own entries in the chart. He's the one charting the information.

Even the next day, ten-thirty and at four o'clock, he writes the entries in there. He's talking to the family. He's the main man as far as the patient's concerned.[15] He calls back at seven o'clock or so after Dr. Bousquet comes in and very well writes out the four considerations for his differential diagnosis [list of possible causes]. [Dr. Bousquet] had four factors.

But what Dr. Bousquet failed to do was make a diagnosis. He just wrote up four things that it might be and said shoot her up with morphine and shut her up until tomorrow. He didn't give her any treatment; he didn't do any diagnostic study. He knew that it might be an epidural hematoma. And what did he do? Absolutely nothing but give her morphine, which would do nothing but shut her up. Tells the nurses to check her.

I don't have any quarrel with the nurses but then, somehow or another, we hear these vagaries that maybe the nurses weren't doing the right thing. There is no allegation that the nurses did anything wrong. Dr. Bousquet was the one responsible to tell them what to do. He goes away. Does not call back or come back until the next morning, and there [Mrs. Roe] is with the problems.

Practicing Medicine By Assumption

There she is with the problems. Dr. Heidary calls up and he says he thought about an epidural hematoma when he was giving Heparin and talked about it to Dr. Howard before he gave the Heparin, but now when she's got the first sign of an epidural hematoma, he calls back up and doesn't ask about her. He tells you what the standard of care is. [Dr. Heidary] swore to you that had he known that Dr. Bousquet considered an epidural hematoma he would have ordered the tests and made sure the tests were ordered then. That's the standard of care Dr. Bousquet should have employed.

But probably more significantly, or at least equally as significant, Dr. Heidary didn't ask. He didn't know what the diagnosis was. He assumed, assumed, assumed, and there's a colloquial thing about assumed—assume what it makes out of you and me—but I'll leave that to you all to think about. Assumptions have no place in the practice of life-and-death medicine.

Assumptions. The practice of medicine by assumption. That's what this whole situation's about, the practice of medicine by assumption in hospitals, where they have MRIs, CAT scans, myelograms, surgeons, all the things that a community could want, are right here to avoid these kind of things happening. And the people entrusted to do the right thing pretended like there was a different standard of care on the weekend after Thanksgiving of 1989, and that's what caused it.

The second element is a breach of their duty. Well, they all breached their duty to the patient. They all dropped the ball.

They might want to say, well, you didn't sue Dr. [Douglas] Gresham [who was monitoring Mrs. Roe for Dr. De Haven], you didn't sue Dr. Gouse. Well, we could have sued, I guess, everybody in sight, and then they'd be saying, well, you shot with a shotgun and you didn't have your case and you didn't know what your theory was.

We brought to you the three defendants that the medical consultants said were responsible for this lady ending up like she did, and it's just that simple. Get this! Dr. Bousquet is so concerned, he calls Dr. Howard and Dr. Osteen, because he's so concerned. They're anesthesiologists like he is. The testimony is clear. They can't do anything except make him feel good. There's nothing they can do for the patient.

Why didn't [Dr. Bousquet] spend that time calling a neurologist or calling a neurosurgeon? He wanted to feel good himself. Self over patient. Well, you ask yourselves, why did he call Dr. Howard and why did he call Dr. Osteen and not call a neurosurgeon or somebody that could do something about it? Maybe when his lawyer gets up, he'll tell you what he was doing, talking to them.[16]

The failure to do the duty was the proximate cause of the injury. Well, proximate cause sounds pretty awesome. You know, what is proximate cause? What it means is, it wouldn't have happened if they had done what they were supposed to do, but their negligence, acts of omission—they failed to do what they were paid to do. This isn't any charitable situation here. This is paying them to do things. Paying them to have a duty. Paying them to be responsible to the patient. And they take the money and don't do the job.[17]

You know, it's very much like if I had thought this case would be over last week—I hoped it would, I didn't think it would—but if somebody had called up and said, "Tommy, we've got a serious case starting Monday morning," or maybe, say, starting Wednesday morning at nine o'clock, "and we'll pay you a pot of money to come back to Atlanta and defend this person or do this thing for this client, and we'll send you some of the money now or we'll just promise we'll send it if you'll just promise us that you'll take this responsibility in your hand and come up here and save this person from a bad fate at the hands of a fine jury. Come up here and do this."

And I say, "Well, I'm committed to Mrs. Roe right now, but I think I can be there and, you know, go ahead and get everything ready and I'll fly in the night before, and I'm sure I can do the job." And then I don't bother to call them last night and say, "Hey, you know, I'm not going make it."

I would be breaching my duty. I would be breaching my duty as surely as a truck driver who says he'll come and get a perishable load and he doesn't show up to get it and the load perishes. He's breached his duty. And under our system of justice, we're all responsible. We're all responsible. This isn't a case of a truck driver driving on the wrong side of the road. This is a case of a truck driver not showing up.

The judge will charge you that the presumption in such cases, medical cases, is that the physician exercised reasonable care. And that sounds like it's a problem for a plaintiff. But that's true in every case. Every defendant is presumed to have exercised reasonable care. Every defendant motorist who's on the wrong side of the road is presumed to exercise reasonable care, because the plaintiff has the burden of proof.

If the plaintiff doesn't carry the burden of proof, then that presumption saves every defendant. But we come into this courtroom, Mrs. Roe and her lawyers, come into this courtroom saying we've got broad shoulders, but even if our shoulders ain't very broad, the facts in this case will show you that it is more likely than not.[18]

That's all we've got to do is, show you it's more likely than not that these defendants departed from the standard of care ordinarily employed by reasonably careful physicians under the same or similar circumstances, that they were careless, that they didn't do what people have a right to expect them to do.

And we don't have to prove it absolutely. Some of you have had experience on criminal juries and you told me you knew about the burden of proof beyond a reasonable doubt. No such burden [exists] in a civil case. I'll show you a way that you might want to consider that.[19]

Forgive my lack of artistry again, but just think [of] this [as] a scale, the old fashioned kind of scale with a needle on it, and the needle tips over, just a little bit off-center. We don't have to knock the needle way down here. And that's preponderance of the evidence, that it preponderates to one side or the other. If the needle's dead center at the end of the case, then the plaintiff loses, but if it's just ever so slightly over to the side on any issue, then the plaintiff wins on that issue.

The same analogy, the young folks today, maybe some of the older folks as well, know about these digital readouts, or the digital things on the front of a stereo set, where the lights light up. If you want your speaker on the left-hand side to play louder than the one on the right-hand side, then you turn a knob and then these dots will light up. The further you turn it, these will go out. It's a balance meter. Well, all we've got to do is light up one dot. You don't have to light up all the dots.

And the traditional example is the Scales of Justice. If the scales are even as they start out, just flat even, then the plaintiff hasn't carried the burden of proof, or whoever has the burden on that issue. But if it's tilted so slightly, a feather's weight, not way down here like this—beyond a reasonable doubt in a criminal case—but just a little bit, then the plaintiff has carried the burden of proof.

Proximate Cause: One Grain of Sand

And there may be more than one proximate cause. The judge is going to tell you that the negligence of several people can come together and cause an event. [It] doesn't mean just one. It doesn't mean the closest one. It means all of the participating factors that result in the condition complained of. We complained that Dr. Heidary knew better. He summoned Dr. Bousquet.

Dr. Bousquet came in, considered the condition, did nothing about it, said give her the pain medication. Dr. Heidary calls back, doesn't even bother to find out. Then when it's there to see for everybody the next morning, they call Dr. Wirth and he doesn't bother to come. Until six forty-five, almost twenty-four hours after they consider that she might have the problem? Twenty-four hours later?

On this issue of proximate cause, I think that you could perhaps analogize it to a sack of sand. If you took all the negligence there was, the finite quantity, 100 percent of the negligence, and you had it in a sack of sand, and then you decided, well, we're going to dish out of this sack of sand the negligence that each of these defendants is responsible for. Under our system of justice, if one grain of sand is in the lap of any one defendant, then your decision is simple. They, too, receive your verdict.

One grain of sand. If that one grain of sand is negligence that proximately contributed, even to the slightest, in the end result, they are responsible. So, you probably will be relieved to know that you're not going to be expected under our system of justice to say, well, this one was 60 percent at fault and this one was 30 and this one was 10. But if it broke down where one of them's 1 percent responsible, another one is 90 percent responsible, and the other one is 9 percent responsible, then your verdict is simple. Your verdict is against all three.

Only if you find that a physician named as a defendant is totally blameless would he have the benefit of your verdict in his favor. Totally blameless. And even if there are others unnamed who are responsible, that would be of no benefit to these defendants—no benefit at all. Because if they had one grain of sand of negligence that contributes to this injury, they are responsible. That is the way our law works.[20]

I would like to take a minute and show you the verdict form

that you will have out with you.[21] Ladies and gentlemen, this is the first page of your verdict form and your verdict is, "We, the Jury, find for or against the plaintiff as to Dr. Heidary and his P.C." That's the first question you'll be called upon to decide. You would either strike through the "for" or strike through the "against." If you want to find for Dr. Heidary, you would strike through the "for," so it would be against the plaintiff. You can see it's that way with every one of the defendants, the same circumstance with the plaintiff against Dr. Bousquet and his P.C., and the same thing with Dr. Wirth and the Neurological Institute.

And then you decide general and special damages in the amount of—and I'll talk to you about the difference in general damages and special damages in the final portion of my summation. But the amount you find in damages is the same, regardless of whether you find all three defendants responsible, or whether you find one or two responsible. We suggest the evidence clearly shows that all three of these defendants had at least one grain of sand of responsibility.

And then you would fill in the amount here, after you indicate that the plaintiff will receive a verdict against the defendants. Then, on paragraph 2, "We, the Jury, find for the plaintiff, Grace Roe, as Executrix of the Estate of Donald S. Roe, against the defendants above indicated." So you would have already indicated the defendants against whom you returned your verdict in the upper paragraphs.

But this amount is an amount that you award the estate of Donald S. Roe. Mr. Roe was alive at the time that his wife was paralyzed on November 26, 1989, and he lived until April 9, 1991, without the benefit of the wife he had, [who] was caring for him before. This is an amount of money that only the enlightened conscience of the jury can determine.

[Mrs. Roe] recognizes her duty as the executrix of the estate, to the heirs of the estate—the children and herself—to continue on with the claim, at least for your consideration. You might decide that Mr. Roe wasn't entitled, or maybe you might want to decide she wasn't a good wife and he didn't lose anything by her paralysis. But you might recognize that this relationship had value, had meaning, [and that] he was entitled to enjoy these last months with a wife who could at least get out of bed and cook him breakfast. But, instead, he lost that and he died a very lonely man who—you know the circumstances. But, anyway, it's not a long time, but it is a matter for which the plaintiff, as executrix, is entitled to compensation.[22]

I will have an opportunity to speak with you again. The evidence is very clear in this case. Just on damages a bit—she has already spent, incurred bills [of] approximately $250,000 that will be out with you. By my count, there have been thirteen different people who have been involved in her health care, and she has used her own funds to provide this health care. She can't get out of bed without help.

I'll talk to you about what she is entitled to get. Maybe one of the defendants' lawyers will suggest to you what is an adequate amount of money, what is an adequate life care plan for Grace Roe, what should she get. Not to enrich her at the expense of anyone else, but just to give her fair compensation for what she has to face.

I, like you, will be interested in the approach the defense counsel have, to probably what is the most difficult issue for you to decide in this case. I think the issue about who is responsible is very simple and very straightforward. All three defendants share some responsibility in this tragic outcome.[23] We do not have to prove [the defendants] intended for it to happen or that they are bad people. That's not part of the plaintiff's burden. Just that they didn't do that which they were paid to do, exercise reasonable care.

After he was called, [Mrs. Roe's] son gets from Tennessee back to this hospital in this fine community before the only doctor in town—except one other one who doesn't have a beeper—and his partner [Dr. Wirth] doesn't even know his telephone number, doesn't even know his address, right here in this county. And looking after all these emergency rooms, not just here, but all around the area. And [he] goes out there in this county to his beach house and can't even be talked to by [Dr. Wirth], and this kind of thing happens.[24]

Concluding Argument

My closing argument followed eloquent and lengthy arguments by three excellent attorneys. I was required to respond to liability arguments that I normally cover in the opening. Ordinarily, I spend most of my time in closing discussing damages.

Exhibiting the Plaintiff

MR. MALONE: If it please the court, ladies and gentlemen of the jury, some of you will notice that Mrs. Roe has decided she wants to come out from behind her corner over there. She was questioning me about not being able to look at everybody. I thought that now would probably be the appropriate time for her to be a little bit more participatory with us because, after all, this is the part of the summations or the argument that will really address her and her needs. She's just as interested as anybody else in the courtroom.[25]

The first thing I'd like to do is respond to a couple of inaccuracies that Mr. Painter [Dr. Wirth's lawyer] shared with you, and I know he wouldn't just stand up and tell you something that wasn't true, so I guess his mind slipped or maybe he just didn't know, but the annuity mortality table that you will have out in evidence with you is the annuity mortality table that Dr. [Robert] Coston [plaintiff's economist] referred to. [It] can be found in the Georgia law books at O.C.G.A. § 24-4-45(A-2), for any lawyer who would care to open the Georgia law book up and take a look. That mortality table is there to be seen by any of us. This is a copy of that mortality table that appears in the law book, and I want to just take a moment and tell you about mortality tables. There was a brief bit of testimony, but companies in our society—people [who] make decisions, big important decisions every day—rely on mortality tables to make a projection as to what may happen in the future, and it is a reliable, customary way for those kinds of decisions to be made.[26]

And these tables are made up of studies of sick people, well people, everybody, from all walks of life. And [the mortality table] is an average which permits a reasonable projection. The plaintiff brings you this table, not as the gospel or an absolute, but as an aid to you in making a determination that we believe you'll have to make. In order to decide what she's going to need for the rest of her life and the amount of money that will be required to produce the things that she needs, you're really going to need to have a starting place. How long do you anticipate those needs will exist? How long will she live?

And one way that it is approached in our society to answer this question is by using the mortality table, and it's very simple to use. You just take the age of a person, any one of us. You can take your age and look over to the side. If you're a male, it will tell you what your life expectancy is, that is to say, the reasonable number of years that you might or any person might be or should be able to reasonably expect to live.

Mrs. Roe, at seventy-three, has 12.11 years of life expectancy remaining. And you just look up the age in the column and then you look at whether it's male or female and then look down and you can see what the reasonable life expectancy is, and that's all a life expectancy table is. But it is so valuable that there is a law in our state passed by our legislature that says it's admissible in evidence without any other proof because it is an accepted way to project life expectancy.[27]

After this case began, a lot of strange things started developing. For the first time on Tuesday morning, I guess it was, when we made the opening, I heard for the first time that Dr. Bousquet was mistaken about what he had sworn to under oath. His deposition has been filed. He didn't make any changes in it. But now, rather than say he was expecting Dr. Wirth minute by minute, or every fifteen minutes, he says, well, he's mistaken about that and he tells you that, actually, he knew at one o'clock Dr. Wirth wasn't going to be there for several hours. He didn't change his deposition by giving an addendum or errata sheet. He decided to hold that back to himself and do that favor for Dr. Wirth after this trial gets started.

Everybody knows that somebody is responsible. Everybody knows. But not one of them stands before you and says, "It's not me, but it's him. It's not me, but it's him." None of them do that. They all say, "It's not me, and I don't know about the others, but it's not me."

That brings us to this suggestion, that somehow the nurses might be responsible. There's some hint that Dr. Gresham should have been sued. When we talked about that sack of sand and the responsibility, it doesn't make any difference if there are a bunch of sacks. A bunch of grains of sand on the laps of other people who are not here to defend themselves, and what a tacky thing for doctors to do, to start blaming it on a nurse that's not here to defend herself.[28]

But you will have the medical records out with you and if nobody takes the yellow page out, you can look to that yellow page that you see is pretty far back in there. I'm going to display for you a copy rather than tearing that apart, and let you see what the nurses' notes actually say, and you can look. This is the critical care flow sheet at the top.[29]

It's 11/26/89. It's a critical care flow sheet that has that yellow page on it and right down here, this is physical appearance, patient assessment, extremities move, "MAE times 4" [meaning] moves all extremities times four. And that's the patient assessment done by the nurses for this time period, and there is a similar report documented by the nurses for every hour, or every period of time after Dr. Bousquet gave the orders to monitor her.

So there's really no suggestion, and I submit to you, no reason for anybody to suggest that the nurses didn't do their job. If anybody had any thought about that, it would have been easy enough to bring the nurses in. So I suggest to you that is, to borrow Mr. Franklin's phrase, another red herring.[30]

A Team Without a Captain

Dr. Heidary says Dr. Bousquet was leading the team. It's important to understand that there was a team. There was Heidary and there was Bousquet. There may have been lesser players, but they were the ones who were really monitoring [Mrs. Roe's] postoperative condition. And that's what this is, it's a postoperative condition brought about by the withdrawal or insertion of that epidural catheter.

Heidary, interestingly enough, bypassed Dr. Bousquet and called Dr. Wirth himself at two o'clock and then again at five. [Heidary's] a player. He's not somebody there just waiting for Dr. Bousquet to do something and not being involved. He, too, could have called directly for a neurosurgical consult. Admittedly, neither he nor Dr. Bousquet were going to be able to handle the problem. That's why the complaint is they didn't call in the neurosurgeon soon enough.[31] Dr. [John] Patton [plaintiff's expert witness, an anesthesiologist] said they should have called on the day before, on the 25th. [That] is when a neurosurgeon should have been consulted.

And we submit to you, had a neurosurgeon been consulted, Dr. Wirth or one of his partners would have come over, done a myelogram, and they would have found—forgive my lack of artistry again—but on the 25th, it's reasonable to think she had this blood thinner in her and that she was bleeding. Everybody, all the witnesses, have agreed [that] is the mechanism by which this [spinal] cord gets compressed.

But she's obviously bleeding a little bit on the 25th, and as the hours pass, the blood goes up and down from the site where the bleeding occurred. So her condition is made more serious by the passage of time without the intervention. Had they come over on the 25th, maybe there would have just been a small area, but it just makes common sense that, [as] time passes, thin blood continues to bleed.

Dr. Heidary says, quite appropriately, careful doctors rule out anything that might be causing the pain problem. That's the standard of care. He counted on the anesthesiologist to make the diagnosis. The point is, the anesthesiologist [Dr. Bousquet] gives you four things he considered but he didn't make any diagnosis. He gave her the morphine.

What does the evidence show that he diagnosed the problem as being? [Dr. Bousquet] thinks it might be just localized point tenderness and that it might be a compression fracture, which, by the way, if it's compressing the [spinal] cord, it's just as serious a situation as an epidural hematoma.

Then he thinks a less likely possibility is an epidural hematoma and even, very significantly, he thinks another possibility is a retroperitoneal bleed. That's not down where Dr. Heidary was doing his surgery. The peritoneum is up here [in the abdominal area] and a retroperitoneal bleed is a bleed behind the peritoneum, which could mean that she could bleed out at any minute and die from blood loss.

But nobody did anything to rule that out. Actually, Dr. Heidary, through his examination, had ruled it out before Dr. Bousquet came in and considered it might be one of the less likely possibilities. So it just shows that they were not communicating. The doctors who were paid to care for the patient, they say they were a team, but they obviously were a team without any true captain, or no true communication between themselves.[32]

Mr. Franklin [Dr. Bousquet's lawyer] said somebody lateralled her off—they lateralled her off like a football to Dr. Wirth. But the truth is, they weren't handling her as careful physicians should have handled her—as a team. Dr. Heidary called the hospital after he went home to make sure Dr.

Bousquet had checked on Mrs. Roe's back pain, but he never inquired as to what the cause of the back pain was.

Now, Mr. Pinson [Dr. Heidary's lawyer] did an excellent job trying to say we're trying to paint [liability] with a broad brush. Well, I suggest to you, the brush doesn't touch the nurses, it doesn't touch Dr. Gresham. The brush that we paint with is the brush that the medical consultants said constituted the physicians who departed from the standard of care that was ordinarily expected of them.

And to touch on what Mr. Painter [Dr. Wirth's lawyer] said, he says you have to look at the circumstances and conditions then existing which faced Dr. Wirth. Well, that is exactly what the law requires. And we say that no one better than Dr. Wirth knew the circumstances and conditions existing when he got the first call.

And the evidence is clear from even Dr. [Jerome] Modell [chairman of the Department of Anesthesiology at the University of Florida, a defense witness], the fine gentleman Mr. Franklin brought, that the neurosurgeon has a duty to take over the neurological care at that point.

Dr. Wirth assumed, we now know erroneously, that he would be available in a timely fashion, and that assumption led him to another disastrous assumption, and that was that his partners were all out of town. Now, had he not made both of those erroneous assumptions, then [Mrs. Roe] would have gotten the neurosurgical care to which she was entitled.[33]

Justice for the Right Reason

It probably makes little difference as to who is held accountable, other than justice demands that you hold those people accountable that are responsible. And we submit to you that the evidence shows that all three share in this responsibility, and you don't let one of them out because he's got a better bedside manner, or hold one of them in because he's got a worse bedside manner. That might be the right defendant in the case, but it would be justice for the wrong reason. And we want justice—Mrs. Roe wants justice—for the right reason, and I know everybody in this courtroom wants to participate in the administration of justice for the right reason. The right reason is, these gentlemen, as nice caring people as they ordinarily are, dropped the ball, if you will, and did not comply with the reasonable standards of care.[34]

Mr. Painter made another misstatement. He said that we were limited to the testimony of Dr. [Gary] Lustgarten [plaintiff's witness, a neurosurgeon]. Well, that's just absolutely not true. You ladies and gentlemen have taken an oath to look at all the evidence, and that includes the testimony of Dr. [J. Paul] Ferguson [defense witness, a neurosurgeon]. [Mr. Painter's] own witness said that they were all part of the team and Dr. Wirth was the leader of the team. I think that would be unfair to Dr. Wirth to say that he's got the total responsibility of a patient belonging to two doctors, who could have known about the problem on the afternoon of the day before. It's just not fair to saddle him with the total responsibility by himself.

That would be justice, but it would be a measure of injustice, and it would be justice for the wrong reason. It would be incomplete justice. The plaintiff might have her total recovery, because that's the way the law works, but it wouldn't be fair to Dr. Wirth. So that should be considered.[35]

Mr. Pinson would suggest that I maybe did something wrong by originally suggesting that the theme of this case was money. Well, ladies and gentlemen of the jury, that is exactly what it is. Exactly what it is. That's our system of justice, when someone by their careless act, causes harm and suffering to another, they must respond in money damages.

And if they hurt somebody big time, they have to respond in big time money damages. So I make no apology for being here before you talking about money. That's all there is to talk about. That's what our system involves. And all of you, under oath, said you could deal with it, and that's why we're all here together.[36]

[Mr. Pinson] would suggest to you that I tried to conceal her preexisting problems. I'm the one [who introduced] the videotape showing you those respiratory problems. And if I said it once, I must have said it ten times, does that have anything to do with her paralysis? And he's accusing me of trying to mislead you. We went right on down the chart. None of the preexisting problems had to do with her being in a wheelchair.

Now, ladies and gentlemen, please understand, Grace Roe is not here seeking one penny of compensation because she's got some respiratory problems. She is not seeking one penny of compensation for this back that has served her very well for these many years. She had back pain, but she did what she wanted to do.

She told you that she could do what I'm not about to attempt, that she could bend down and touch the floor with her hands before this happened to her. Now, that might be an osteoporotic back, but it's a pretty good back and it's serving her well—until they stuck that catheter in her, they pulled that catheter out, they caused that epidural hematoma, and they paralyzed her by not acting promptly.[37]

Now, this isn't a condition like cancer got her, or some illness or God got her or something like that. Very simple. They did it with that catheter. Make no misunderstanding about that.[38]

Mr. Pinson says irony, Dr. Heidary is sued because he was at Memorial Medical Center and responded immediately as he had a duty to do when called to [St. Joseph's Hospital to] treat [Mrs. Roe's] key problems. That's not irony. That's his duty.

And that's the same duty Dr. Wirth had, but Dr. Heidary shows you what the standard of care is by a consulting surgeon. They come promptly. Exactly what Dr. Lustgarten said, exactly what all the other witnesses said. I don't think there's any question about it. Truth is, Dr. Wirth was contacted, he didn't come promptly, but he was contacted a bit late.

Now, Mr. Pinson said back pain is common like Mrs. Roe had. I don't think there's any indication that the back pain she had is common. Reality is, Dr. Heidary recognized he was dealing with a problem beyond his expertise. Well, everybody knows that. The complaint is he didn't get somebody in who could handle the problem. Dr. Heidary told you the duty was to get a neurosurgeon as soon as the mechanism [blood building up in the epidural space causing pressure on the spinal cord, producing pain] becomes apparent. If Dr. Bousquet and Dr. Wirth had been handling this properly, then the patient would not have this problem.

That sounds like our case, you know, at least against the other two. And that's what Dr. Heidary is forthrightly telling you, that Dr. Bousquet considered his responsibility to monitor [Mrs. Roe] from 6:45 P.M. [Saturday] to 10:00 A.M. [Sunday]. Well, the problem is, Dr. Bousquet didn't do what he should have done and Dr. Heidary just said if he knew the facts, he would have ordered the studies. He would have gotten a neurosurgical consult if he had known the facts.

We criticize Dr. Heidary, not because he isn't a fine man, but because he didn't find out what the facts were so that he could do that which he tells you he would have done. It's just failure to find out, failure to know about what's going on with his patient. And, of course, Mrs. Roe said she was pleased with Dr. Heidary. Everybody's pleased with Dr. Heidary. He's a great vascular surgeon. He did a good job of vascular surgery, and Mr. Pinson said there was not one single vascular surgeon that took the stand to say anything unkind about Dr. Heidary because we couldn't get one anywhere in the country.

The criticism of him is basic to all branches of medicine; that is, he did not get the proper neurosurgical care or the proper test in a timely fashion, and his patient ended up paralyzed. And in this case, there is no criticism about his activities as a vascular surgeon. It is a criticism basic to all branches of medicine, and we felt that Dr. Lustgarten, Dr. Patton, Dr. Modell [plaintiff's neurosurgical expert witness], Dr. Ferguson, and others had certainly established what the standard of care common to all of them would be at that time.

It's Unpleasant to be Sued

It's never a pleasure to be sued for the many, many dollars the plaintiff is seeking. Well, certainly it's not. But how that can be voiced on a same level as the life that she has in store for her—you know, they just are apples and oranges. You know, certainly it's offensive to be sued. I'm sure none of them—all of them wish they'd never met me, probably wish they'd never met Mrs. Roe, you know, and it's not pleasant.

But to try and equate in some basis that it's unpleasant to be sued—my God, look at what it is for the people who are put in the situation of suing. There is no evidence, nor could there be, that she's the kind of person that wants to sue people. She don't want to sue people, she wants to walk. Unfortunately, she won't ever walk again. So our system of justice requires that she bring a lawsuit. But let's not be persuaded with that.

[Mr. Franklin said] when you get sued, it's a bitter pill to swallow, and no good deed goes unpunished, and Frank Bousquet is the victim. How they can stand before you in the presence of this paralyzed lady and talk about pills to swallow and talk about being a victim is beyond me, but, fortunately, I don't have their jobs to do.[39] I've got mine to do. We don't have to prove that any physician was uncaring.

It was interesting that Mr. Franklin said [Mrs. Roe] needs the things Mr. Malone will be talking about. He agrees that she needs these things. He said, "We shouldn't have to pay for it." But then, Mr. Painter gets up and candidly tells you, "I'm the designated hitter."

Well, the team is still strong, ladies and gentlemen. Three members of the team are seated right there with their excellent counsel, and the designated hitter got up and did the dirty work that nobody else wanted to do, and that was try to take away from [Mrs. Roe] the lunch for her companion. Take away from [Mrs. Roe] the hotel room to cover the cost for her companion if she ever gets to take a vacation.[40]

She doesn't want to have somebody along with her all the time but, unfortunately, if she's to go anywhere, she can never do it alone. And we're not asking you, and Dr. [Jack] Sink [plaintiff's life care planner] did not ask you, to pay for [Mrs. Roe's] lunch or pay for her motel room or pay anything for her that she otherwise would have been spending anyway. It's this additional care, this additional responsibility that she's got through no fault of her own.

I don't suggest to you that the information of Dr. Sink is the gospel. I would not use that term and do not suggest that to you. Dr. Sink is a professional life care planner, a gentleman who is of high integrity and high standing in his profession. He charges a good bit of money, but I felt it was my responsibility in trying to handle her lawsuit, which is the only chance she'll ever have, to get adequate compensation to justly compensate her.

I knew I didn't know what she needed. I wasn't a professional life care planner. I knew her treating doctors didn't come out and look at her house and know how she has to live and know all the things that she would need. So I got a true professional in the field. And Dr. Sink, interestingly enough, told you he testifies more for defendants than he does plaintiffs. Certainly there are life care planners available for defendants, if they want to get a life care planner and come in and 'fess up to their responsibility, and then we can talk about what she really needs and what she doesn't need.[41]

There [are] no workers' compensation benefits, there is not any Social Security paid now, there are no health benefits. These ladies [Mrs. Roe's caregivers] have to look after [Mrs. Roe] out of the goodness of their heart and for the four dollars an hour. [Mr. Painter] said, well, it's really a lot of money because it's four dollars an hour, because they [work] a lot of hours. I don't think there are any doctors and very few lawyers who will say, "Well, I'll give you a reduced rate because I get to work more hours."

I've never heard of any discounts like that in the professional field, but maybe when it comes to minimum wage folks, maybe they're supposed to knock off some of their little old change because they have to work so many hours. That just doesn't seem to me to make good sense, and I don't think four dollars an hour according to Dr. [Robert] Coston [plaintiff's economist] is even minimum wage today.

My point is, if these ladies are so good, they at least deserve health benefits. They at least deserve that if they, in lifting her, hurt their back, that they have their medical benefits paid.

But if they can't feed their family because they've got an injury and they know that they're covered by the [workers'] comp law, even though there aren't [workers'] comp benefits, they can get a lawyer that would require Mrs. Roe to pay for those benefits. They might not want to do that but in order to feed their famil[ies], they might be in a situation of having to do it. So at least on the minimum wage thing, you must add to that health care benefits, workers' compensation benefits, Social Security, maybe bookkeeping, things of that nature.

Let me show you, if I may, what we think the evidence has shown. The evidence has shown these expenses. This is Plaintiff's Exhibit Number 2 [a loose-leaf notebook summarizing all Mrs. Roe's expenses, tabbed and indexed so that under each tab the jury could see the total bills of any given provider]. This notebook—I was going to present some of this, but I won't take your time now; if you want to see what all of these items are, there are about thirteen different people who have been home health care providers.

When I said home health services, what I'm referring to is somebody like these ladies who come and tend to [Mrs. Roe's] needs in the home rather than hospital-type personnel. And all these expenses have been covered by either Dr. Sink or by Dr.

De Haven [plaintiff's treating physician], and, you'll recall, I got Dr. De Haven to estimate what percentage of the original hospital bill was related to paralysis so that we could present a fair amount.

I put $250,000 on the board. This is money that's already been spent [on her medical and home care]. Make no misunderstanding about that. This isn't asking for something in the future. This is money and these are the documents here that we will show that it's all been paid.

Now, Dr. Sink and Dr. Coston say that it will take $2,252,000 paid down today to produce this life care plan for her. Admittedly, the largest single item, and that's the only thing they had any complaint about, was this $155,000 per year for home care, and Mr. Painter suggests $36,000 will do the job. I don't tell you this is the gospel. I tell you that the professional man says she needs professional care and gave the reasons why.

Dr. De Haven says she doesn't really need what the professional is saying, she can get by with what she's got. I don't know. That is a decision for you ladies and gentlemen to reach. You decide what she needs and you decide a number that will provide it. I don't know. But I know that we retained a professional to come and give you his honest, objective opinion as to what her needs were. This is the plan, at no small cost, that [Dr. Sink] took the time to work out about what she needed. He had no suggestion for me about pumping it up. He is just giving you what he says the lady needs. Dr. Coston, who is the economist, reduces it to present cash value, so that's $2,502,000.

I would suggest to you that if you don't cut her life short—Dr. [J. Michael] Hemphill [plaintiff's treating neurologist] didn't. Dr. Hemphill said she was entitled to a reasonable life expectancy. Dr. De Haven said he couldn't guarantee she'd be dead in seven years.[42] If you short-cut her on the money and she's still here ten, eleven, twelve, fifteen years from now, she can't come back and say to another jury, you know, "The other jury made a mistake and we ran out of money and I'm here now asking you to give me the difference because I'm still alive." So the responsibility is to make sure there's enough money to do the job you think is appropriate to be done over her reasonable life expectancy.

And that's just in our system. Juries answer those questions. We cannot answer them. No one of you, no one judge, as brilliant a jurist as we've got, he can't answer these questions. Under our system, it takes twelve jurors, fair and impartial jurors, to answer the question.[43]

Those are what we call special damages. And I want you to notice, you will not see any word up here called consequential damages, nor will the jury say anything about consequential damages, because consequential damages are not involved in this case. We have special damages and we have general damages.

General damages are for physical and mental pain, suffering, and disability. Past compensation, I took 955 days and that's how many hours you've got; $25 an hour is $573,000. I would suggest to you, to be resigned to a life of forever in a wheelchair, $25 an hour is not much. She hasn't even taken a bath. Has not had a shower since November 26, 1989, because she can't get in a bathroom. That $25 an hour, I would suggest to you, is a very reasonable amount of money. If I wanted to make—talk about it being $5 million, I could take so many minutes in an hour and put some money on that and make a bigger figure, but I think $25 an hour is reasonable.[44]

She spent 113 days in the hospital due to the paralysis. She was in there less than thirty days, and the hospital charged $41,000. I would think that to put up with being in a hospital, $500 a day is not an outrageous amount of money. But, once again, you consider it and you decide what's fair for her to be in that hospital through no fault of her own. Just compensate her for it.

The future? We've got 11.82 years. That's how many days, that's how many hours, at $25 an hour. Now, that comes out to

$600 a day or a little over $2.5 million—$25 an hour is $600 a day. Think about this, if you want another way to approach what is fair for her on general damages, the pain and suffering that she's been through.[45]

Indignity and Humiliation

The testimony is that in order to urinate, this fine lady has to have somebody, friends or strangers—they start off as strangers and become friends—remove her clothes, expose her private parts, and take a catheter, six times a day, and run it up in her private parts so that she can urinate.[46] $100 for each one of those experiences? $100, that's $600 a day.

[Mr. Painter] says that anybody can roll over in bed even if they're paralyzed. You saw the film. God knows she wishes it was easy just to roll over in bed. She gets pulled and yanked, and that's another thing about not having a professional.

Nobody in this world loves anybody more than Jackie [Mrs. Roe's adopted daughter, whom Mrs. Roe met while serving in the Peace Corps in Nicaragua] loves Grace. I'm sure of that. But you notice, she didn't even have the bed rail up when she was pulling her back in? Grace could have tipped back over and fallen on the floor. [Jackie] is not a professional, and loved ones are not the right people to be delivering this kind of care. Thank God, she's got her, because she hasn't had any help from anybody else.

There you are. It's a number over $5 million, $5,720,000. The defense says if you go the twelve years, a million. So maybe somewhere in between those numbers is where your verdict ought to be. On this thing about the executrix [the loss-of-consortium claim], I don't know what to tell you there, but I know Mr. Roe was entitled to the loving wife that he had before she became paralyzed and some number should go there. I wish I could help you, but there is no way that anyone other than the enlightened conscience of twelve fair and impartial jurors to assess that dollar amount.[47]

Whatever your verdict is, just let it speak the truth of this case. Let this lady, the kind of lady who has worked as an educator, saved her money, had a wonderful life ahead of her in what they call golden years, the kind of lady that would go down and volunteer in Nicaragua and adopt a Nicaraguan and bring [her] back after starting that shelter and telling that [dictator] Mr. Samosa, "You ain't looking after your children like you ought to. You ought to be ashamed of yourself."

This, ladies and gentlemen, is a special lady. A special lady who is entitled to a fair measure of justice. She seeks no sympathy. She seeks no cash reward, no winning ticket, anything like that. This is what the professionals say, this is a fair amount of money and, admittedly, it's big.

But if a drunk lawyer were to run across the centerline of a road and run over somebody and paralyze them and put them in a wheelchair so they had these same needs, would there be any doctors around saying, "You know, that's too much money"? I don't think so.[48]

That is a just and adequate amount of money. We asked you if you could deal with $5 million and we explained to you why $5 million is not unreasonable, but I'll tell you, whatever you do, you take care of her. She and the entire system of justice will be rightly appreciative. Thank you very much.

Endnotes

*Born in 1942, Thomas W. Malone completed his undergraduate work at the University of Georgia in 1963 and received his LL.B. from Mercer University's Walter F. George School of Law in 1966. A member of the State Bar of Georgia since 1965, Mr. Malone was president of the Georgia Trial Lawyers Association in 1980–81. Mr. Malone has won eight verdicts exceeding $1 million. He has written several articles as well as the book *Maximizing Damages Through Voir Dire and Summation* (The Harrison Company, 1988).

1. The phrase "If it please the court" shows respect for the judge and the judicial process. Also, addressing the jurors and my client in a somber and respectful manner captures the gravity of the moment. On

the other hand, the folksy "hootin' and hollerin'" comment shows that I am a plain south Georgian, like the jurors, and not a slick Atlanta lawyer.

2. I see no reason to berate any counsel in the jury's presence. To show a basic disagreement, which leads to no conclusion other than one side is truthful and the other is not, can be done without direct insults.

3. The jurors need to understand the solemnity of their responsibility. They are special people, each of whom has survived a lengthy voir dire examination and the challenge process. Each juror should be proud of the fact that he or she has been handpicked to represent the conscience of the community.

4. In this day of attacks upon the basic fabric of our society by tort reformists and others who would change our system of justice, it is essential in a medical negligence case to remove those who disagree with our justice system. A commitment to our system was obtained from the jurors in voir dire.

5. With proper expert testimony and demonstrative aids, even the most complicated medical matter can be explained to the average juror. That is trial counsel's job. At the conclusion of plaintiff's case, every listener knew an epidural hematoma was a condition that demanded urgent discovery and treatment.

6. My remark was a not-so-subtle reference to the first Rodney King trial, which resulted in a not guilty verdict and rioting in Los Angeles. An eye for an eye and a tooth for a tooth could be mentioned along with the concept of self-help in order to stress the importance of the rule of law. In our enlightened time, a victim does not inflict bodily harm upon the person who caused his injuries. Money is awarded to compensate for such wrongs.

7. Winning medical negligence cases in small communities is extremely difficult. The only way to overcome the jury's bias in favor of the local doctors is getting the jurors to recognize that they, and they alone, are the foundation upon which the rights of all free people depend.

8. Average people do not come into the courtroom thinking they have the right or the ability to judge the professional actions of neurosurgeons, anesthesiologists, and vascular surgeons. In voir dire they learn such judgments are within their province, and in summation they are reminded that they agreed to hold physicians responsible for their acts of carelessness.

9. If the evidence demands no conclusion other than a defendant has

lied or has committed a gross act of carelessness, then it is appropriate to call a liar a liar and a butcher a butcher. The anesthesiologist testified during his deposition that he was expecting the neurosurgeon minute by minute as time passed. Courtroom testimony suggested otherwise.

10. An analogy that puts the juror in an understandable situation similar to that of the parties is an appropriate and effective means of simplifying the medical issue. The physicians all knew the deadly risk of letting an epidural hematoma go untreated.

11. Medicine has become a big, highly specialized business. Many strangers are involved in the delivery of health care to any hospitalized patient. The Dr. Welbys of yesterday are few and far between. As the close, almost family-like relationship between physician and patient has disappeared, so too has the protection that existed for a careless but concerned doctor.

12. The defense argued that an MRI had to be performed on Mrs. Roe before she could undergo decompression surgery. The defense was trying to suggest that decompression was justifiably delayed because of the problem associated with getting an MRI. However, the medical evidence showed that a myelogram was the appropriate test and that Dr. Gouse could have performed one at any time.

13. Plaintiff's counsel has the opportunity to anticipate and therefore diffuse standard defense arguments. Sympathy and windfalls are frequently the subject of defense rhetoric.

14. Many lawyers feel it is inappropriate for counsel to discuss the law with the jury as this is the court's province. However, in cases involving professional negligence, products liability, and other complex principles of law, discussion of confusing principles with the jury is essential to avoid verdicts based upon an erroneous interpretation of a legal principle.

15. Dr. Heidary was a fine physician who cared for his patient and took steps to have her treated properly. We gave serious consideration to dropping Dr. Heidary from the lawsuit following his deposition testimony. However, had he been dropped from the suit, the "empty-chair" defense could have proved fatal.

16. I anticipated and hopefully diffused the empty-chair defense. I used rhetorical questions to get the jury thinking and anticipating a response from defense counsel. When defense counsel fails to answer the question, many points are scored for the plaintiff's case. Any juror is a potential patient and does not like the idea of a doctor putting his own interests before his patient's welfare.

17. Proximate cause can be confusing and needs to be explained to the jury in an understandable manner. Also, the jury needs to be reminded of the fact that modern physicians make a great deal of money and should be held responsible when they don't do the job that they were paid to do. Certainly, if the doctor were acting as a good Samaritan, or working for less than full pay because of some charitable motivation, the defense would continually remind the jury of that fact.

18. The presumption of care can be fatal if not explained. Juries do not understand, without help, the difference in a rebuttable presumption and an absolute presumption. This charge is frequently given and is simply a restatement of the plaintiff's burden of proof. Moreover, in his opening statement, Dr. Bousquet's lawyer had first mentioned that Dr. Bousquet had broad shoulders and could accept whatever responsibility was appropriately his. However, counsel continued to maintain that his client had no responsibility. My mention of broad shoulders was designed to remind the jury of counsel's opening statement.

19. I now draw the three examples—a needle scale, digital readout, and Scales of Justice. One mark on the needle scale, one dot on the digital readout, and a slight tilt on the Scales of Justice is all that is needed to carry the burden. The jury remembers when they hear and see how small a burden the preponderance represents.

20. There is no more confusing principle of law than proximate cause when more than one actor is involved. In explaining the principle to the jurors, I try to use some of the same language I expect the judge to use.

21. Here, I used an opaque projector to show the jury the actual verdict form. I call it an "underhead" projector because, unlike an overhead projector, it does not require transparencies and does not have an overhead lamp. The projector permits me to take any photograph or any document and project it upon the screen much larger than any typical blowup used in courtrooms today. I use a laser pointer in conjunction with this projector.

22. The plaintiff's husband had suffered a stroke at the time the suit was filed. We gave some thought to dismissing the loss of consortium claim after he passed away during the pendency of the litigation but decided that leaving the claim in place would permit any compromise faction on the jury to have something they could deny the plaintiff.

23. This challenge puts tremendous pressure on the defendants. It would have been dangerous indeed for the defendants to ignore the damages in this case. However, to discuss the damages almost amounts

to an admission that they are appropriate.

24. No stronger factual comparison could be drawn than that between the duty of the son to the mother and the physician to the patient. Mrs. Roe's son traveled from Tennessee to Savannah quicker than the neurosurgeon could travel across town. Dr. Wirth assumed none of his partners were in town when the evidence actually showed one partner was at his beach home in nearby Tybee Island.

25. In many cases it is appropriate to leave the plaintiff out of the courtroom during the entire trial and have her appear only to testify. Such is the case with burn victims, closed head injury plaintiffs, and many others whose presence, in the judgment of trial counsel, would tend to offend the jurors or condition them to the injury. A great risk is involved in having a severely injured person present in the courtroom throughout the entire trial. This delightful lady would not have missed a minute of her trial, and I did not want the jury to become conditioned or hardened by her presence. Therefore, she was placed in the courtroom just outside the normal view pattern of the jurors. The final summation was the opportunity to personalize her so that the jury would remember her wonderful testimony and consider her situation fully.

26. Defense counsel should be forever mindful that plaintiffs have the right to close. Mr. Painter said that the annuity mortality table for 1949 is not the law in Georgia, it is just a table found in a book which the jury could ignore. By pointing out the inaccuracy, counsel's credibility was jeopardized.

27. The greatest problem of the trial arose when Dr. De Haven, who cares for Mrs. Roe on a daily basis, refused to project her life expectancy beyond seven years. One of Mrs. Roe's other physicians did say that he saw no reason why she should not live out a reasonable life expectancy if she was afforded proper care. Moreover, I cannot imagine a circumstance where I would not introduce and rely upon a mortality table. My experience has shown that the Annuity Mortality Table of 1949 Ultimate is as good as they get and provides a reasonable figure for projecting damages. The more modern tables require the testimony of an economist to lay the foundation, and not every case requires an economist.

28. Dr. Bousquet's direct change in testimony from deposition to trial ruined his credibility with the jury. Also, the defense failed to give the jury a satisfactory explanation of how Mrs. Roe ended up a cripple. The jurors wanted to know who permitted this unexpected event to

occur. Subtle suggestions by physicians that somehow the nurses or some consulting, lesser-involved physician have the responsibility simply will not stand before an objective jury.

29. Here, I used the opaque projector and a laser pointer to display the nurses' notes from November 26, 1989, the day after the surgery to decompress Mrs. Roe's epidural hematoma. The yellow page was a sheet I took from my legal pad to mark the place where the jury could find the nurses notes, which contained the critical care flow sheet.

30. The critical care flow sheet revealed that the nurses had done all that was expected of them. No harm comes from defending the innocent, and the jury does not appreciate the physician trying to lay responsibility on a nurse, without proof to back it up.

31. Dr. Heidary was honest and straightforward in his testimony. When first called, he came to the hospital in a timely fashion to treat the blood clot in the patient's left leg. He testified that prompt response was the duty of a consulting surgeon on staff at the hospital. On a technical, medical/legal basis, it would seem impossible to extricate Dr. Heidary from the responsibility. However, the jury knew the anesthesiologist was in charge and that an anesthetic complication brought about the need for neurosurgery. The verdict included an expression of compassion for Dr. Heidary as well as the plaintiff.

32. The preceding three paragraphs succinctly state the liability case prior to the neurosurgeon's involvement. Jurors today expect physicians to follow up and diagnose problems that they document. The anesthesiologist considered compression fracture, epidural hematoma, and retroperitoneal bleed as possible causes of the Mrs. Roe's pain. All three of these conditions can lead to paralysis and even death if not treated in a timely fashion. Nothing, however, was done.

33. When Dr. Wirth, the neurosurgeon, was first contacted, the jury recognized that his duty was either to explain he was not available or to respond promptly. And Dr. Wirth assumed none of his partners were available although one partner was at his nearby beach home.

34. I am trying to give the jury an opportunity to find in favor of Dr. Heidary. The jury has awesome power and under our system of justice can "do the right thing," even if it does not strictly comply with the evidence and the judge's charge. The argument "justice for the wrong reason is injustice" comes from the great New York City attorney Mo Levine, now deceased.

35. It was important that the jury find against both the neurosurgeon, Dr. Wirth, and the anesthesiologist, Dr. Bousquet. We had reached a

high-low agreement (high of $1 million) with the anesthesiologist's insurance carrier, and if the jury had not found the neurosurgeon liable, the plaintiff would not have received full satisfaction of the verdict.

36. One of the most difficult challenges I ever faced involved amassing enough nerve to stand up in a courtroom and talk about millions of dollars. If you cannot comfortably discuss millions of dollars with the court, opposing counsel, and the jury in a catastrophic case, you should not expect such a recovery. In voir dire, jurors must be asked if they would hesitate to award a multimillion-dollar sum, assuming the evidence and the law justified it. In summation, I reminded the jury of the commitments they made in voir dire.

37. I used the projector to show the jury the list of Mrs. Roe's preexisting problems to indicate that none of them had anything to do with her confinement to the wheelchair. Counsel should bear in mind that people suffering from preexisting disabilities have a certain quality of life, which can be projected and shown to the jury. Jurors tend to admire and respect those who function well under adverse, preexisting conditions. If the plaintiff's life was full and complete despite preexisting problems, jurors should not be expected to shortchange her.

38. Health care providers who fail to intercede and arrest a disease process that they did not cause make the most difficult medical defendants. However, if the health care provider actually caused the problem, recovery is much easier. Thus, I pointed out that the health care providers caused Mrs. Roe's condition.

39. Mr. Pinson had stated that it was not a pleasure to be sued for the many dollars the plaintiff was seeking. In past years, I have seen this argument work effectively to protect the careless doctor who was looked upon as a pillar of the community. It is designed to invoke sympathy for the doctor, who was merely trying to serve humanity, and to cast aspersion toward the victim of his carelessness. The plaintiffs and their counsel were looked upon as undeserving, unclean, or simply greedy people trying to take advantage of an unfortunate situation. The argument sometimes works, but can be extremely dangerous before a truly objective jury.

40. Defense counsel had argued that the jury should not award sums to cover the incidental expenses associated with her caregiver.

41. The defense's attack on the life care planner gave me the opportunity to remind the jury that this was indeed an expensive trial, which the defendants could have avoided if they had lived up to their responsibility. Life care planners are invaluable witnesses in appropriate cases,

and I use them along with economists to answer the jury's difficult questions regarding how much money paid down today is needed to provide the plaintiff with the kind of life that she deserves. I would suggest that the life care planner always communicate with the primary care physician so that the life care plan can become a joint project of the primary care physician and the life care planner. Unfortunately, in this case the life care planner's testimony differed from the treating physician's testimony. Defendants frequently employ life care planners in an effort to come up with a more conservative plan. However, that was not the case here, and I'm confident defense counsel was concerned about making a tacit admission that Mrs. Roe was entitled to recover.

42. By using the underhead projector, I graphically put the special damages argument before the jury. The jury understood $250,000 had been spent on her medical and home care, and they could follow the battle line being drawn between the cost of home care at $155,000, as the plaintiff contended, or only $36,000 annually, as the defense alleged. I did not call Dr. De Haven in our case because of his opinion regarding Mrs. Roe's life expectancy and the adequacy of her current caregivers.

43. As obvious as it may seem, jurors cannot be expected to know that the plaintiff is not allowed to come back for more if the circumstances change. They must be told and must fully appreciate their power and the finality of their verdict.

44. The increment of time argument effectively shows the reasonableness of a large figure. General damages awarded following an increment of time argument are not reducible to present cash value, as are special damages.

45. A review of the damages in summary form displayed before the jury on a board or a projection screen is most helpful in bringing the numbers together. The jury had been asked in voir dire if they would hesitate to award a sum as large as $5 million if warranted by the evidence and the law. Here before them were those large numbers clearly supported by the evidence.

46. Every four hours the plaintiff was catheterized in order to urinate. As delicate as this subject was, we had to bring home to the jury the indignity of Mrs. Roe's situation.

47. The jury made no award for the loss of consortium to which the estate of Mr. Roe would have been entitled. We made no real issue of an entitlement to damages on that claim, thereby presenting the jury

with an opportunity to rule against us. Counsel should consider arming the jurors who are on his side with some concessions that can be made to the other jurors in order to reach a satisfactory plaintiff's verdict. This was one of those opportunities.

48. In these final paragraphs, I attempted to remind the jury of this wonderful lady who had testified many days before. She and her husband had volunteered for the Peace Corps in Nicaragua, and Mrs. Roe had established a day care center there for underprivileged children. She testified about how she bathed, fed, and clothed the children before sending them home. Jackie was one of those children. The Roes brought her back to the United States. Mrs. Roe also testified that she visited Samosa's palace and complained that he was not doing enough for the children. As for the drunk lawyer analogy, I wanted to give the members of the jury something they could use to explain to other members of the community why they awarded Mrs. Roe a very large sum of money.

Stubblefield v. Ford Motor
No. C-32204 (Fulton Super. Ct.)

Result: $9.3 million verdict
Plaintiffs' Counsel: Foy R. Devine of Foy R. Devine, P.C. (Atlanta), Irwin W. Stolz Jr. of Gambrell & Stolz (Atlanta), and Albert Sidney Johnson of Johnson & Montgomery (Atlanta)
Defense Counsel: Ben L. Weinberg Jr. of Long, Weinberg, Ansley & Wheeler (Atlanta)
Judge: Philip F. Etheridge
Date of Verdict: November 24, 1982

Chapter IX

Trading Lives for Profits: The Mustang II Case

Introduction
By Pearl S. Schaikewitz

On July 10, 1977, Linda P. Standley's 1975 Ford Mustang II burst into flames after it was smashed in the rear by a Pontiac Grand Prix. The Mustang's backseat passenger, Standley's fifteen-year-old daughter, Terri J. Stubblefield, received third-degree burns over 35 percent of her body. Miss Stubblefield survived for fifty days in Grady Memorial Hospital, where she died on August 29.

Standley and her ex-husband, William O. Stubblefield, brought a wrongful death and survival action against Ford Motor Company, which manufactured the Mustang II, alleging that the vehicle's fuel tank was negligently designed, that Ford knew the tank was unsafe, and that Ford marketed the car without adequately warning the public of the danger that the tank might explode upon rear-end impact. The plaintiffs claimed that the Mustang II's design caused the fuel tank to jam into the rear axle when struck from behind.

The jury sided with the plaintiffs, awarding $8 million in punitive damages and $1 million in compensatory damages to

Mr. Stubblefield as administrator of Terri's estate, and $300,000 to Ms. Standley on her wrongful death claim. The judgment, entered on December 28, 1982, added $533,589 pursuant to the Unliquidated Damages Act, $450,000 as attorney's fees, and $38,137.90 as litigation expenses.

In affirming the award, the Georgia Court of Appeals[1] held that the evidence authorized the jury's findings that Ford negligently designed the 1975 Mustang II, that the company marketed the car knowing that it was unsafe, and that Ford failed to warn the public of the danger. At trial, the court noted, Dr. Leslie Ball, a safety systems scientist, testified for the plaintiffs that based on his review of hundreds of Ford's internal documents, Ford's decision-making process was unreasonable from a safety science management standpoint. Similarly, the court pointed out, Frederick Arndt, an engineering expert who had worked in research projects devoted to postcollision fires, testified that, based on his extensive review of Ford's crash tests, the Mustang II's design was not reasonably safe.

The appeals court rejected Ford's contention that the amount awarded for punitive damages was "shockingly excessive." Ford had premised its argument on the fact that no appeals court in the country had ever affirmed an award that large in any personal injury suit arising out of a manufacturer's negligence. The court held that $8 million was an amount necessary to deter Ford from repeating its conduct—deliberately waiting to install a safety device in order to protect its profits. Ford's internal memoranda, the court stated, showed that Ford knew about the problem of postcollision fires as early as 1968, but chose to delay implementation of protective hardware for the car's fuel tank until required by law, enabling Ford to save $20.9 million. The opinion, penned by former judge John W. Sognier, notes that Ford finally installed a polyethylene shield in the fall of 1976 on the 1977 model, but did not warn owners of older models of the dangers the fuel tank posed.

In Mr. Devine's closing, he repeatedly hammers home the

point that Ford was willing to trade its customers' personal safety for increased profits. He reminds the jury that Ford's president and chief executive officer, Lee Anthony Iacocca, and Ford's chairman of the board, Henry Ford II, met with President Richard M. Nixon on April 27, 1971, and suggested that the President lean on the Department of Transportation to "cool it" on requiring car manufacturers to install safety devices. And Mr. Devine utilizes, with great success, the "send a message" argument so popular with the plaintiffs' bar.

Opening Final Argument

MR. DEVINE: May it please the court, ladies and gentlemen. I know this has been a long and sometimes trying time for you, and I want to begin by thanking you for your patience and your attention throughout the entire course of this trial, and to bring you the news that it is not going to be too much longer before you will have the opportunity to undertake the responsibility that you have in this case, aside from listening to the evidence as you have already done, that is, making a decision.

First, I would like to begin by simply reviewing the issues that are going to be before you to decide when his honor instructs you as to the law of the case. And I have prepared a summary of those items for the screen, and I hope that everybody can see those. Essentially, the case will be before you in five counts, and each count will deal with a particular item or question for you to decide.

The first question is whether to compensate Terri's father for the hospital and funeral bills, which have been stipulated as to amounts. And those figures, if my math is correct, [are] $18,832 and some cents.

The second item for you to deal with will be to compensate the estate—that is, Terri's estate—for the personal injuries and the pain and suffering which she endured between July 10, 1977, and August 29, 1977, a period of fifty days before she died.

The third item for you to deal with is the question of whether to compensate Terri's legal representative for what is known as a wrongful death action for the value of her life lost. Essentially, that is the value of Terri's life which was lost on August 29, 1977, projected into the future, as you heard some testimony here during the course of this trial.

The fourth item is whether to require Ford Motor Company to pay additional damages, or punitive damages, for the purpose of deterring Ford Motor Company from repeating the kinds of decisions and conduct which the evidence has shown to you in this case, and to encourage, if you will, Ford Motor Company to protect the people who buy their cars.

And the last item is whether to require Ford Motor Company to pay attorneys' fees and other expenses of litigation which were incurred by Terri's estate in bringing this action. Those are the five questions which will be before you.

Now, I will simply tell you that with regard to item number one, there is no dispute as to the amount. That is agreed upon as being $18,832. As to item number five, you will not have the responsibility of determining that amount, but merely making a decision as to whether or not Ford Motor Company should be required to pay those expenses. His honor will tell you a little bit more about that later. With respect to items two, three, and four, that will be a matter for you to determine as to the amount.

Plaintiffs in this case are not, have not in their complaint, prayed or asked—[prayed] is a legal term—for a specific dollar amount. They have prayed in their complaint, in each of those three counts, for pain and suffering, for loss of life, and for punitive damages, in such amount as you as jurors in your collective and impartial consciences feel is fair and appropriate and right.

Now, that is not to say that we will not suggest to you some things that you might take into consideration. In fact, during the course of the arguments here I expect [co-counsel] Mr. [Albert Sidney] Johnson to suggest to you some thoughts and considerations and approaches that you might take in attempting to determine what is fair and appropriate in trying to value Terri's life.

[Co-counsel] Mr. [Irwin W.] Stolz [Jr.] will also suggest to you some approaches and considerations to take into account in trying to determine how to value the pain and suffering during that fifty-day period. And I will suggest to you some approaches and some considerations to take into account in trying to determine a figure that would be fair and just and right for punitive damages.

Now, just to tell you a little bit about what's going to happen. After I finish talking to you this first time, [defense counsel] Mr. [Ben L.] Weinberg [Jr.] is going to come on and talk to you for a period of time, and then I will come back to respond to some of the things that Mr. Weinberg said, and in addition to that probably talk to you about some ways to deal with the question of punitive damages in terms of amount, if you feel that it is appropriate and just and right in this case to determine punitive damages.

After I talk, Mr. Stolz will talk to you, as I said, about pain and suffering, and an approach to take and suggestions in that regard. And Mr. Johnson, finally, will talk to you about the very difficult question of trying to put a dollar value on life.

With that preliminary statement about what we are going to be doing this afternoon, I would like to begin by saying that we anticipate that after we argue this case to you that his honor will instruct you as to the law in the case. . . .

Duty of Reasonable Care

And I anticipate that one of the things that his honor will tell you is that an automobile manufacturer has a legal duty or responsibility to use what is known as ordinary care or reasonable care—reasonable efforts to design the car so as to protect the people who are in that car in the event that that car is involved in a foreseeable incident, including collisions, and that those efforts that the manufacturer has the duty to follow must be reasonable. In other words, he must make a reasonably safe product, reasonably safe in the context or in the environment or on the highway as that car is going to be used, as every manufacturer knows.

Now, we submit that the evidence will show and that you should find from the evidence that Ford Motor Company knew when they undertook to design this Mustang II that gasoline is dangerous. [A Ford vice-president] Mr. [T. J.] Feaheny said he knew about that a long time ago. Gasoline is dangerous. It is a very volatile substance, and when it gets out of the fuel tank it has a propensity to mix with ... ignition sources and there can be a fire. Indeed their own document, specifically Plaintiffs' Exhibit 13, shows that in 1968, in October 1968, [Ford's executive engineer of safety research] Mr. [John] Versace informed the people in the company and talked about the risk of fires. And among the things that he talked about [were] that on an annual basis some 20,000 persons were exposed to 10,600 vehicle fires. ... And that in addition to that, of those people who were being exposed, that some 600 to 2,200 people a year were being burned to death on American highways. And this document went to a number of people in the company, including [Ford's automotive safety director] Mr. [J.C.] Eckhold, whose name is signed to all these documents that were submitted to the federal government, and [Ford's director of safety] Mr. [H.L.] Misch, whose name was being mentioned as head of automotive safety.

In addition to that, not only were there a number of people who were being burned to death, but—and this is part of P-13—the likelihood of a fire increases considerably with an accident's severity. And as you will remember from [plaintiffs' automobile engineering expert] Mr. [Frederick] Arndt's testimony, that makes sense. Not only does it make sense from the standpoint of there being a possibility of rupture of the fuel tank in a high-speed impact, but when it ruptures [fuel] comes out and mixes with air. The higher the speed of impact, the more likely to get ignition sources, the more likely to get a fire. So, the high-speed impact had to be dealt with. Ford knew all this.

In addition, Ford knew this kind of vehicle that was being designed, the Mustang II, had a failure mode with respect to fuel tanks when they were struck in the rear. The tank got pushed into the rear axle; it would rupture and fuel would come out. That was a failure mode known too well to the engineers. . . .

Did they know of ways to correct it? Unquestionably, yes. On November 10, 1970, their own engineering department and power sources systems said essentially there are three ways. You remember Mr. Arndt talking about three levels of protection? Nothing new. Ford engineers were telling them this in November 1970, "We can go with the tank over the rear axle. Now, we have a problem with the three-door models in getting the tank over the rear axle, or we can put the tank behind the axle, but we can design the frame rails so that when [the tank] crushes it moves up and over the rear axle so in a high-speed impact we have the same thing as over-the-axle tank. Or, thirdly, we can do the last of the lowest level, the minimum level of protection, and that is put some sort of protection or shielding between the tank and the axle to prevent this puncture that's going on.". . .

Now, the third level of protection that was suggested in Plaintiffs' Exhibit 15, on page 2, was to add shields for protuberances adjacent to the fuel tank for the Mustang fold-down model. You ask, did that work or would that work? Well, [Ford test engineer] Mr. Gegesky, as we pointed out during our evidence, was working with a similar car, the Pinto. And he was, in October of 1970, sliding that tank down an incline sled into the rear axle housing to the point where he had gotten holes punched in the tank just like it looked in the crash test. And he tried a couple of things. He put a crash shield between the tank and axle. The car was tested using the same configuration as the above tank failure, in other words, to cover the areas of tank failure the shield or flak vest was made of quarter-inch, this Goodyear Plylon two-ply conveyor belt. He took some conveyor belting and cut out a piece and he glued it so the vest completely covered the side of the tank that was covering the axle and it successfully protected the tank.

Now, he also made some suggestions in this document, which is P-38. He made some suggestions in October of 1971. Mr. Gegesky said—incidentally, that is spelled, G-e-g-e-s-k-y—said, "In the first place these crash shield or flak vest methods of protecting fuel tanks from sharp underbody objects in crash situations has merit in high-energy situations, high-speed impacts, and it should be considered as an alternate to bladders and fuel cells. . . ." He suggests, again, "An austere molded version of the flak vest should be designed, casted, and tested." Okay. Also, "Polyethylene liners should be used as an alternate material to the conveyor belting presently considered for shielding." Mr. Gegesky in October 1971 knew exactly how to correct this problem. He was telling the company the direction to go.

Now, as we indicated to you earlier with [Dr. Leslie] Ball's [plaintiffs' expert, a systems safety scientist] testimony, the question is, what is it that the company is going to do about providing some protection to prevent fuel tanks from getting ruptured by rear-axle housings, especially in Mustangs, Pintos, where it is clear, and they know that if that car is hit in the rear that there is going to be a puncture? . . . So what were the alternatives that were being considered?. . .

Now, the next level of protection that they were considering was what the government was proposing at that time and that is a thirty-mile-an-hour fixed barrier, and again Crash Test 1615 gives you a feel for the kind of crush that a car takes when it gets hit with a fixed barrier at thirty miles an hour.[2] The rear of that car gets crushed all the way up to the rear axle, and the rear tires get flat, but with an over-the-axle [fuel tank] design, or as Crash Test 1680 showed, if you design the tank to move over the axle it is perfectly within the realm of what the engineers were capable of doing, because this Capri was a regular production car. No special features on that car. On the highway, being sold to the public, manufactured by Ford in their European, or English, area. Not here in the United States. That's the car that Mr. Feaheny told you that in his opinion was inherently dangerous.

Deferring Safety, Saving $20.9 Million

Now, you recall that on March 4, 1971, as the engineers were looking to the top management of Ford Motor Company for some guidance [on] how hard we design these cars to be able to withstand an impact, Mr. Feaheny and other members of top management met in [Ford's general product development head] Mr. [Webster] McDonald's conference room there at Ford Motor Company in what is known as a product review meeting. These are weekly meetings where the top members of management sit around a conference table and they set policies for the company. And the question came up, what must we do? What do we do right now as a result of our November product review meeting when the government proposed standards came out of thirty-fixed? We made a decision we would begin in 1974 to have our cars meet a thirty-moving, and the car that is going to have to meet that is the Mustang. That will be the first year that the Mustang is introduced.

But they say: Now, wait just a minute. We have had a chance to look at [what] the industry—GM, Chrysler, et cetera—said in response to 70-20. We have had a chance, and those [responses] indicate that a corporate thirty-movable barrier objective for all cars by '75 may be too severe and overreactive. In other words, we may be ahead of the industry. We may be making our cars safer than General Motors, we may be making them safer than Chrysler, and what would be the effect of that?

Oh, my goodness, "lower performance level may be pursued within the industry which would make Ford competitive in variable cost and tooling and facilities expended."

We may be spending too much money on safety here, and we don't want to spend any more than GM or Chrysler or American Motors, so let's take another look at this thing. So the direction that they gave in that meeting, on the front page of Plaintiffs' Exhibit 27, is to "review the status of financial impacts of fuel system integrity programs at the April 8 product review meeting." So, no decision was made in that March meeting.

Along came April 8. They didn't meet then. They met on April 22, the record shows, and on April 22, in that same conference room that Mr. McDonald has at Ford Motor Company, they talked about this problem and they said: To meet a thirty-mile-an-hour moving barrier test we are going to have to put some sort of flak suit, some sort of shield, or maybe a bladder, in the tank; and if we do that, it is going to cost us at least $4 a car, it might cost us $8 a car. We are going to start doing that in 1974, and we are going to start putting them on the Mustang II in '74, but if we do it in 1974, we are going to spend that $4 a car, $8 a car, and it is going to cost us some money, so let's put it off. Let's defer it. Let's defer it. Let's not adopt that safety design at $4 a car, and let's not do it until 1976 in order to realize—realize, put in our pocket—"$20.9 million as compared to incorporation of the safety designs in 1974." That was the recommendation from the product review meeting on April 22, 1971, which Mr. Feaheny attended along with several other persons.

Now, four days later Mr. Feaheny signed what is called a General Product Development Safety Program letter, dated April 26, 1971. And what did Mr. Feaheny do? Did he defer the adoption of those flak suits? He not only deferred them until 1976, he went a step further. Mr. Feaheny said, "actual hardware will not be added until required by law. Add-on items such as flak suits will not be adopted until required by law."

The Nixon Tape

Now, we ask, why that change, why that change? Is it possible, while Mr. Feaheny was signing that letter on April 26, that he was aware that Henry Ford II and Lee Iacocca, the president of the company, were packing their bags to go to Washington to meet with the President of the United States? Because on the very next day they go into the White House and they talk with President [Richard M.] Nixon and they tell him, Mr. Iacocca—and this is at the bottom of page 18 of Plaintiff's 32. Mr. Iacocca says: "If inflation abates, what safety is doing to us is going to make inflation, in my opinion, look like child's play." And he continues to talk, and he says to the President: "I am in a position to be saying to Toms"—Mr. [Douglas] Toms [director of the National Highway Traffic Safety Administration], who came here and testified, and Mr. Volpe who is the secretary of transportation—I'm saying to them: "Would you guys cool it a little bit, you're breaking us." And they say, that is Toms and Volpe: "Well, hold it, hold it, people want safety." And I say, "Well, what do you mean they want safety? We get letters, we get about thousands on customer service [saying] you can't get your car fixed. We don't get anything on safety." [Iacocca] is telling Toms and Volpe we don't get anything on safety.

So the President says: "What do you want me to do?" And Mr. Ford says to him: "I think there are many things in DOT, Mr. President, that could be done if industry—that you could do by just calling them up, and just say, let's get some cost effectiveness." And the President says: "I want to find out, I want to find out what the situation is. Is cost effectiveness the word?" Mr. Ford says: "That's right. [We] want some cost effectiveness in these safety standards."

Now, we submit to you that the reason they don't get letters on safety is because the people assume that when they buy a car they are buying a safe car. When you get on the elevator out here in this courthouse you don't go around and look to see how many cables there are holding that elevator up. And if you did, would you know that you were looking at enough cable and that they were big enough? Do you know enough about elevators to know whether that is going to hold all the people that are on there? I'm ignorant about such things, and the people who drive cars are ignorant about such things.

If anybody climbs up underneath a car like this without the advantage of having heard all the testimony in this trial, they are not going to know whether that fuel tank gets rammed into the axle housing when it gets hit in the rear, because Ford Motor Company keeps the people ignorant about what happens and about the dangers involved. They don't want us to know. And the reason they don't get letters on safety is because people don't know that the cars they are putting out aren't safe, as in this Mustang II. It's no wonder.

Now, did the admonitions, the pleas to the President of the United States and Department of Transportation to "cool it on safety," have an effect? Mr. Toms said he understood that there was a point of view from Ford Motor Company and others that he should listen to the other side of the safety question. But the facts are clear. It took six years to get a standard that would require a rear-end crash test. Six years. And when [Federal Motor Vehicle Safety Standard No. 301] came into effect it was half as strong or protective of the people as the original proposal. Six years and 60 percent watered down.

I don't blame Mr. Toms. He came here and told you what he was trying to do. He didn't work for the automobile companies, he didn't work for Ford. He is doing his job as best he could, but he depends on many automobile companies, specifically Ford Motor Company, to give him the information that he needed to do his job properly. Ford Motor Company repeatedly gave Mr. Toms [and NHTSA] incorrect or half-truths, incorrect information, or only part of the information. . . .

From this emerges an attitude towards safety on the part of the top management at Ford Motor Company. And the attitude is, essentially, do only what is necessary to comply with the law. If we can put off the effective date of the law and we can water it down, then we can put off into the future when we have to really protect them. And in the meantime, whether it is '74 or '75 or '76, while we hold them off we can be putting more and more money into our pockets. We can increase the company profits on an annual basis, as, for example, [was discussed at] the product review meeting of April 1971. We can improve profits by $20.9 million by putting off for two years, '74 and '75, putting in the very minimum level of protection between the tank and the axle. In just two years we can save $20.9 million. It turns out they bought themselves another year with their efforts to lobby the government, because it wasn't until the 1977 model year that they actually put those shields on the tanks.

In addition to that, they were perfectly willing to give to the government only that information which supported their argument to postpone or delay or water down the standard. And they withheld the information which they knew would be supportive of higher, stiffer standards, better safety, better protection for the people.

Basically, Mr. Feaheny sat here and said: We did not want to do anything to make our cars safer, until we knew what we were going to have to do by law. Well, the answer to that is: Do what you know you should do for safety and do it first and do it foremost and don't worry about the law.

You go out on the highway and there is a fifty-five-mile-an-hour speed limit and everybody knows that. That's just a rule. The rule is, operate your car at a safe speed for the circumstances. And if you are in a driving rainstorm and you can't see more than fifty feet in front of you, don't drive down the road at fifty miles an hour and say, well, I'm five miles an hour under the speed limit. You might even pull your car over to the side because you can't see. The law requires everybody, including top management at Ford Motor Company, to be responsible, to look out for other people, to do what's right and what's reasonable, to make the cars reasonably safe. Don't stand back and say: We don't have a responsibility to make the cars safe until the government tells us how we are going to make them safe. And that's essentially what Mr. Feaheny was here talking about. And that is Ford Motor Company's top management.

Now, why do they want to keep us in the dark? Why do they want to keep us ignorant about the dangers of postcrash fires? Why have you never seen . . . a film showing what happens when a car crashes and is on fire in the rear end like you saw in the evidence presented by the plaintiff in this case? Because the Ford Motor Company doesn't want you to see that. They don't want you to see the dangers of that. Why did they not give the information to the government? Why do they want to keep Mr. Toms ignorant? Why do they want to keep Mr. Nixon ignorant? Because they didn't want those people to know, because if you and I know and the people know and the government knows about the dangers involved and availability of alternate designs which can eliminate this problem, we are going to demand a safer car. If we demand a safer car, oh, my goodness, it just might cost them money in profits, which is going to cost Mr. Feaheny more bonus money, more stock options, and other things. It's the profits that are paramount, the highest, the most important to these men.

In short, their attitude is: What you don't know won't hurt you. But what they really mean is: What you don't know won't hurt them as long as people are kept ignorant of the problem and ignorant of the fact that the motor companies can change things and make these cars safe. Then, as long as the people are kept ignorant, then they are not threatened to make a safer car at the potential expense of a company profit.

But it hurt Terri and it hurt her parents. And the reason why is because that car, that Mustang II, was dangerous as they manufactured it and put it on the road, and they knew it was dangerous. Even Mr. Feaheny and [Ford design analysis engineer] Mr. [Jack] Ridenour and [accident reconstructionist and automotive design expert witness] Mr. [John] Habberstad all admitted that the car is safer with a shield on it than without. And yet, knowing of the danger, knowing of the risk, knowing of the failure mode, knowing of several ways to correct it, and knowing that it could be done for as little as $4 a car, they made a conscious and deliberate decision to withhold putting those safety devices on the car in order to increase company profits by $20.9 million for the '74 and '75 years.

Perfuming the Pig

Now ... Ford would have you believe in this case that the shield wouldn't have made any difference. Oh, my, this impact was just so hard that it wouldn't have made any difference, and any car manufactured would have caught on fire in this impact. That's what they would have you believe. Now, Ford Motor Company, we submit, is doing a little of what Mr. Feaheny would refer to as "perfuming the pig," when they try to tell you that the shield wouldn't have made any difference.

In the first place, this was a three-car collision involving seven people, and it couldn't have been all that horrendous when six of them walked away. The only person who had to be hospitalized was Terri Stubblefield, and if there had been no fire, she would have been able to recover from her injuries completely. Not only would she not have been killed, she would not have been permanently disabled. So this is not one of those horrendous impacts from which no one can survive. This was a very foreseeable impact.

Yes, it involved high speed, sure, no question about it. I didn't get into arguing with Mr. Habberstad about how you arrive at this figure. High speed, yes. Damage to the fuel tank, no. Would the shield have made a difference? Well, just from a crash-test standpoint—Plaintiffs' Exhibit 10 lists crash tests.... And in every one of those, in every single one of those with the exception of one test, there was a shield on the tank and there wasn't any rupture....

Now the only thing that you can conclude is that in April of 1971, top management of Ford Motor Company, knowing of the danger, knowing of the failure mode, knowing of alternatives, made a deliberate and conscious and considered decision to do nothing. To do nothing to make that car safe, but to sell it anyway to the public in order to put $20.9 million in their pocket. And they knew when they started selling those cars, they knew that sooner or later somewhere there would be a rear-end impact to one of those cars, and that fuel tank would get rammed into that differential housing and it would rupture, just as their crash test showed. And when that happened, there is a possibility of fire, and if there is an ignition there would be fire, and if there was fire somebody would get burned, and if there was burn there had to be pain and suffering.

They had to know that, just as you would have to know when you drive [too fast] down a rainswept highway, if you do it long enough, you're going to run into something and hurt something. The only question those people had, if they ever bothered to think about it, was where will it happen, when will it happen, and who will it happen to. There could not have been any question in their minds that it would happen. It was a certainty....

[Ford] began putting shields on cars in August of 1976, almost a year before Terri was burned, on the '77 model cars. They would have you believe that they waited to do that. They didn't put them on the '74 model, they didn't put them on the '75 model, they didn't put them on the '76 model. They did put them on the '77 model. They would have you believe it was because they were busy trying to develop some fancy new type of material to put between the tank and the axle. They waited, because it wasn't until 1977 model cars that the federal government made them do something. That's when they put the shields on the cars. They deferred the adoption of those shields until required by law, exactly as management desired to do in April of '71. Exactly.

And even after they started making them a part of the '77, '78, and '79 model cars, they didn't make any effort to tell the people who were driving '74s or '75s or '76s that they didn't have a shield in their car, that they could come in and have one of those shields put on in something like thirty minutes. It would cost $1.31, or maybe, if you believe Mr. Feaheny, as much as $5 to have it put on the car. They didn't do that. They kept everybody ignorant of the danger, knowing full well that it was there.

Now, I want to say a word, too, about punitive damages. Punitive damages, as his honor will instruct you, have a special purpose in our law. They are to deter, as his honor will instruct, the wrongdoer from repeating the misconduct.

Now, deterrence means—and this is the dictionary definition—"to discourage, to turn aside, to prevent from acting, as by fear." That's one of the reasons why as a society we punish. I want you to understand that we are not talking here about punishing personally anybody at Ford Motor Company. Not Mr. Feaheny, not Henry Ford II, not Lee Iacocca, not anybody like that. Those people are not involved in this case. They are not a party to this case. The only party to the case is Ford Motor Company. They designed the car, manufactured the car, they sold the car to the public, and Ford Motor Company is the defendant that we are asking you to return a verdict against. And whatever you do in this case, it will not speak in terms of the individuals, but those individuals will know what you do in this case and they are watching, and what you do in this case is going to affect what they do in the future. That's what punitive damages are all about. . . .

Now, I'm going to give way to Mr. Weinberg here for a while and then I will be back to talk with you after he has spoken with you, and as I indicated I am not going to be very long that time, and then I will be followed by Mr. Stolz and Mr. Johnson and you will finally have your opportunity, after listening to the charge or instruction from the court, to get about the business that this has been all about for two weeks. Thank you for your attention.

Concluding Argument On Punitive Damages

MR. DEVINE: The first thing I want to say to you is that I want to agree with Mr. Weinberg entirely. None of these plaintiffs, not Bill Stubblefield, not Linda Standley, none of the attorneys representing them want you to be influenced by sympathy. They do not ask for your sympathy. They ask you to be fair to all parties, to do what is right in this matter. I don't want you to be under the impression that we feel any differently about that than Mr. Weinberg.

Something else that I want to say real quickly. Mr. Weinberg opened and closed with some reference to Hollywood production. Well, I tried to find out how much it would cost to get a document blown up and posted like this, and it was $40 or $50 per document. I tried to find out how much it would take to get a photograph blown up and posted, instead of a photograph like this, [and it was] close to a hundred dollars. I tried to find out how much it cost to get a fine car that is perfectly runable, exactly like the car involved in this case, and cut it up and bring it into the courtroom, and couldn't find one. I had to end up getting a wrecked car where the front end was torn up, the rear end was still okay, and it turned out it was a '74 instead of a '75. Maybe what we have done is make it easier for you to understand the facts. That was the purpose. But in terms of spending money to present those facts to you, the money has been spent by Ford Motor Company, when they were unwilling to spend even $4 a car to improve safety.

Mr. Weinberg [says] they want us to wave a magic wand, they want us to put a man on the moon in less than eleven years. That's no magic wand. That's not putting a man on the moon. Pure and simple, [a safety device was] suggested by an engineer as early as 1971, and the only reason they didn't pursue it earlier was because of the conscious and deliberate decision of Ford Motor Company to defer putting those devices on cars until required by law. When the law required it to be done in 1977 models, then they developed it, put it on....

"Nobody else had shields before we did," [they say.] "We were pioneers in safety." Well, what they are really saying is that everybody does it, everybody else makes the car this way. Don't blame us. Don't say that we are negligent, because everybody makes them this way.

Well, in the first place, all these other cars had axle housings that punched holes in tanks. You don't think for one minute that they would have failed to bring you crash tests in here to show you that the kind of car that Mr. Arndt drove, or the kind of car [Dr.] Ball drove, had the failure mode that they had in the Mustang II? Sure they would have brought that in here and showed it to you....

I anticipate that his honor will instruct you with respect to what other manufacturers do. Basically, it is no excuse to say [that] we do it like everybody else does it. We anticipate that he will instruct you that such matters [as] industry practice, both in the United States and in foreign countries, together with technological development as shown by patents or other evidence pertaining to design features of the automobile fuel system, are relevant—yes, sir—relevant for you to take into consideration, but not conclusive. In other words, just because everybody else don't put a shield on it doesn't mean that it is not negligence. If the car crushes and it needs a shield, put a shield on it. And the question of whether or not Ford Motor Company exercised ordinary care is to be determined by you based on all the evidence. Industry custom [or] practice is relevant, but not conclusive.

Put Away These Childish Defenses

Now, very quickly, all these defenses that Ford is talking to you about sound very much like the child who has gotten caught misbehaving: I didn't do it, somebody else did it. Somebody else made me do it. Everybody else does it. I couldn't help doing it. They made me do it. Go easy on me, because it's no big thing. Terri had cystic fibrosis; she would only have lived to be twenty. What the top management at Ford Motor Company needs is to change their values. They need to understand that human life, that suffering, pain, is more important, more important than profits. That's what they need to understand. They need [to think] like the biblical passage says: "When I was a child I talked like a child and I acted like a child, but when I got to be a man I put away my childish thoughts" [1 Corinthians 13:11]. They need to put away these childish defenses, these childish thoughts, and place values where profits are more than human life and suffering.

What can you do about that? The jury system and the system of punitive damages permits you to send a message to Ford Motor Company management—to men like Mr. Feaheny—to send them a message that the people will not tolerate the kinds of decisions made in this case, that the people will not permit deferring a safety decision in the interest of company profits. That people will not permit a knowingly dangerous product to be put on the highway and continue to be sold to the public for three years running, without any word, without any warning, without any opportunity for people who use the product to go into their dealership and get one of these [shields], to put it on their car at a very minimum, even if they have to pay for it themselves.

... Regardless of what you do in this case it is going to affect what [Ford's top officials] do in the future. If you return a verdict that does not contain punitive damages or contains punitive damages that they consider to be a marginal amount of money, it is business as usual. They are going to go right on, and the people that are out there on the highway right now driving these cars will never know, because Ford is not going to tell them. But if you return an amount which these men respond to, which they listen to, it will affect their decision. That I can guarantee.

There may never be another opportunity, and there may never be another jury that will have a case where the documentation of a decision that was made by Ford Motor Company management is so clear and so direct between the decision being made in 1971 and the horrible agony and pain and death of a little girl in 1977, six years later. That's a long time, and there are a lot of miles between Detroit and Atlanta, and the direct cause and effect between those two points may never be that clear again.

But don't you think those decisions aren't made on a regular basis. Look at the very documents in which they made this decision. Not only did they decide to defer the flak suit on all affected cars until 1976 to realize $20.9 million in savings, but right before it they decided to defer all the rollover hardware until 1976 to realize the design cost savings of $10.7 million for '74 and '75. And up before there they say that the estimated total financial impact on company profits of the entire fuel system integrity program over '73, '74, '75 and '76, four years, is to—and I am quoting—"reduce company profits by $109 million."

Unless you return an amount which is sufficient to make it such that they don't want to run the risk of getting caught again. Because, if they get caught again, it is not just a matter of giving out what they put in their pockets, it is giving up more than what they put in their pockets. Unless the figure you arrive at is sufficient to get the message across, it is business as usual. I will leave the figure to you.

I suggest that you look at Plaintiffs' Exhibit 29, because that is the document where the decision was made, and that tells you the kind of things that move these people to make decisions one way or the other.

At this point, I am going to thank you for your patience, and I am going to defer to Mr. Stolz.

Endnotes

*Born on June 29, 1942, Foy R. Devine graduated with honors in 1964 from the University of North Carolina at Chapel Hill, receiving a B.A. in history. He obtained an LL.B. from the University of Virginia School of Law in 1967, where he was a member of the law review and attained the honor of Order of the Coif. Mr. Devine was admitted to the Virginia and District of Columbia Bars in 1967 and to the Georgia Bar in 1970. He was an associate with King & Spalding from 1969 to 1972, a partner in Fierer & Devine from 1972 to 1978, and president of Devine & Morris from 1978 to 1988. He has been president of his own professional corporation since 1988.

1. *Ford Motor Company v. Stubblefield*, 171 Ga.App. 331 (319 S.E.2d 470 (1984).

2. According to Devine, there are two ways of testing the effects of vehicular impacts: fixed-barrier tests and moving-barrier tests. A fixed-barrier test involves towing the car into a concrete barrier at a certain rate of speed. The problem with that test is that the severity of the impact is substantially dependent upon the weight of the vehicle. Therefore, the moving-barrier test is more commonly used. That test involves placing a plywood-over-steel frame on the front of a truck body and towing the rig into the stationary test vehicle. The rig weighs about 4,000 pounds, which is the average weight of all vehicles on the road. Thus, the only variable element, aside from speed, is the design of the test vehicle.

Moseley v. General Motors
No. 90-V-6276 (Fulton St. Ct.)

Result: $105.24 million verdict
Plaintiffs' Counsel: James E. Butler Jr. and Robert D. Cheeley of Butler, Wooten, Overby & Cheeley (Columbus)
Defense Counsel: Fred H. Bartlit Jr. of Kirkland & Ellis (Chicago)
Judge: A. L. Thompson Jr.
Date of Verdict: February 4, 1993

Chapter X

Sounding Forth the Trumpets: The *Moseley* Reprise

Introduction
By S. Richard Gard Jr.
Reprinted from Side Impact *(revised)*
Copyright 1993, American Lawyer Media, L.P. All rights reserved.

The jury foreman's reading of the verdict in *Moseley v. General Motors* cracked the courtroom's silence and shattered every big-verdict record in Georgia. But even before the trial's stunning conclusion, before the lawyers quoted Lincoln and Shakespeare and a Civil War hymn, before a policeman wept describing how flames drowned a teenager's screams for life, before the judge pounded his gavel and the clerk called the case and the lawyers announced ready, before the events of a midnight crash ever exploded in a cramped Atlanta courtroom, the case was destined to be one of the generation's great civil trials.

The jurors would hear testimony no other jury had ever heard before—an insider's allegations about the safety of several million American trucks on the road. The drama would combine human tragedy with boardroom thriller, and the lawyers, two of the country's most skilled, would give performances that legal practitioners, students, and observers will long study and second-guess.

Both sides played for national stakes. As trial got under way, the National Highway Traffic Safety Administration (NHTSA) continued its investigation of the product design in dispute, side-mounted fuel tanks on 1973 to 1987 full-sized Chevrolet and GMC pickup trucks. At the time, a recall would have dealt an estimated billion-dollar blow to a company that, after special charge-offs in 1992, posted the biggest losses in the history of American business. To plaintiffs' lawyer James E. Butler Jr.,* a recall threat dealt the trump card he needed for punitive damages. The greater the verdict, he told jurors, the greater the pressure for NHTSA to pull the trucks off the highways.

The award they gave him, $105,241,612.84, marked Georgia's first nine-figure victory and one of the nation's largest for a product liability case. *Moseley* dominated the *Daily Report*'s headlines for most of January and into February of 1993. It was the country's most significant civil trial at the time, and Court TV covered the proceedings live for a national audience. At the courthouse, a crush of onlookers spilled over into an extra courtroom equipped with closed-circuit television monitors for the scores of local lawyers who had come to see the World Series of torts trials.

A Morality Play

Shannon C. Moseley, 17, burned to death in suburban Gwinnett County, thirty miles northeast of Atlanta, shortly after midnight October 21, 1989. Drunk driver David Ruprecht ran a red light and rammed into the driver's-side gas tank on Moseley's 1985 GMC Sierra. If other lawyers regard the courtroom as theater, Butler sees his trials as morality plays. In *Moseley*, he pieced together evidence of document shredding, clandestine crash testing, and institutional dissembling to portray twenty years of corporate villainy. GM had not simply made a poor design decision, he tried to show the jury, but an evil one.

If Butler presented a saga, GM counsel Fred H. Bartlit Jr. set out to debunk. He tried to reduce the case to two essentials: The speed of the other vehicle, not the design of the fuel tank, killed Moseley, and it killed him instantly. Under Georgia law, any award of punitive damages hinged on a finding that Moseley lingered before death. Bartlit staked out pain and suffering as the last line of defense where he would repel Butler's onslaught, if only to keep the damages to a minimal amount of millions.

Two factors set *Moseley* apart from the some 120 other side-impact suits filed against GM. First, Butler's clients, Thomas and Elaine Moseley, stayed true to their vow to see the case through judgment no matter how many millions of dollars GM threw their way. Second, Butler had Ronald E. Elwell, GM's own fuel tank safety expert turned disgruntled retiree turned whistle-blower.

Elwell was Butler's star witness if ever a lawyer had one. For nearly three days Elwell educated the jury on the problems he perceived in GM's having mounted gas tanks outside the frame rails of full-sized pickups. And he lent credence to Butler's conspiracy theory, telling how GM allegedly kept from him the results of a series of crash tests and how that testing program indicated high-level panic at the company.

Butler had another former company insider helping him make his case, only this one did so less willingly. More than a year before trial Butler had demanded to take the deposition of then-GM Chairman and Chief Executive Officer Robert C. Stempel. It was a long-shot request, typical of the plaintiffs' lawyer's combative tactics. To the defense lawyers' chagrin, a part-time magistrate substituting for Fulton State Court Judge A. L. Thompson Jr. ordered GM to make Stempel available. He ended up enduring two hours and twenty minutes of Butler's grilling. He held his ground, but never before as the chief of a company that is routinely dragged into car wreck cases had Stempel had to sit for such an indignity.

Knowing Butler planned to show the jury the videotape of the deposition, Bartlit on the third day of trial arranged for

Stempel to sit at counsel's table as the company's personal representative. The surprise entrance instantly boosted the national magnitude of the trial. And what was to come would leave an indelible impression on the jurors. Butler not only played the videotape the next day, but the following week put Stempel on the stand, if only so the jury could hear him repeatedly refuse to take responsibility for the death of Shannon Moseley and the dangers GM's pickups supposedly posed to the public.

Butler gave his $105.24 million closing argument in three parts—the first coming before Bartlit spoke, the second in rebuttal, and the last, reprinted below, during the punitive damages phase of trial.

When the jury returned with $4.24 million for Moseley's life plus $1 for pain and suffering, the punitive phase began. Neither side presented any evidence, instead opting for a final round of arguments. Bartlit went first, admitting the jurors had dealt his client a crushing blow and assuring them of GM's commitment to mend its ways. Unfortunately, during the lunch break, a company spokesman had just issued a press release insisting on the safety of the pickup trucks and discrediting the jury for reaching a verdict based on emotion, not fact. This sends Butler to new heights of indignation, building to a crescendo that all but had the gallery mouthing the glory hallelujahs from the "Battle Hymn of the Republic." The jurors gave Butler $1 million more than he requested; GM has appealed the judgment.

Sounding Forth the Trumpets
Concluding Argument on Punitive Damages

MR. BUTLER: Ladies and gentlemen, cases should be decided based on evidence and based on what witnesses say. I said this once before and let me say it again now, after that moving address by Mr. Bartlit, who is a lawyer, who is not General Motors. Cases must be decided based on the evidence and not on what lawyers say, no matter how profound it might seem.

Tom and Elaine Moseley didn't crawl into this courtroom seeking sympathy. We don't need it, we don't want it. They've got their family and their friends and they've got three years' worth of sympathy. They didn't come here—they didn't fight this case and have us fight this case for them for three years to get sympathy from General Motors, which has never been expressed except inside this courtroom in your presence, I might point out. We don't need it now. It doesn't help. It won't save anybody. It won't even help General Motors itself.

Mr. Bartlit says this has been a crushing blow. He says General Motors respects it and accepts it. He says, "It will make us a better company," and he says, "General Motors is going to get an independent lawyer to investigate this. You can take that to the bank."

Ladies and gentlemen, the thing has been investigated in over 120 lawsuits. You can take that to the bank. . . .

Ladies and gentlemen, focus, please, in this part of the case, not on what we lawyers say but on what the evidence is. And here's what the evidence is right now on this part of the case, which is about the amount of punitive damages. The evidence is that General Motors elected to present no evidence. The evidence is that nobody from General Motors is even here. It's fine and good, and I hope not compelling, however, for Mr. Bartlit, a lawyer, to say to you that General Motors accepts and respects your verdict. But there's nobody from General Motors here even to receive your verdict.

He says that we respect the jury system. General Motors has already issued a press release about this case. Why don't they give you the press release and see if that tells you that they respect your decision?

BARTLIT: Your honor, I object to that as going far outside the record and I—

BUTLER: I'll withdraw it and get it over [with].

"There's no one here from General Motors, nobody here from upper management of General Motors. You've heard the evidence. You've heard [former GM engineer] Mr. [Ronald E.] Elwell's undisputed testimony that it's upper management who has to decide that there's a defect. It's upper management. You heard [GM engineer] Mr. [Robert A.] Sinke in his deposition, Mr. Sinke saying only upper management can order a recall.

Where is somebody from General Motors? All we have is Mr. Bartlit. This is a serious matter. It ought to be taken seriously. Can you logically conclude that it's taken seriously when General Motors elects to put up no evidence on the amount of your verdict for punitive damages? General Motors doesn't even have anybody here to receive your verdict.

There's nobody here—did you hear these words, ladies and gentlemen? A hundred and twenty lawsuits. Your verdict now. The Insurance Institute for Highway Safety, you've heard about what they say. The Center for Auto Safety, you've heard about what they say. The National Highway Traffic Safety Administration, you've heard about what they've said thus far. All of that is behind us. This is not the beginning of an investigation of this defect. All of that is behind us.

Did you hear even the lawyer General Motors sent here say, "We accept responsibility"? It's easy. David Ruprecht said it, what, three times—in his opening, in his testimony, and in his closing. It's real easy. We teach our children to do that. If you're wrong and you're obviously wrong, the first thing you do—and if you're going to get up and say it's a tragedy and we have sympathy—the first thing you ought to do is say, "We accept responsibility." That's what grown people do.

That's not a criticism of Mr. Bartlit. He's doing his job. He's doing what General Motors has instructed him to do, and he's done it very well.

BARTLIT: Your honor, I resent that, and that should be stricken. I don't do what anybody tells me to do, nobody.

BUTLER: Judge, he's had his argument and I'm entitled to mine.

BARTLIT: That's personal, your honor. That's just flat not true.

BUTLER: That's the opposite of personal.

THOMPSON: Have a seat, Mr. Bartlit. Move on.

BUTLER: Thank you, sir.

Have you heard anybody come before you and say that we will even acknowledge that there's a problem? Not a soul. Not a soul.

Where does General Motors—not Mr. Bartlit—where does General Motors stand today with respect to this defect that you have found and the danger that's posed to people riding in— and who happen to collide with—the other five million trucks still on the road? Where does General Motors—not Mr. Bartlit— stand with respect to those matters, the lives that are at stake? Where do they stand with respect to automotive safety? Where do they stand with respect to simply telling the truth and accepting responsibility?

They don't have anybody here. They stand where [former GM chairman] Mr. [Robert C.] Stempel told you they stood. Admit a problem? No. Does Tom and Elaine—did Tom and Elaine and Shannon and all the rest of us have the right to know? No.

You see, Mr. [GM engineer Michael] Juras has the right to his opinion and, you remember when I had him on the stand, I told him I respected that. He thinks the trucks are safe. He's got that right. Mr. Stempel has the right to his opinion that the trucks are safe. Everybody has got a right to their opinion.

But, ladies and gentlemen, that's not the point. The point is that Tom and Elaine and the people have a right to form their own opinions—just like Mr. Juras and Mr. Stempel have that right—based on the facts. And it is wrong for General Motors, not only to withhold the facts, but to shred evidence and to deceive and to mislead, which is what they've done for twenty years. That's wrong. That is a monstrous, monstrous wrong, and that's what the amount of punitive damages addresses.

I want to thank you for your efforts. We all do. You have been a meticulous jury. You have also scared us to death, I might add that. Two days [of deliberations during the first phase of the trial]—it's not the worst two days I ever spent in my life, but it's right up there.

We thank you from the bottom of our hearts for your verdict. We thank you most of all for the last thing you said, and that was, "Yes [to whether punitive damages are called for]." That's the second best "yes" I've ever heard in my life. It's awfully important because that's why we came here. That's the only— we told you that and I hope you believed us. I think you did. That's the only reason we came here was to hear you say "yes" and then to ring the bell loudly, and that's what we're after. We didn't have to be here.

A Line of Victims

You have found—well, let me, before I say that, I—the case weighs heavily on us, and I'm sure it does on you. You know, you cannot miss—or I have not been able to get away from— a haunting vision of a line of victims that stretches back into the past for twenty years and that, unless we do something about it, will stretch on into the future. That's the vision that I've had in my mind about this case since we first started uncovering some of this evidence that had never been heard before, that line of victims. And it's haunted us.

But the case has gone beyond that now, because what you've heard tried and what you've got before you are not only that line of victims and stopping it now, I hope, but some fundamental issues about automotive safety and the responsibility of manufacturers. And, you know, people are important. But that's even more important than the people that burn and die because of one product.

And even beyond that, we've gone further in this case, because you've got a transcendent issue in this case that's affected by the amount of your punitive damages verdict. And that is, how must corporations behave?

Why was there an attack upon [accident witness] Teresa Stabler, on Officer [Bruce R.] Higgins [the first police officer to arrive at the scene], on somebody at my table, me or [co-counsel] Bob [Cheeley] or Tom or Elaine or somebody? Why was there an attack upon those people? And the reason is this: It is so much easier for us as human beings to be critical of the guy next to us, you see, and to doubt the guy next to us, than to understand and appreciate what a faceless, soulless corporation is doing. What we see here—the reason we see those attacks is to try to reduce the case down [to] the level, so that it becomes citizen against citizen. That's what that tactic is.

You see it in every case involving punitive damages. Set the folks of the jury against Teresa or "Boomer" Higgins or Tom or Elaine or Jim [Butler], you see, and then they won't focus on what General Motors has done, or on the manipulations engaged in by General Motors over two decades. You see, that's what that's all about: Take your eyes off what this case is really about.

I hope—I think from your verdict that it didn't work. I think from your verdict that you focused on what this case is about. And let me talk about that just a minute. You have found that there is clear and convincing evidence of the need for punitive damages to be imposed against General Motors. We applaud your courage. All that's left now is the amount, and I want to talk about that.

I want to say first to you that you've gone this far, please don't shrink from the task at hand now, because this is what's really important. This is what makes history.

The judge is going to charge you about the measure of punitive damages, and he's going to tell you that—I've already told you once and I'm going to mention it again—they are not to compensate, you see. Don't let General Motors set citizen against citizen. Don't get wrapped up in who gets what. It doesn't focus on Tom or Elaine or Shannon any more. It focuses only on General Motors, who is absent. Nobody from General Motors is here. But the focus necessarily must still be on General Motors in punitive damages because that's what they're for.

The purpose of them—there's three purposes: to penalize, punish, or deter. That means three different things. You penalize or punish past conduct. I must tell you frankly we're not real interested in that. I mean that's important, but the next purpose of punitive damages is what really brings us here and that's deter, D-E-T-E-R, deter.

What deter means is to stop, and that's why we're here. It's the line of victims stretching into the future that haunts us most of all. Deter means to stop, and that's why we ask for punitive damages: to stop the misconduct, to stop the dying from these trucks, to stop the General Motors attitude toward automotive safety that you've seen, to stop the corporate mentality that you've seen that would respond.

Now, please, ladies and gentlemen, think about what you've seen. What is General Motors' corporate culture? What is their response? I told you it wasn't just Tom and Elaine and Jim and Bob saying this was a dangerous product; it's the Insurance Institute for Highway Safety. They're not my friends. I represent victims, and they call me a plaintiffs' lawyer. That group is not my friends. It may be the first time in history they've ever said a product needed to be recalled. [It's also] the Center for Auto Safety.

Deter means to stop. And the measure of damages—the measure of damages—how much? Here's the standard, and I can't do anything about it because this standard will weigh you down, sure enough. The measure of damages is "the enlightened conscience of a fair and impartial jury." Judge Thompson will tell you that. Now, that's tough. I can't help you with that, because it's up to you. All I can do is tell you what I think is material to that decision.

Never Again

I will say this, that whatever else you do, ladies and gentlemen, when you go back there to consider the amount, think about the purposes. First, think about the fact that it focuses on General Motors. Second, think about the purposes: penalize, punish, or deter. And don't be swayed from that. Don't let anybody let some improper influence alter your course. Nothing matters except the amount that is sufficient to punish, penalize, or deter. He's going to tell you that—Judge Thompson will. It's the amount that is sufficient—that's the word. And again, I focus on deter, which means to stop.

How much is sufficient to stop—not make risky, not slap their wrist, not make it unpleasant, not make them think twice, not make them appoint some more lawyers to investigate? That ain't the point. How much is enough to stop General Motors from continuing this misconduct about these trucks and their attitude about automotive safety and their attitude about telling the truth and telling the public the facts? How much is enough to stop it? That is the measure of damages.

It doesn't do any good to say we'll appoint somebody. See, that derogates from your job, because your job now is to decide how much is enough to stop it—not make it risky or unpleasant—but, by gosh, to stop it. Never again. That's what it means. That's what it means to me. Stop means never again. After 120 lawsuits, the Insurance Institute, the Center for Auto Safety, this trial, your verdict—

BARTLIT: Your honor, I object to the 120 lawsuits for about the fifteenth time. There's no foundation for that. It's improper.

BUTLER: May I proceed, your honor?

THOMPSON: Move on.

BUTLER: Eighty lawsuits is what they admitted first. A hundred—I don't remember the evidence. You will. Does it make much difference whether it's 80 or 100 or 120 or 200? At some point it's got to stop. Ladies and gentlemen, make it stop now—not tomorrow, not somewhere else. Right here, right now.

Even those who may be philosophically opposed to large punitive damages—and we know many people are—have to agree that at the very least, if nothing else, people have a right to know. And if you hide facts from the people, if you mislead the people, that, too, has got to stop. That cannot be tolerated.

Let me mention something about the evidence that's been hidden from the people: the crash tests successfully hidden for ten years. They say the purpose of them was to improve, make improvements. Mr. Bartlit said earlier that if you penalize us, then corporations won't test to the limits, they won't do that kind of crash-testing program. Think about it. You probably already have.

One of the things I forgot to say earlier, think about it, ladies and gentlemen. If you conduct a testing program to find a problem and you fix the problem, that's fine. But no corporation is going to be deterred or discouraged from testing products and fixing products by a large punitive damages verdict. What they'll be deterred from is testing products and then not fixing them, and then misleading the public about whether there's a problem, with stuff like stone shields and confidential memos to the sales staff.

I submit to you, ladies and gentlemen, that GM's approach to this case and [to] your job was the opposite of responsibility. It was the essence of willful misconduct. That's what the—I submit to you that the way they've handled this for twenty years, the way they handled this trial, proves beyond anything else the need for a large verdict of punitive damages. It's not just what one lawyer says. It reflects the corporate mentality of General Motors, the way they respond to their critics going back for thirty years.

We join—those of us at this table who have a terrible accusation hurled at us—join in some very august company: "Boomer" Higgins, Teresa Stabler, who are attacked, and you are told that they are lying. "Boomer" Higgins, [Bartlit] puts on a chart and says, "paid-for testimony." We all join some mighty celebrated company in American history because we have now been attacked simply because we disagree with GM. I am proud to be in the company of those people, because those people are the ones who created automotive safety, and they did it going after GM.

Ladies and gentlemen, the only—let's get back to evidence, not lawyer talk. What is GM really concerned about? Remember Mr. Juras's memorandum from 1985? Did you see in there any expression of concern that people were burning? No. His concern was that there was an increase in post-collision, fuel-fed fire litigation.

Remember Mr. Stempel's videotape? Did he express concern that people were burning? No. He was concerned about an increase in litigation.

That's their concern. They don't accept your verdict. They don't propose to do anything about your verdict. And they won't do anything because of your verdict unless it absolutely, indisputably, forces them to do so and puts an end to it. You know that from the last thing Mr. Sinke said, the last piece of evidence you got.

And I'll tell you again: The reason we're here is to force a recall, either by GM, because your verdict makes them do it, or if they won't do it, from NHTSA, because your verdict makes it impossible to say, "We're not going to force a recall." That's why we're here.

You heard it all through this trial about—whenever we would talk about some other cases, GM would say, "Oh, that's not relevant, because they're not substantially similar." Ladies and gentlemen, every single one of those people who burned to death were in a GM pickup truck with an outside-the-frame-rail fuel tank. And it is appalling to me that GM would conduct this trial as it has, would respond to your verdict [by] not responding, when every one of those people—every one of those souls stirring in heaven—was in one of their trucks with one of these fuel tanks.

Why Did They Shred Evidence?

I know I'm being long-winded. This is not going to be like the other day where we talked all day. I'm going to wrap up pretty quick. I appreciate your patience in listening to me. It's awfully important. Tom and Elaine have waited for three years for somebody to stand up there and talk about this, the most important subject. It's preyed on their minds for three years, and I've waited a lot longer than three years. I'll try to be brief, but I appreciate your listening to me.

How does GM expect anyone, any reasonable person, to believe that they accept and respect your decision when they don't even bring witnesses to defend the case and they don't bring witnesses to tell you that? GM's got plenty of people they could bring down here to put on the stand and say, "We understand. We acknowledge the problem. We'll work with NHTSA. We'll tell NHTSA. We acknowledge the problem. We'll do a recall. We'll fix it."

Ladies and gentlemen, it doesn't take a rocket scientist to figure out how to drastically reduce the danger of these pickup trucks. You put on the steel shield that Mr. Elwell told you worked in the seventies in crash tests. That's unrebutted. You put in a bladder tank. One of the other witnesses mentioned a bladder tank. That's like they used to use in the military inside the steel tank so if the steel tank gets punctured, you've got to also puncture the bladder, the rubber tank, before you get any leaks, you see. And rubber tends to seal. So if you get some leakage, it won't be bad. It's easy. That doesn't cost a whole lot of money. Or you can move the fuel tanks inside the frame rail and put a shield around the drive shaft.

It's not—it's easy to fix this problem. The problem is not what to do upon recall. The problem is getting this mammoth corporation simply to accept responsibility, and that's why we're here. At risk, ladies and gentlemen, from your verdict—that's why the last two days have been so stressful for us, because of the stakes involved.

And I probably shouldn't say this because y'all have had enough stress on you already—but the risks are enormous. There are not just the lives that are at stake; it's that what you say will speak volumes about what's required in the field of automotive safety and about what is acceptable and what is not acceptable corporate conduct, about what a corporation's mentality should be about safety, about telling the truth to the public, about shredding evidence.

Where is the rebuttal evidence to what Ron Elwell told you—"indefensible"? Where is the rebuttal evidence to what [GM engineer Theodore] Kashmerick told you? What was GM's response twelve years ago when these cases really began to percolate up? It was to send the lawyer staff and engineers to Ted Kashmerick, get his documents, and start shredding them. And yet we're here today, and GM, through a lawyer, says they accept your verdict, they respect your verdict. Why did they shred evidence?

There are some, I am sure, that would say, let NHTSA do it, the National Highway Traffic Safety Administration. We've talked about that before. Ladies and gentlemen, do not abandon your responsibility as General Motors has abandoned theirs. You must tell them, you must teach them—NHTSA and GM—what will and will not be accepted.

Hearing the Trumpets

I woke up—I'm always hesitant to say something like this, but I'm going to tell it to you anyway. I woke up at three o'clock yesterday morning. I figured y'all would be coming back yesterday. And I woke up with a tune in my head, and it was about trumpets. And you will recognize it, because I remembered most of the words but not all of them. And I went out to get a hymnal to look them up, because this is what we seek in this case. The hymn goes like this, third verse [reading], "He has sounded forth the trumpets that shall never call retreat. He is sifting out the hearts of men before His judgment seat. Oh, be swift my soul to answer Him, be jubilant my feet" ["Battle Hymn of the Republic"].

Ladies and gentlemen, that's what we're asking. That's what we're asking. This is a historic opportunity to make a difference like no jury I've ever looked at has ever had.

I want to talk to you about the amount, but I want to tell you some things about the amount first. Keep this in mind. Judge Thompson has already told you that the purpose of your verdict is to speak the truth. Collection is not your concern, who gets what is not your concern. That the verdict is, quote, "sufficient to stop it," that's your concern.

What is "it"? The line of victims from these trucks going into the future, the attitude toward automotive safety, and to stop misconduct of this giant corporation. That's what "it" is. What your concern is, is a verdict that speaks the truth about how much is sufficient to stop it. Don't let them set citizen against citizen.... I know nobody is envious of Tom and Elaine, but a lot of times people reduce their verdict because they get fixated on who gets what.

Ladies and gentlemen, that's not your concern. As a practical matter, it's not even ours. The judges are going to decide that. They'll look at your verdict. Your decision is, in your mind, what's the truth? How much is enough to stop it—forever?

How much, is up to you, ladies and gentlemen. We ask for a verdict that will make them do right, a verdict of not less than $20 per truck, and there's five million of them on the road. That is $100 million in punitive damages. The verdict is strictly up to you, but that is a verdict—if you return a verdict of not less than $100 million—we can guarantee you that your verdict will stop all three of the "its" I've talked about.

Collection is not your concern, that's up to the courts.

I'm at the end. My last note says, "The End." I have to use notes because, frankly, though I've waited a long, long time for this, I'm too nervous not to. I'm afraid I'll forget something.

The power of an idea can move nations. Please, ladies and gentlemen, give us a verdict that says, "Never again." Stop the dying, stop the misleading, stop the abandonment of responsibility. If for no other reason, ladies and gentlemen, do it for seventeen-year-old boys who do not deserve to die or be maimed or be crippled simply because General Motors' executives think they know what's best for us and think that whatever they decide is the gospel. If you don't do it for anybody else, do it for the seventeen-year-old boys like Shannon and their parents.

We ask those of you who believe in the cause, when you go back there [to] do what Judge Thompson has already told you to do, listen to your fellows, but hang tough. This is what we came for. This is what we, and I think much more than just we, all of us, need out of this case.

Remember, you come to court for justice. Not half-justice, not a piece of justice, but full justice. And when you render your verdict on the amount of punitive damages, ladies and gentlemen, ring that bell so loud that nobody, nobody anywhere, can fail to hear it.

Thank you very much.

Thank you, Judge Thompson.

Endnote

*Born in Atlanta on March 25, 1951, James E. Butler Jr. attended the University of Georgia, receiving an A.B.J. and a J.D. (cum laude) in 1977. During law school, he was a member of the law review and the moot court team. Mr. Butler, a principal in Butler, Wooten, Overby & Cheeley, has won four of the ten largest verdicts in Georgia's history. *Moseley* tops the list.

Rithmire v. Southern Railway
No. D-12904 (Fulton Super. Ct.)

Result: Defense verdict
Plaintiff's Counsel: Thomas W. Thrash Jr. and Baxter Finch of Finch, McCranie, Brown & Thrash (Atlanta) and E. Graydon Shuford (Atlanta)
Defense Counsel: Edgar A. Neely Jr. and Eric J. Spitler of Neely & Player (Atlanta)
Judge: Don A. Langham
Date of Verdict: September 22, 1986

Chapter XI

Derailing a FELA Case

Introduction
By Edgar A. Neely Jr.*

Plaintiff Robert A. Rithmire alleged that he injured his back on November 17, 1983, while working in Southern Railway Company's shop. Mr. Rithmire sued Southern Railway Company under the provisions of the Federal Employers' Liability Act (45 U.S.C. § 51 et seq.) (FELA).

FELA provides the exclusive remedy for injuries suffered by railway employees engaged in interstate commerce or in the furtherance of interstate commerce. Under federal case law, almost every injured railroad worker is deemed to have been engaged in the furtherance of interstate commerce.

The basis of railway liability under FELA is negligence and causation. As to negligence, the duty of the railway is to exercise ordinary care. It is not required to furnish a safe place to work or safe tools, but only to exercise ordinary care toward these ends. If the railway fails to exercise ordinary care, the plaintiff need not show proximate cause. Liability exists if the railway's negligence causally contributes to the injury.

The employee, however, is under a duty to exercise ordinary care for his own protection. If both parties are negligent, then plaintiff can recover, but his recovery is diminished in proportion to the extent that his negligence contributes to the injury. This differs from non-FELA tort cases in Georgia, in which a plaintiff's equal or greater contribution of negligence to his own injury bars recovery.

What the Parties Contended

Mr. Rithmire alleged that he injured his back while working the "bench" job in Southern Railway Company's shop. Mr. Rithmire's job involved removing worn parts from a safety hanger and replacing them with usable, nondefective parts. A safety hanger is a support system that keeps in line the brake rigging in a locomotive. The bolts on the hanger would break off, and Mr. Rithmire would redrill the holes and put in new bolts.

At the time of the incident, Mr. Rithmire was holding a safety hanger that weighed approximately ninety-seven pounds. Mr. Rithmire said that he was putting the hanger down on the work bench when he "felt [his] back pop." Plaintiff contended, among other things, that Southern Railway was negligent because it had failed to furnish to him a jib crane to lift the hanger, that the hanger was too heavy for a man safely to lift and carry alone, and that no one helped him transport the hanger to the bench.

The company, of course, denied all of the allegations, contending that Mr. Rithmire failed to exercise ordinary care for his own protection. Southern Railway also contended:

• that the sole proximate cause of Mr. Rithmire's alleged injury was his negligent failure to request assistance;

• that plaintiff negligently ignored defendant's rules, warnings, and instructions not to engage in this kind of lifting;

• that there was a serious question whether plaintiff's alleged injury resulted in any disability;

• that plaintiff performed physical labor for others for pay during his alleged disability;

- that plaintiff's back operations on March 19 and 25, 1985, were unnecessary;
- that the alleged injury was unrelated to the 1983 incident but was directly related to a 1978 injury which the parties had settled; and
- that plaintiff chose the more unsafe of at least two methods of doing his job on November 17, 1983, resulting in his alleged injury.

Mr. Rithmire's Admissions

It was indeed true that at the time of the alleged injury, Southern Railway had never furnished either the jib crane or any other electric or mechanical device to anyone then employed on the bench job for the purpose of lifting or transporting a safety hanger. However, Mr. Rithmire made a number of admissions that the company contended barred his recovery on the ground that he failed to exercise ordinary care for his own protection. These admissions were:

1. On a number of occasions before the incident in question, Mr. Rithmire had been an acting foreman on the same job.

2. On those occasions, Mr. Rithmire had the same duties and responsibilities that a full-fledged foreman would have had.

3. One of those duties would have been to instruct all personnel working under him that one of the requirements of the particular job was to furnish help to co-employees whenever requested.

4. On the date of his injury, Rithmire was not acting as foreman. However, before the incident he fully understood that whenever any employee needed additional help of any kind in his work, such employee was duty-bound to call upon a fellow employee either directly or through the foreman for that help. The called-upon employee was required to furnish that help.

5. Mr. Rithmire's co-employee, James Edward Stover, was very close by before and at the time Mr. Rithmire began lifting the safety hanger. However, at the time of the alleged injury itself, Mr. Stover had gone to wash his hands.

6. Although Mr. Rithmire and Mr. Stover were good friends and had helped each other out on numerous occasions, always involving heavier or more awkward objects than the safety hanger, nevertheless, at no time did Mr. Rithmire request any help in connection with the safety hanger.

7. The reason that Mr. Rithmire did not ask for help was that he considered the lifting, transporting, and setting down of the safety hanger well within his physical capacity. In fact, without asking for help he had successfully, safely, and without injury lifted like safety hangers by himself on many occasions.

8. On the occasion in question, Mr. Rithmire had already by himself lifted nine safety hangers, put each separately in the vice, and worked on them individually. The alleged injury involved the tenth safety hanger. Further, it was not at all in the lifting and transporting of the tenth safety hanger that the injury occurred. Contrary to what Mr. Rithmire's neurosurgeon, Dr. Exum Walker, had testified that Rithmire had told him, Mr. Rithmire swore that in lifting and transporting the safety hanger there was no problem whatever and that it was only when the pressure was released and he was putting the safety hanger down that he felt a sharp back pain. He swore that he did not know what caused the back pain to hit him.

9. Mr. Rithmire swore that he was fully familiar with the rules emphasized by Southern Railway as to how to lift and transport objects (use the legs rather than the back, hold the object close to you, etc.) and had followed those rules to the letter in performing the key operation.

What the Evidence Showed

Mr. Stover was a key witness at trial. He testified on direct examination that he was on the "press" job—putting bushings, or sleeves, into the holes in the hangers—when Mr. Rithmire was injured. Mr. Stover also testified that he and Mr. Rithmire had mentioned the need for a jib crane to their foreman, Leroy Gates. They had been told that it would be installed as soon as possible.

On cross-examination, Mr. Stover said that someone had ordered the wrong material for the jib crane installation. He did not know whether the right material was on hand ready for installation at the time of Mr. Rithmire's asserted injury.

Mr. Stover said that the true weight of the safety hanger in question was ninety-seven pounds. Mr. Stover testified that when he returned from washing his hands, Mr. Rithmire was all bent over and appeared to be in pain.

When Mr. Rithmire applied for the bench job, he knew that no jib crane was available. Also, he voluntarily left a job with ample crane facilities—the press job—which required no manual lifting of any kind. In fact, three cranes were available at the key time for lifting and transporting on the press job.

When Mr. Rithmire reported to Mr. Stover that he was hurt, the two men were located very close to one another. Mr. Rithmire never at any time asked Mr. Stover for help. The shop is a cooperative one and had Mr. Rithmire asked Mr. Stover for help, it would have been Mr. Stover's duty to help Mr. Rithmire. All Mr. Rithmire would have had to do was to ask Mr. Stover or another co-employee to help him in lifting, transporting, and handling the safety hanger. Mr. Stover and Mr. Rithmire had helped each other out many times before the incident.

On re-direct by plaintiff's lawyer Thrash, Mr. Stover said that in the seventeen years he had been with Southern Railway, he never had failed, to his knowledge, in getting help when he asked for it.

When Mr. Rithmire came back to work after August 17, 1985, the situation had been changed and he had available cranes, if he wished to use them, to do every part of his job.

Plaintiff brought in a scientific lifting expert, Mr. Gary Orr. Co-counsel Eric Spitler cross-examined Mr. Orr, who agreed that the formula for lifting developed by the National Institute of Occupational Safety and Health (NIOSH) incorporated the following four factors:

1. How far away (from the lifter) is the load?

2. How far must the load be lifted?
3. Where do you start your lift from?
4. How many times do you lift?

Mr. Spitler even let the expert portray the facts in the best light for the plaintiff. Under the evidence, the formula came out with a 50-pound bottom minimum level. This meant that 99 percent of the population could lift 50 pounds without risk. Twenty-five percent of the adult population can lift more than 150.3 pounds. If a worker asks for help to lift a 97-pound object, the risks are minimal. Despite his agreement with the NIOSH literature and formula, Mr. Orr contended that a person could lift no more than 90 pounds safely. Mr. Orr's only explanation for his 90-pound figure was that it came from his "experience." In his portion of the closing argument, Mr. Spitler pointed out that this weight was conveniently 7 pounds less than the safety hanger Mr. Rithmire lifted.

Mr. Rithmire had sworn in effect that after November 17, 1983, he had never done anything which could possibly be deemed work, except at Southern Railway until Dr. Exum Walker told him to quit. However, because the company had statements and records, Mr. Rithmire was forced to retreat (though reluctantly and partially) from this position.

Southern Railway had records showing each time Mr. Rithmire drove a truck delivering pulpwood he sold to a company. The defendant also introduced videotape of Mr. Rithmire cleaning up brush and cutting limbs from trees.

Although the jury returned a defense verdict on liability, it is noteworthy that Mr. Rithmire did not have a strong case on damages. Dr. Walker's own records on numerous occasions showed that Mr. Rithmire was virtually neurologically intact before and after his operations.

Moreover, Dr. Walker did not conduct any myelography before operating on Mr. Rithmire. Instead, Dr. Walker relied upon myelograms performed on Mr. Rithmire in connection with his prior low-back injuries. Thus, the defendant argued that whatever Mr. Rithmire's condition may have been, it did not result from the incident at issue.

A Winning Formula

Eye contact with jurors is an essential ingredient of any first-rate final argument. When talking directly to a jury, an attorney can sense what ought to be emphasized and what should be discarded. No part of a final argument should be read.

There is also the question of time, either limited by the court or by good judgment and thoughtfulness for the jurors. Frequently, a lawyer, however able, will take too much time on a few issues and leave out equally important ones. This is not a matter of policy. It is a matter of attorney error, which occurred in my final argument. Good final arguments, like the Gettysburg Address, should be relatively short. This final argument for the defense did not meet that test.

Why, then, was the final argument for the defense in the *Rithmire* case an effective one? First of all, the defense's opening statement had laid out in detail what Southern Railway expected that the evidence would show, either by its own witnesses or by examination or cross-examination of Mr. Rithmire and his witnesses. That opening statement invited the jury to test the evidence actually adduced against the defense's expectations. Fortunately, the actual evidence came sufficiently close to Southern Railway's projections to make final argument a lecture in confirmation rather than in excuses and explanations.

Second, I passionately believed what I was arguing. Thus, though many sentences were convoluted and long, the honesty and sincerity shone through.

Third, this was a case which the defendant deserved to win. Many such cases are lost. This is particularly true where, as here, plaintiff had a splendid and persuasive attorney who attacked with emotion and logic.

Lastly, Mr. Eric Spitler had made himself a scientific champion on the question of manual lifting and transporting of weights, had destroyed plaintiff's expert, and opened final argument in a persuasive manner.

Closing Argument: Part One

MR. SPITLER: Ladies and gentlemen, I am going to talk to you for just a few minutes this morning. Mr. Neely is going to talk to you then about some specifics. But I am going to talk to you a little bit about a few generalities that you and I have already observed in this case, and that I think have a significant bearing upon this case and upon the issue of whether or not Southern Railway was negligent in this case.

One of the plaintiff's contentions in this case is that this job was dangerous for anyone, not just Mr. Rithmire, but that lifting ninety-seven pounds was dangerous for anyone. You remember they brought in Mr. Gary Orr [plaintiff's scientific lifting expert] to testify to that fact: that lifting ninety-seven pounds was dangerous. Mr. Orr talked to us about a lot of things, and I think you all remember his testimony. We talked about psycho-physical factors and biomechanical factors, and we talked about using cadavers for testing, and we talked about a whole lot of things. Maximum limits and action limits and the whole thing, and we talked about numbers. And part of what this case involves, and part of what is involved with the negligence of the railroad in this case, is numbers. And numbers today are becoming more and more part of our life.

I think you all remember when we were choosing a jury there was one individual in particular who, as his name was asked, each time responded that his name was Juror Number Nineteen. We don't want numbers to take that kind of [control] in life. But they set limits sometimes, and statistically they can show us where dangers exist. And in this case we had some statistics to work with, and we had some numbers to work with. And when the plaintiff brought in Mr. Orr to tell us that this job was dangerous, he gave us some numbers, and I think we need to take a close look at some of those numbers.

Now, you recall we used a formula, and that was just a long nasty formula, but it was from the National Institute of Occupational Safety and Health. The National Institute of Occupational Safety and Health: their sole purpose, their sole job, is to protect workers in the work place, and so they do studies, and they develop guidelines. And in this case they developed a guideline and a formula that took into account variables for lifting. And the formula was long but it was very simple. It boiled down to four things.

How far away is the load? How far do you have to lift it? And you will remember in that case that as we went through the numbers, when we got to how far do you have to lift it, we got to the situation where Mr. Orr said, well, you need to give the plaintiff a little more space in there, and so we gave him eight inches. We gave him the complete benefit of the doubt there. It depends on, third, where you start your lift from, and how many times you lift. When you bring all that together, the National Institute for Occupation Safety and Health's formula gives you, for a specific lifting task, a formula, and some numbers that set some limits for you. I am not going to go through the math again, and I know that's a relief to everyone.

But there are a couple of bottom-line things that I want you to remember as this case develops. I want you to remember that when we did all the math—and at no time did Mr. Orr say, no, that's wrong, except for when we added eight more inches. When we did the math we came out with a 50-pound bottom minimum level, and remember what that meant. That meant that at lifting 50 pounds at this kind of a job, 99 percent of the adult male population could do that lifting without risk, 99 percent. And that's about as good as you are ever going to do with scientific studies, because you are rarely going to find one that will give you a rating for 100 percent.

Remember we then went up to a maximum 150.3 [pounds], and you need to remember a couple of aspects about that. At 150.3 pounds that doesn't mean that as soon as somebody walks outside there and tries to lift 150.3 pounds they are going to get hurt. That number means, in fact, that 25 percent of the adult male population can lift above that weight.

But the most important factor, ladies and gentlemen, is, if you get help, you are under the level that allows 99 percent of the males in this country to lift with safety. That's an important thing to remember, because if you ask for help the risks are nominal. The risk barely existed that [Mr. Rithmire] would be hurt under these statistics. Mr. Orr told you where the statistics came from, a wide range of scientific study. But what this bears on is when it is stated and contended that Southern Railway should have known that this job was dangerous for anyone, not just Mr. Rithmire, with help, [when] 99 percent of the adult male population would not suffer an injury.

We talked about administrative controls, and you remember what Mr. Orr said about administrative controls. He said the problem with administrative controls is that a lot of times people don't pay attention to them. Now, we know what the rule in the shop was. You have heard testimony to that effect. It was: get help. If you need it, get it. And nobody ever said that they wouldn't give it.

Mr. Rithmire said that when he was a relief foreman he ordered people to get help, and ladies and gentlemen, that is an administrative control. The rule to get help is an administrative control. It says, this makes the lifting safer. And Mr. Orr was right in this case. One of the problems with the administrative control is that Mr. Rithmire failed to follow it, and we have an injury as a result.

Now, one other thing I want you to remember is that Mr. Orr came in and he talked about a 90-pound upper limit. No lifting above 90 pounds was safe. I may have missed something, but I don't know where that 90 pounds ever came from. At no point did we ever come up with a 90-pound figure on the chart.

You all remember the chart. On this chart 90 pounds is in the administrative control range. It is not the upper limit. [Mr. Orr's] only explanation for the 90 pounds was the fact that 90 pounds was based on his experience. Now, ladies and gentlemen, the National Institute of Occupational Safety and Health has its limits. Mr. Orr says his experience puts it at 90 pounds. But he didn't contest the math, and he didn't put at any time a different number. He didn't ever tell us where that 90-pound limit came from, and the only thing that we know about [that figure] is that it is conveniently 7 pounds lower than the weight of the safety hanger.

Now, that [90-pound limit] didn't come from the chart, didn't come from the math. I don't know where it came from. But what we know according to the National Institute of Occupational Safety and Health, according to its figures and its formula, using the variables in this case, all [Mr. Rithmire] had to do was ask for help and the risk of him getting hurt barely existed.

I am going to turn it over to Mr. Neely now.

Closing Argument: Part Two

MR. NEELY: I am going to talk to begin with, ladies and gentlemen, a little bit about the law, because my brother [Mr. Thrash] started off, and, of course, he will make his factual argument following mine. I do tell you that once I have sat down I am known as "handcuffed Neely." I cannot get up and say, "No. That's wrong, Mr. Thrash. You are incorrect, Mr. Thrash." Because he has the final argument. As he has said, the reason is that he has the burden of proof on the main issue.

Now, first of all, my brother [Mr. Spitler], who just spoke to us, is absolutely right about what he said. Under the NIOSH [National Institute of Occupational Safety and Health] figures, why he even gave eight inches, as I recall it, to the plaintiff, in working out the formula. So, [the results are] really far better than that, and as [Mr. Spitler showed the chart], it went up, as I recall it, to 150.3 [pounds as being the maximum which could be safely lifted by 25 percent of the adult male population]. But I want to make perfectly plain, you are not bound by the NIOSH figures at all.

You can disregard any expert's testimony, if you wish, or give it just such weight as you wish, just like any other testimony. You are not required to believe any expert of any kind, medical or otherwise. But you are required to listen, of course, and weigh it. I just [say] that in passing because I do want to respond somewhat to what Mr. Thrash said in opening statement.

Defining the Railroad's Duty

First of all, [Mr. Thrash] did correct it, but he, at first, said that the duty of the railroad was to provide employees a safe place to work. That's not the duty at all. Under this law, as I believe his honor will charge you, the duty is to exercise ordinary care to the end of providing a safe place to work.

The sole burden upon the railroad is not to furnish something great or furnish something safe, but only, as his honor will charge you, to exercise ordinary care. [Judge Langham] will define ordinary care for you pretty much like this: it is just such care as an ordinarily prudent person would exercise under the same or similar circumstances.

Negligence is a matter solely for you to determine, and when you determine it you have just got to say to yourself, well, now, what would an ordinarily prudent man do? Ordinarily prudent. Not a fellow that's great or anything like that, but what an ordinarily prudent man would do under the same or similar circumstances.

Now, the second thing that [Mr. Thrash] was somewhat mistaken on—and I am sure he didn't mean to, and it may be that he didn't realize it—there are two separate factors that are involved here. One is the question, did the railroad exercise ordinary care or did it not? And the other is the question, if [the railroad] did fail to exercise ordinary care, was there any causal connection between that failure, if any, and the injury to the plaintiff?

So, you will see that those are two important factors. Now, what [Mr. Thrash] thought he was saying, I am sure, was that if the causation were not great why, then, you are entitled to bring in a verdict. But what he failed to point out was that it is not a question of small negligence. Negligence sits at a high level, high or medium level. We are not insurers of the safety of an employee, as his honor will charge you. But [negligence] sits at a medium level. What an ordinary person would do under these circumstances, whether an individual [or] a corporation. The only duty resting upon us at any time is the duty to exercise ordinary care under the same or similar circumstances.

Now, the second thing, though, and [Mr. Thrash] is right about that, if indeed he does prove that there was negligence, then what did the failure do? Was there a causal connection? On causal connection it is true that the FELA has now [been] interpreted [to] say that the causal connection need not be great, and I think it says the causal connection may be small. But the big point is that you have first got to get through with the question of whether or not either party failed to exercise ordinary care before you move into the causation area.

Now, the next thing [Mr. Thrash] said was, well, he gave this example. Suppose that 1 percent of the causation was Southern Railway's, and 99 percent was Mr. Rithmire's, then under those circumstances Mr. Rithmire could still collect 1 percent of his damages. That's true where you are dealing with contributory negligence, where both parties are negligent, which means failing to complete the due care standard. If both parties were negligent then, where that negligence does contribute [to the alleged injury], then even though 99 percent of the contribution was Mr. Rithmire's, he could still collect 1 percent of his damages, if [he was] otherwise entitled to recover.

But what [Mr. Thrash] left out was a very, very important thing, and that is not the question of contributory negligence but the question of sole negligence. Because if you should find from the evidence in this case, that the sole proximate cause was the negligence of Mr. Rithmire, if you find that he was, in effect, the author of his own misfortune, then he can't recover at all.[1]

The Great Law of Self-Justification

I did want you to know that there is a law that doesn't appear on the books. It is known as the great law of self-justification. It is an ethical principle. It is a psychological principle. That law says, in effect, that every person automatically, whether honest or not, favors himself. He favors himself in terms of what happened, of how badly he was hurt.

The longer a fellow goes from the time he is hurt, from the time he hires a lawyer to the final end of the case, why he becomes more and more a prisoner of the case. Because the case becomes to him [his] whole [life]. The longer he goes, the more he believes fully and truly that the accident happened in fashion A; that it was caused by B; and that he is injured to the extent of C. That is something that just is automatic.

Now, let's see how and in what way the real law matches what I have said, and please listen closely to the charge in any of these things because I want to be right.

First of all, his honor will charge you as to the credibility of the witnesses and as to the verdict, and in charging you about the credibility of witnesses he will say, you have the right to take into consideration their interest or want of interest. In other words, what interest does anyone have in a verdict one way or the other? Obviously nobody could have a greater interest in the case than the plaintiff himself. Particularly one who has gone all this time, since November 17, 1983, living, in effect, for this case. So, when the court charges about interest or want of interest, listen closely.

But there is one more principle the law realizes than what I said about the greater interest of the plaintiff, and I think his honor will charge you that the testimony of a party where vague, equivocal, or self-contradictory is to be construed most strongly against that party. If the judge does charge you that, then remember that in evaluating the testimony of Mr. Rithmire.[2]

How Do You Say No to an Injured Man?

Now, you know I have been at this court for fifty-two years, and back in the old days the jury would go in and there would be paper-thin walls, and you would hear something from the jury room: "He's hurt, isn't he? Give him some money. He sure is hurt, and they can afford it."

You would hear somebody say, "He has got to pay his lawyers something. Give him a little extra money."

You would hear something about, "Well, why don't we all do this. Let's just add up all twelve—everybody put a figure down. Say three of us put a figure zero. So many put the figure so and so, and let's divide it by twelve." That's what is known as a quotient verdict. You would hear all this sort of thing. You would hear someone say, "Hey folks, it's getting dark. Let's get out of here and go home."

So, you would hear all of these various things. You would hear them, in times past, and I did, because they would come right through the walls. Fortunately we have a different [situation] today. I mean, isn't it wonderful that everybody, if they want to, can take notes about what is going on, and that everybody is listening closely and wants to reach a correct conclusion, no matter what. That is the status that we have finally reached today.

Of course, it is true that the psychological burden is really on the defendant. We all like a contender. We believe in the contender rather than the champion, and we have sympathy, and sympathy very frequently plays a large part. But as I believe the court will charge you, neither one of those things can possibly play any part in whatever verdict is rendered.

The real burden is sort of like this: Somebody comes up to you and says, "Hey, you owe me $10," and I say, "No, I don't owe you $10." They said, "Yes, you do," and I say, "Well, prove it. Prove it." So then he has got to prove that [I owe him] the $10, or whatever it may be.

The same principle is applicable here. Mr. Rithmire has got to prove Southern Railway Company owes him $10, or whatever it will be. That is the real burden.

Very frequently a plaintiff's lawyer will hope that lightning will strike, that he will get some big, big verdict, and so he is likely to ask for a thousand times more than he really expects to get because then somebody will say, "Well, heck, if we cut him down to one-thousandth of that we have made a good verdict." Not so.

The verdict has got to be your verdict, and it has got to be based upon your evaluation, and it has got to be unanimous.

Now, it takes real courage to say no. It is a difficult thing to say no to an injured man. It is a very difficult thing. It is wrenching. You will have to go out after this thing is over, and [ask] why did you render a verdict for the defendant? Well, you would have to say, I just had to follow my oath and the facts as I understood them, and the law as it applied to those facts. But it still takes an awful lot of courage to see the disappointment on the face, particularly of an injured man. So, please bear that in mind.

Now, one of the favorite final words from the plaintiff is this. He will say, ladies and gentlemen, this is the last chance for poor old Robert Rithmire; this is the very last chance. He will never get another chance. Well, now, that statement is really an effort to change the law as to the burden of proof. The burden of proof remains on him. So, please don't listen to the last-chance doctrine, and [don't] let that change your [mind] about what the verdict is.

All right. It takes twelve persons to reach a verdict in this case, and each one must make it [his] verdict. Each of you has the right, after listening to the evidence and after listening to the charge of the court, after consulting with your fellow jurors, to maintain his personal opinion. Because under Georgia law the verdict must be unanimous. So those of you who agree with me that the verdict should be zero in this case, please stick with me.

Destroying Plaintiff's Credibility

I want to call your attention to a couple of things. One of them is the requests for admissions.

I am so long-winded sometimes. It got boring, I am sure, listening to those requests for admissions. But the questions that were asked related to a previous deposition, as well as to facts that occurred before the deposition was taken, and the questions that were attached there were, in effect, these [Mr. Neely reads from Mr. Rithmire's admissions]:

"Now, Mr. Rithmire, I know that you say you have not received any money for anything that looks like work. You have told us that. But, Mr. Rithmire, tell me about what you have done that anyone might even consider in the vaguest way as being work."

And he is under oath at this time, and signed [his responses to interrogatories and requests for admissions] again. So, twice under oath, and what he said in substance, was this:

He said, "Well, I did the timing on a couple of cars. But that didn't require any stooping, bending, or anything of that sort."

He said, "I did a brake job, and I really didn't do it all. I showed somebody how to do it." And he said, "That's the limit on what I did that anybody might consider work."

Well, there wasn't any chance about his misunderstanding [the question]. We were talking about free work when we asked the question. That's why we put this request for admission on, number ten, which, among other things, asked him whether he hadn't said that, and then limited it. Then we went to other questions.

Well, I realize that a man can be forgiven for misunderstanding. But this went through his then-attorney [E. Graydon Shuford] who was running the case, and it was answered, "Yes, I agree that that is what I said—that that's all I did."

Then we get down to questioning Mr. Rithmire about, well, "What did you really do in addition to all of that? Did you drive a truck?" And in his answers for request for admissions he said yes. Well, you know, that kind of looks like work, which he had not revealed to us under oath. Then, I said, "Did you drive a pulpwood truck down to Fulco?" Which was a place where they unload the truck, and he said, "Well, yes, sometimes." He said, "The only reason I did it was to relieve the boredom." Him being a totally disabled person, or words to that effect.

And then we kept on going about that driving down to Fulco, and ultimately Mr. Rithmire said that, "You are wrong, Mr. Neely, about all the times that you say that I was—that you don't say, but that you are asking me about—that I went down there and drove the pulpwood truck, you are wrong about that. But at the same time I don't believe that lady there, she only came in on Fridays. I don't think she could have seen me more than four or five times." [The lady referred to is the bookkeeper at Fulco. She did not testify but the defense had the records.]

Well, if [the bookkeeper] came in on Fridays, and couldn't have seen him more than four or five times, that still would add up to a lot of trips, a lot of trips.

And then he went on and said, "Well, in addition I used to take a load down there at night and leave it," where she couldn't see him on such occasions. Then, I said, "Mr. Rithmire, tell the jury how many times you went down there." He said, "Well, I can't really tell you. Between one and a thousand. You kept after me, and finally I gave some figures, but I couldn't really tell you. Between one and a thousand."

Now my question to you, ladies and gentleman, is this: if you were asked what free work you have done, that is, what you did that looked like work, wouldn't you think driving a pulpwood truck [and] on one occasion getting up on the top there and swinging those chains, binding the load and unloading it, wouldn't you think that that fell under the general classification of work? He wasn't forced to perform free work.

Under oath, he answered to a couple of minor, nothing things that couldn't have involved any bending, couldn't have caused any work. [And he said] this is the only free work I have done. Then it develops that he has done a lot of free work.

We developed that the driving of the truck had to be fairly frequent if he said [the bookkeeper] could have seen him only four, five times. Don't you think that that was being unfair to the jury?

Insofar as what we called the credibility factor is concerned, that is, the believability factor, I think his honor will charge you that if you believe from the evidence that somebody has told something that is not true, then you are entitled, if you want, to disregard other portions of his evidence upon the grounds that maybe if what he said on one occasion was not correct, then something else [he said] might not be correct.

The Medical Evidence: Everything Is Chicken Down in Dixie

Now, let me go to some other things right quick. Before surgery, according to Dr. Exum Walker [Mr. Rithmire's neurosurgeon], on many occasions—this is after he started treating [Mr. Rithmire] on November 18, 1983—on many occasions this man was quote "neurologically intact." I told you at the beginning of our discussions that what neurologically intact meant, I thought—and you will recall that when I asked Dr. Walker about it, he agreed with me—that, in effect, it means that everything is chicken down in Dixie insofar as the neurology is concerned. That's a foolish way to put it, but it means everything is all right as far as the neurological signs and symptoms are concerned. Then, he also said that he had used old myelograms, you see. He used two sets of myelograms.

Two doctors [Dr. Walker and Dr. Robert Wells, an orthopedist] said that one of the myelograms didn't show any pathology, didn't show any bulging at L-4. One of the doctors said he couldn't see anything. But both Exum Walker and, I believe, Dr. Robert Wells said that. But in any event, that wasn't the entirety of what caused Dr. Exum Walker to operate. But it had a good deal to do with it because he said, "I can look at these and see that this fellow has from way back some disc pathology. I can't tell about it all."[3]

Now, Dr. Exum Walker did not comment at all upon [Mr. Rithmire's] ability to do work other than to say there might be some connection between his 20 percent impairment and some impairment in income. But he didn't say a word about what this man could do other than, "I don't think he can go back to the railroad." So that the only position taken by Dr. Exum Walker on that was that he felt that this man could not go back to the railroad, and that if he did he might last six months. He might last a year. He might last three years. But he would ultimately regret it.

So, what I am saying is that in this connection if you have considered damages, and I hope to goodness you won't, but when you consider damages remember that there is no evidence as to what this man could do or could have done—well, on the few little jobs that he did in the neighborhood or could have done other than the railroad.

Mr. Macho Authored His Own Misfortune

Now, let's look a little bit at what I call the plaintiff's admissions. A good many of you have taken notes, so if I am wrong about it, why then change me.

[Mr. Rithmire] said, "I never asked for help in lifting any safety hanger." In effect he said—this is number two—"I knew that help was available." Three, he said, "I have worked as a relief foreman, and I have instructed others to help out." Four, he said he thought the safety hanger was about sixty-five to seventy pounds, and, of course, the reason he thought it was less than ninety-eight pounds was because he was a husky 220 or 230 pounder, six feet three, and just, you know, Mr. Macho insofar as big is concerned. He said, "I have on occasion helped but I never, myself, asked for help."

Now, then, this is very important, he said, "I have bid on that job." Now, what does bid on a job mean? That means Mr. Southern Railway Company, if there is a job opening, here is my application, and I want that job.

You will hear something, I think, in the charge about assigning a man a job. This man assigned himself [the bench job]. He said, I want that job. I am going to have that job. I have got the seniority, and, of course, he was, in effect, saying, I have got the vigor.

[Mr. Rithmire] said [the bench job] is the easiest job in the shop. And when he took it, what did he know about the job? It may well have been that he said, well, listen, we ought to have a jib crane in this job. [He] was responsible for that. But he knew it when he took the job; he knew there wasn't any jib crane. It [was] a lifting situation.

He knew that he had [James Edward] Stover [a co-employee]. He knew if he didn't have Stover, [he could ask] his good friend, the foreman Leroy Gates, who said that this man [Mr. Rithmire] ought to be a foreman himself, and certainly believed he should be a relief foreman. [Mr. Gates] wasn't pushing [Mr. Rithmire] or anything. [Mr. Gates] knew [Mr. Rithmire] was having no problems whatever, and [Mr. Rithmire] knew all he had to do was say, "Somebody help me lift this thing."

Oh, no. [Mr. Rithmire] determined [the scope of] that job. [Mr. Rithmire] was going to lift [the hanger]. Now, of course, if he wanted to say, well, listen, I don't want to work in there without a jib crane, that would be one thing. But the point is, and I think Mr. Watson [a supervisor] finally made it pretty clear, he said, well, yes, there is a strain on your back if you don't have a jib crane. It would relieve the strain if you had one. But he said there is another type of help, and that's called human help. There is a rule in the shop, which you heard from person after person, which was if you don't think you can lift, get help.

So, what I am saying right quickly in this connection is that this man knew precisely what his duties were. He knew precisely what his opportunities for getting help were, and he chose voluntarily to do all the lifting himself.

Now, [Mr. Rithmire had] his eyes wide open, and saw the whole picture. He had an opportunity to measure the risks, if any. He was under no compulsion to go ahead and strain himself, none whatever, because you know darn well his good friend [Leroy Gates] is not going to say, "Come on. I have got to get this done." He had all the time in the world, and he decides, by God, he is going to do it himself.

Now, frankly, I think [Mr. Rithmire] could lift one and a half times [the hanger's weight] if he had to, and [his injury] wasn't from the lifting. According to him the lifting just didn't do it. He said, "I had [already] lifted . . . nine [safety hangers]." He said, "I had lifted this safety hanger from the cart that's twenty inches high to the drill press, and then I done my drilling." And then he said, "I am going to walk over here and I am going to put this on the workbench." And there is a vise on this workbench. And he said, "I had fixed up something on that workbench that had the vise on it where it wouldn't be any problem. If I laid it down it would stay there."

I don't know whether you remember this—I think it was just a statement, and we read it in the investigation. [Mr. Rithmire] said, quote, "and that's where I get help. That's where I get help. That's the point where I get help," which meant that here is a man who said, I never asked for help in my life, and then in the investigation right after the accident he said, this is a point where I get help, anyway. So, what I am saying to you is that that man, in my judgment, was the author of his own misfortune.[4]

Now, there will be a lot of talk about why we would let this fellow do what he did [lift the safety hanger by himself]. Here is a man who has recovered, so far as anyone could ascertain, and even before he recovered—well, Dr. Wells said, here is a man recovered, and gone several years in great shape, vigorous as he can possibly be. And they say, well, the railroad in the exercise of ordinary care ought to have known that we had a defective fellow here, a fellow who has proven himself time after time, for three years, to be as strong as a bull. Strong as he can be. For he is and was a man in every sense of the word. There is just no question that we acted as a reasonably prudent person would have acted in letting him do this work, particularly where we are telling him, and he knows, he gets all the help he needs.

So, what I am saying to you is, and this is very important, sure a jib crane makes it easier to lift. Although [Mr. Rithmire] said that, by golly, even when he was on [the press job], that when he sought to pick up two hundred pounds, even with a jib crane, he had to sort of fool around and [hoist] about a hundred pounds. I think you will remember that. I said to myself, how can that be?

The Mental A-Team

Now, I'll talk about [Mr. Rithmire's] seniority and his efforts to rehabilitate himself and obtain employment. And then I will sit down.

Please remember this guy was first in his class from 1,260 folks at a mechanic's school. This is a brilliant man. This man makes me look like a skinny scout when it comes to questions and answers.

Of course, I'm old, and can't quite keep up. But you know he is very good. You know he's smart. And what does a smart man do? He says, "Well, if I can't work for the railroad, [still] I'm smart. I have got a good brain. I can read well. I can do a lot of things well." [A smart man] says, "Well, maybe it would be better if [I] tried to obtain some other employment. Because as [Dr.] Exum Walker says, railroad work has a certain amount of hardness to it."

What would you do about trying to get suitable employment? Let's just go back to April 17, 1985, when the doctor says [Mr. Rithmire] has just improved so wonderfully. What would you do about seeking employment? You know that there are laws that say you can't discriminate against handicapped people. There are laws that say you can go and get a good evaluation from the state. Then the state will point out what jobs you can do.

Think about it. Did he do any of those things? No. The only thing he did was go around the neighborhood and ask a few people whether or not they would give him a job. That's all he did, and I am saying he was under a duty of due care to find and maintain employment not just for the railroad. He doesn't own the railroad. The railroad doesn't own him. But when a fellow says that he is in the condition where he can't go back to the railroad, and he is in as good condition as we have seen, [then he has a duty to look for other work].

I cannot speak further. I know that I will be jumping up and down inwardly trying to answer this handsome, this very able gentleman [Mr. Thrash], because the truth of the matter is that this man, Mr. Rithmire, now has the big team. It is the mental A-Team, and they have done a splendid job of trying this case. But if you cut through all this foolishness, and say what would an ordinarily prudent man have done, I believe you will say with me the verdict ought to be zero.

Endnotes

* Edgar A. Neely Jr. was born in 1910 and was admitted to practice in Georgia in 1934. He received an A.B. in 1931 from the University of North Carolina at Chapel Hill and an LL.B. in 1934 from Emory University.

1. In FELA cases, a negligent plaintiff can recover, but his recovery is diminished to the extent that his negligence contributes to his injury. In other words, plaintiff must prove that defendant was negligent, and that said negligence contributed to plaintiff's alleged injury. A plaintiff cannot do that if his negligence or any factor other than the railroad's negligence constituted the sole cause of his alleged injury.

2. As mentioned, the defense's cross-examination of Mr. Rithmire was very effective. In the preceding paragraphs, I remind the jury of his extreme interest in the case and inform the jurors that they must construe his contradictory statements against him. This sets the stage for when I review in detail Mr. Rithmire's inconsistent statements and tell the jurors that if they decide he has been untruthful, they may, if they wish, disregard his entire testimony.

3. Dr. Walker did swear that he thought that the incident at issue was a proximate producing cause of Mr. Rithmire's condition, but the jury was entitled to believe from Dr. Walker's testimony that he based his opinion on what Mr. Rithmire told him; namely, that Mr. Rithmire had suffered an injury while lifting, even though Mr. Rithmire testified at trial that he hurt

himself while setting down the hanger. Further, Dr. Walker's own records revealed that the plaintiff was neurologically intact after he was in Dr. Walker's office. Thus, I argued that prior disc pathology may have been the cause of the alleged injury at issue.

4. During his testimony Mr. Rithmire swore that he never asked for help on any occasion. However, in a prior statement he admitted that there were times when he asked for help and received it.

Acknowledgments

The *Daily Report* wishes to thank the following for their invaluable contributions:

Daily Report publisher Shayla Keough Rumely, who approved the concept and provided insights and moral support; *Daily Report* editor S. Richard Gard Jr., whose expert editing skills sharpened the book considerably; and opinions editor Rachel A. Derrico, whose faithful production assistance helped keep the project on schedule.

Projects editor Yvette Upton, the workhorse who laid out the book and coordinated the production effort; art director J. Allan Stagg Jr., the technology wizard who designed the cover; and freelance copy editor Marian G. Lord, without whose eagle eye and expertise this book could not have been produced.

Pearl S. Schaikewitz